BLOOD MUST TELL

*Debating Race and Identity in the Canadian
House of Commons, 1880-1925*

GLEN WILLIAMS

willowBX Press
Ottawa, Canada

Copyright © 2014 by Glen Williams

All rights reserved. The use of any part of this publication reproduced, transmitted in any form or by any means, electronic, mechanical, recording or otherwise, or stored in a retrieval system, without the prior written consent of the publisher is an infringement of the copyright law.

Library and Archives Canada Cataloguing in Publication

Williams, Glen, 1947-
Blood must tell: debating race and identity in the Canadian House of Commons, 1880-1925

Includes bibliographical references and index.
Electronic monograph.
ISBN 978-0-9937993-0-3 (pdf).–ISBN 978-0-9937993-1-0 (epub).–ISBN 978-0-9937993-2-7 (mobi).–ISBN 978-0-9937993-3-4 (pod).

1. Canada–Race relations–Political aspects–History–19th century. 2. Canada–Race relations–Political aspects–History–20th century. 3. Ethnicity–Political aspects–Canada–History–19th century. 4. Ethnicity–Political aspects–Canada–History–20th century. 5. Debates and debating–Canada–History–19th century. 6. Debates and debating–Canada–History–20th century. 7. Canada. Parliament. House of Commons–History–19th century. 8. Canada. Parliament. House of Commons–History–20th century. 9. Canada–Politics and government–19th century. 10. Canada–Politics and government–20th century. I. Title.

FC104.W57 2014   323.17109'034   C2014-903380-X

Published by willowBX Press, Ottawa, Canada using PressBooks.com

Cover design by Kate McDonnell

CONTENTS

	Acknowledgements	v
1.	Introduction	1
	Anti-Japanese Canadian Policies 1942-1944	3
	Race-thinking and race politics in late nineteenth and early twentieth century thought	10
	Challenges to biological race-thinking and race politics	16
	Anglo-Saxonism, British imperialism, and race-thinking	19
	Outline of the Book	26
2.	Dominion Anglo-Saxonism within the international system	45
	Political Liberty and Moral Mission	46
	The Protection of British Guns	52
	The Defensive, Peaceful Empire	59
	Anglo-Saxonism in Canada-US Relations	66
	Conclusion	74
3.	Dominion Anglo-Saxonism and Canadians of European Origin	79
	French Canadians as British Subjects	81
	The Confederation Compact	83
	Language, Blood and Duality	86
	Immigration	96
	Call of the Blood: World War I and "Enemy Aliens"	104
	Call of the Blood: World War I and the Quebecois	112
	Constructing Canadians	123
	Conclusion	132

4. **Dominion Anglo-Saxonism and Canadians of non-European origin: Native Peoples** — 142
   Jus Soli and the Vote — 144
   Macdonald and the Framing of Native Policies — 146
   Alternative Policy Paths? — 151
   Losing the Franchise — 157
   Infantilized Objects of Bureaucratic Administration — 159
   Controlling the Message — 172
   Conclusion — 180

5. **Dominion Anglo-Saxonism and Canadians of non-European origin: Asians, South Asians, and Africans** — 188
   British Columbian Epicentre — 190
   Royal Commission of 1885 — 195
   Losing the Vote — 198
   Exclusion and White Canada — 203
   Prejudice and Bigotry — 214
   South Asians as British Subjects — 223
   Continuous Passage — 226
   Self-Government and Empire Citizenship — 231
   African Canadians as "sons of Canada" — 239
   Conclusion — 246

6. **Conclusion** — 254
   The British Empire — 256
   Christianity and Liberalism — 261
   Racial Pseudo-Science and Biological Determinism — 266
   Political Representation — 274

Index — 285

About the Author — 297

Also by Glen Williams — 299

ACKNOWLEDGEMENTS

Some of the material in this book appeared first in a research paper, "Mapping Racial/Ethnic Hierarchy in the Canadian Social Formation, 1880-1914: An Examination of Selected Federal Policy Debates," presented to the 1992 Annual Conference of the Canadian Political Science Association at the University of Prince Edward Island. My co-author was Professor Daiva Stasiulis of Carleton University and I acknowledge here, with deep thanks, my intellectual debt to her contribution to the "Mapping" paper.

Radha Jhappan, my Carleton Political Science colleague, urged me many times over the years to develop the "Mapping" research paper into a broader study and publish it for general use – thank you Professor Jhappan!

I thank as well Emily Andrew and Philip Cercone for their encouragement and advice as well as two anonymous peer reviewers whose comments helped me improve the book.

Carleton University generously granted me a half sabbatical in 2012 to allow me to finish the first draft of this manuscript. Library resources at both Carleton and the University of Ottawa were critical to the success of the project.

Finally, I have been much blessed by the love and support of my family in this assignment as in all my endeavours – Carol-Lynne, Annie and Maggie.

CHAPTER 1.

INTRODUCTION

We must not permit in Canada the hateful doctrine of racialism which is the basis of the nazi system everywhere.[1]
–WILLIAM LYON MACKENZIE KING, 1944.

There is scarcely a government building, bridge or public roadway of significance in Ontario not already named in honour of a former municipal, provincial, or federal political worthy. Today's politicians immortalize yesterday's politicians perhaps in the hope that their political successors will likewise honour them in the future. On occasion, these namings generate controversy. In Ottawa in 2011, for example, the then mayor backed away from naming a city archives building after a predecessor amid accusations that the former mayor had opposed on racial grounds Jewish and Armenian immigration to Canada during the 1930s.

The 2012 renaming of the Ottawa River Parkway in honour of Canada's first Prime Minister was similarly met with charges that Sir John A. Macdonald had delivered especially virulent racist speeches attacking Chinese Canadians. In a series of letters and columns in the local newspaper, defenders of the renaming held that Macdonald had lived in a different, less racially sensitive, age and that his accusers were smugly trying to parade their own sense of moral superiority through inappropriately judging the past by present-day standards. Canadian journalist Richard Gwyn weighed in on Macdonald's side in this debate with an important argument. Contemporary Canada, he said, has become a multicultural "role model among the United Nations' 200-odd member-states of accommodation to and acceptance of difference — cultural, ethnic, religious, racial, of colour." Gwyn then asked the question at the centre of this book: how could Canada's "transformation" from intolerance to multiculturalism "have happened if so many of us collectively and Macdonald personally were all once such racists?"[2]

In seeking an answer to Gwyn's very good question, I begin this introductory chapter with a consideration of a case frequently judged to be a high-water mark of racist politics in Canada as well as a staple in Canadian popular history and media reference – the federal government's policy during World War II of forcibly displacing some 23,000 Japanese Canadians from the British Columbia coast, housing them in internment camps, seizing and selling their private property, and compelling them to relocate outside of B.C. after War's end. There is scarcely a schoolchild in Canada that has not learned of the heart-breaking mistreatment of the Japanese Canadians of this era.[3]

John Diefenbaker, in introducing his 1958 Bill of Rights to the House of Commons, cited post-World War II attempts to deport thousands of Japanese Canadians as evidence that there was a "need of some restraining influence and the declaration of some principle to assure that there shall not be repetition in the future."[4] For his part, Pierre Trudeau deplored the "terrible acts" taken against Japanese Canadians during WWII and believed that his 1982 Charter of Rights would prevent Canadian governments from ever repeating such abuses. "I am certain," he said, "that the kind of actions that we regret would not be justified or condoned by the courts in the future. Therefore, we have brought in redress, for our time and for the future, to the most unacceptable acts which have happened in the past."[5] In 1988, Brian Mulroney offered Japanese Canadians a "formal and sincere apology" on behalf of parliament "for those past injustices against them..." which were "morally and legally unjustified."[6]

ANTI-JAPANESE CANADIAN POLICIES 1942-1944

At first glance it is difficult to find evidence of any coming political transformation from racist intolerance to accommodative multiculturalism in the 1942 and 1943 debates in the House of Commons regarding Japanese Canadians. The governing Liberals and all the opposition parties supported internment. There was no dissent; no parliamentarian spoke in the Commons against any of the wide range of discriminatory policies that were targeting Japanese Canadians.[7] Since the House of Commons typically operates as an adversarial theatre dividing government and opposition opinions along strict party lines,[8] its unanimity here regarding a major policy initiative like Japanese internment[9] is uncommon and needs to be explained. This is even more the case since this book's subsequent chapters will confirm that unanimity was not at all characteristic of the 1880-1925 Commons debates relating to race and identity.

A deeper look reveals a more complex pattern. Despite the consensus on internment for Japanese Canadians, there was neither complete silence concerning their plight nor agreement over the policy's objectives. A debate over racial politics percolating just below the surface was exposed through expressions of liberal equality principles and supportive 'knowledge by acquaintance' testimonials.

"Equal treatment before the law of all residents of Canada irrespective of race, nationality or religious or political beliefs" had been called for in the 1933 Regina Manifesto adopted by the Co-operative Commonwealth Party's founding convention. Still, the B.C. wing of the CCF favoured the "evacuation of the Japanese" from the province's coastal areas and was against their "sudden return" after the war was over.[10] And, so it was in 1942 that CCF member for Vancouver East Angus MacInnis commended the Minister responsible for removal of Japanese Canadians from

B.C. coast – "his department has handled a most difficult job in an efficient manner" – while at the same time reminding members "that a great many of these people are Canadian citizens no matter what the colour of their skins may be, and they are entitled to the treatment that would be accorded to a Canadian citizen whose skin is white. We should also keep in mind that when the war is over, we shall have to continue to live with these people..."[11]

In addition to the formal enunciation of liberal equality principles, as MacInnis was doing here, the chauvinistic generalizations of racist theories were also undermined in Commons debates through anecdotal counter-narratives. These narratives were commonly based on the life experience of an MP or were grounded in his duty to represent and speak out on behalf of his constituents. Japanese Canadians were severely disadvantaged in this later respect as they had been denied both the provincial and federal voting franchise in British Columbia since the 1880s. Nevertheless, in one 1943 'knowledge by acquaintance' exchange in the Commons, a racist generalization by T. Reid, representing B.C.'s New Westminster constituency, was effectively rebutted. Reid began by alluding to eastern Canadian liberal critics of his anti-Japanese opinions – a common complaint of B.C. members dating back to the years immediately following Confederation – before launching into a dare to other members.

> very often people get up in this country, when some of us undertake to speak about the Japanese and to put before the people the facts as they are, and immediately tell us what we should do. I repeat that if any of the Japanese born in this country are to remain in this country, the first step that should be taken should be taken by the Japanese themselves; and no Japanese has so far taken the first step in the direction of real Canadian citizenship, for the reason that everyone of them owes allegiance to Japan, whether born in this country or not. We have never heard one of them stand up and say to Japan, 'You are not our country; we were born here, we are Canadian citizens.' I challenge any hon. Member to show one instance, in the long life of the Japanese in this country, where one of them has made it apparent that he is a true Canadian citizen.[12]

Saskatchewan member R.T. Graham immediately rose to meet this challenge:

> In justice to a very brave man and a very fine citizen of Japanese origin, I cannot let the statement made by the hon. Member for New Westminster go unchallenged. I have in mind a young Japanese who served with distinction in my own company in France [in World War I] and who was decorated by this nation. He saved the life of one of his comrades by performing a very brave deed. He came back and settled in my district where he is now farming and is one of the most highly respected farmers in his particular area. To-day he has two sons serving with the Canadian forces in this war.[13]

So, then, while there may have been consensus on internment and other wartime anti-Japanese Canadian policies of the federal government, there is evidence that a deeper debate on racial politics was taking place at the same time. This debate was informed by six decades of parliamentary dispute on issues such as citizenship, equality rights, and civic culture that we will review in later chapters of this book. Some of the protagonists in this debate, like Prime Minister W.L. Mackenzie King and British Columbia Independent member A.W. Neill were very familiar with each other's positions on racial issues as they had been exchanging their views in the Commons for two decades. For Neill, and most of the other B.C. members, the Japanese attack on Pearl Harbor represented a once-in-a-lifetime opportunity to fulfil a driving political ambition – expulsion of all Japanese Canadians from the province. In their view, this ambition, supported by most British Columbians, had been thwarted by sentimental liberals elsewhere in Canada who had been blind to their warnings of coming catastrophe.

> We who have taken the position that I am now taking have been called all sorts of names. We have been called agitators. It is said that we are willing to exploit the interests of Canada for our own political advantage; that we are rabble-rousers, Jap-baiters, and that we have a very dangerous influence... Yes, we are all bad because we want a white British Columbia and not a place like Hawaii! Fifty years from now, unless something is done to stop it, all west of the

> Rockies will be yellow. I submit, Mr. Speaker, that we want but little; we simply want to be left alone, like New Zealand and Australia. I have no ill-will against the Japanese... I wish to be fair to the Japanese, and I think that if we expatriated them, as we ought to do, they should be given full justice in regard to their property, because I am strongly in favour of a Japan controlled by the Japanese, just as I am in favour of a Canada controlled by Canadians.[14]

King, on the other hand, had no such agenda. In his February 9, 1942 speech describing the measures to be taken against Japanese Canadians he outlined three "legitimate apprehensions" that the policies were meant to address: a) espionage, b) sabotage, and, c) the protection of Japanese Canadians from racial attacks – "the possibility of anti-Japanese riots in which military force might have to be used to restore order."[15] On this later point, King had been receiving reports from his officials in B.C. in early 1941 warning that public "feeling" in the province was "simply aflame."[16] King's sensitivity to the threat to public order had been raised in dramatic fashion earlier in his career when as Deputy Minister of Labour he had investigated the Vancouver anti-Asian riots of 1907. Chapter 5 will show that, in the immediate wake of these 1907 riots, the perceived political climate in the province had been judged so intolerant that the leadership of both the national Conservative and Liberal parties moved opportunistically towards acceptance of the political slogans of "White British Columbia" and "White Canada." King's investigation of the anti-Asian riots left a powerful impression on him: many years later he explained to the Commons that they had taught him of the "obligation that exists at all times to avoid as far as possible the danger of social and industrial unrest, to say nothing of the vaster possibility of international strife."[17]

In his February 9th speech, King promised Japanese Canadians that they would be justly treated and that "their persons and property will receive the full protection of the law." Although King's government did not in the end deliver on these promises, especially concerning property, it is significant that the tone is conciliatory, even respectful, and not confrontational. King concluded this speech with a call for mutual understanding and restraint on all sides:

> It will be recognized that Canadian citizens of Japanese race have been placed in a very difficult position. They are being asked to bear with patience inevitable hardships and losses. A situation of this kind can only be effectively met by an equal measure of tolerance and understanding on the part of the people of Canada generally. In the national interest it is of the utmost importance that the problem should be approached in this spirit.[18]

Ten days later, King again found himself trying to dampen the 'flames' of anti-Japanese Canadian feelings. This was in response to the reading of a telegram in the House sent by the Kelowna municipal council with demands that all male Japanese Canadians of military age be interned under strict supervision.

> Whereas under dominion regulations all male Japanese of military age have to vacate areas west of Cascade range by April 1st; and whereas apparently no supervision or restrictions have been made of this evacuation; and whereas these Japanese are steadily seeping into the Okanagan valley seeking to purchase land, residences and to settle, many of them coming in new automobiles and acting in a very truculent and insolent manner; and whereas public indignation is being roused to such an extent that violence against this infiltration may easily break out and unless stopped almost certainly will break out…

King countered not by sympathizing with the Kelowna council, or thanking their MP for transmitting this warning to the Commons, but by delivering a short lecture on the duty of parliamentarians to promote public order and not set the stage for "anti-Japanese riots."

> In replying to my hon. Friend, I think I ought perhaps to express just a word of caution with respect to the wording of messages and public utterances generally which may relate to the present position of Japanese nationals and other persons of Japanese origin in Canada at the present time. I need not say how critical the situation

is and how necessary it is, if we are to maintain law and order in the different communities and prevent hasty and unwarranted action on the part of individuals who may not be sufficiently appreciative of the effect of their actions, for all to be as restrained as possible in the language used in dealing with these difficult questions.[19]

Until mid-1944, King was pushed along by belligerent B.C. members who demanded an immediate commitment to deport all Japanese-Canadians after the war was over. He did not promise them anything, however, and was prepared to push back to some extent as well. In June of 1942, A.W. Neill accused the government of "pussyfooting" in the early stages of interning Japanese Canadians and voiced suspicion that "two officials at Ottawa" had intentionally dragged their feet. One, he claimed, was known in British Columbia "for his open and passionate advocacy of the Japanese, their rights and their wrongs and their privileges... This man was always ready, in letters to the press, and speeches, and one thing and another, to boost the supposed necessity of certain rights for the Japanese: 'why not give them votes,' and so on..."

King denied that these civil servants "dictated" wartime government policy regarding Japanese Canadians while at the same time defending their liberal perspective on human rights to Neill and the other B.C. members who were pressing for deportation: "There are gentlemen in the Department of External Affairs – fortunately – who have humane feelings in their breasts – which they are entitled to entertain..."[20] This prompted a fuming response from Neill in which he shows his contempt for King's "humane feelings."

> It is the feeling of the people in British Columbia, and it would be the feeling of the people in the rest of the country I am sure, if they were wise and informed, that at the close of the war these men [Japanese Canadians] should not be sent back to British Columbia but should be expatriated. The Prime Minister (Mr. Mackenzie King) talks about feelings of humanity, but I suggest that our duty is first to the people of Canada. This has been a canker all along and it will become worse and worse – it is nothing but a canker

in the heart of the country. These people are breeding rapidly, and they have but one mind: first and last they are Japanese. This is the time to take the necessary action in regard to them, when they are but 22,000 or 23,000 and not when we are overrun with 200,000 or 300,000.[21]

But King's endorsement of "humane feelings" for the interned Japanese Canadians struck a resonant chord with R.B. Hansen, then leader of the Conservative Opposition.

> ...with respect to the humaneness of the attitude of this government, I think that the people of Canada will sustain him in the principle has is endeavouring to enunciate. It must not be said that we departed from the spirit of British fair play with respect to a matter of this nature, not so much because of fear of reprisals... but, if I may say so, for our own self-respect.[22]

By mid-1944, with the campaign in the Pacific going well, King was prepared at last to show his hand on B.C. members' demands that all Japanese Canadians be deported after the war. His answer was not just a 'no' but it was a stinging repudiation of their demands firmly anchored in a liberal equality rights discourse.

> ...while problems of assimilation undoubtedly do present themselves even to loyal Japanese in Canada, nevertheless they are persons who have been admitted here to settle and become citizens, or who have been born into this free country of ours, and that we cannot do less than treat such persons fairly and justly... For the government to do otherwise would be an acceptance of the standards of our enemies and the negation of the purposes for which we are fighting... We must not permit in Canada the hateful doctrine of racialism which is the basis of the nazi system everywhere.[23]

Other members joined King in drawing a line between their liberal vision of racial equality and the 'discriminatory' and 'prejudiced' opinions of those B.C. members who they now denounced in no uncertain terms. M.J. Coldwell asked what was behind their raising "the problem of the citizens of the Japanese race who are in our midst"?

> I do not know why this problem is always called 'the Japanese problem'. We do not speak of the second, third or fourth generation of Germans as creating a German problem, but we speak of the Japanese problem... in my opinion it is copying the policies of Hitler to discriminate against any people because of their race, colour or creed.[24]

Toronto labour lawyer A.W. Roebuck lectured the B.C. members on citizenship, justice and rights.

> I hope that the hon. Member for Comox-Alberni (Mr. Neill) will not expect those who follow him in this debate to take part with him in his discussion of the Japanese question, and certainly not to follow him in some of his logic or attitude. It seems to me that the hon. Member loses a little of the influence he might otherwise possess in this house and in the country by too evident a dislike for the subject of his remarks. What he fails to appreciate in the policy of the Prime Minister is that it is guided not by likes and dislikes. We all have a right to like whom we please; kissing goes by favour, but statesmanship is based not upon favour but upon justice... It is not whether we like the Japanese or dislike them; they are human beings and have certain rights, and these rights must be respected, not for their sakes but for our own sakes... They are not Japanese: they are Canadian citizens of Japanese origin... when it comes to dealing with Canadian citizens born in this country or nationalized by us in a solemn way by legal process... these people are Canadian citizens and have a right to be treated as Canadian citizens... I am the champion of democracy, of justice and of right, applied to anybody; and I am not going to imbibe here the violent prejudices of the hon. Gentlemen from British Columbia.[25]

RACE-THINKING AND RACE POLITICS IN LATE NINETEENTH AND EARLY TWENTIETH CENTURY THOUGHT

The infamous case of the Japanese Canadian internment during World II is an excellent jumping off point for our book's survey of race-thinking[26] in the debates of the House of Commons during the near half century between 1880 and 1925. When we first began our review of Canada's wartime internment policy, parliamentarians appeared unanimous in their disregard for the human rights of Japanese Canadians. But a closer look at the Commons debates soon uncovered a vigourous dispute between those who promoted a collectively-based race politics against those who defended a counter narrative of individually-based liberal equality rights. Chapter 5 will document in considerable detail that this profound division over the political rights of Asian Canadians can be traced back to the 1880s and had subsequently proceeded without interruption over several decades.

Politics reflects social conflict and determines who gets what, when, and how. Japanese Canadians were significant losers at the beginning of Canada's Pacific war and British Columbia's anti-Asian members of the House of Commons were temporarily ascendant. In the end, however, their victory proved pyrrhic because as the hysteria created by Pearl Harbour faded into the background, their political opponents discredited them as prejudiced racists and linked their ideas with those of the odious Nazis. This terrible event was later to catalyse Canada's political progress towards its multicultural future.

As this book will focus on debate in the late nineteenth and early twentieth century Commons regarding race-thinking and race politics, we would do well at this point to consider the intellectual origins of these concepts. Scholars link the development of modern racism in European thought to its Enlightenment and Scientific Revolution of the 16th to 18th centuries. The Enlightenment turned away from the religious world view of Christianity focusing instead on rationality – the ability of reason to perfect the organization of human society. The companion Scientific Revolution drew inspiration from the older Greek philosophy of natural law which held that the universe is fundamentally orderly and can be understood by the application of human reason.

Before the Enlightenment, European collective identities were typically grounded in historical and religious categories: Christian, pagan, Muslim, and Jew. These categories were mutable to the extent that religious conversion could transform, say, a pagan into a Christian.[27] But with the process of consolidation of feudal political entities into larger territorially-based states along with the global expansion of European trade and colonization beyond the confines of Europe, new and more fixed group identities rooted in space, culture and biology began to emerge in relation to the social and military conflict that attended these upheavals and transformations. Biologically-grounded race-thinking did not spontaneously self-generate but rather took several centuries to mature.[28]

Racism is closely associated with military or economic struggles between peoples as stereotyped group identifications harden in the process of confrontation. Racism becomes formalized as an ideological justification for the domination of one group by another: As Bonilla-Silva observes, "historically the classification of a people in racial terms has been a highly political act associated with practices such as conquest and colonization, enslavement, peonage, indentured servitude, and, more recently, colonial and neocolonial labor immigration."[29] Haney Lopez stresses that the political process that forms or 'fabricates' races is reciprocal in nature – "races are constructed relationally, against one another, rather than in isolation," he says.[30]

Race is a relatively modern and fundamentally political idea, then, that relates to the internal and external power balance between social communities. Today's scholarship affirms that race is a socially constructed category without any meaningful biological basis. As Smedley and Smedley summarize, "the consensus among most scholars in fields such as evolutionary biology, anthropology, and other disciplines is that racial distinctions fail on all three counts — that is, they are not genetically discrete, are not reliably measured, and are not scientifically meaningful."[31] Or, as Kidd puts it; "a wide range of evidence drawn from the biological and medical sciences directly contradicts the layperson's assumption that external indicators of race are biologically meaningful. Race is quite literally no more than skin deep, as well as scientifically incoherent."[32] Beasley observes that "the 'races' familiar to us in the modern West were invented and elaborated" in the period between the early nineteenth century and "the maturity of modern genetics in the middle of the twentieth." And so, "the idea that there *are* biological human races in the more familiar sense, that blacks, whites, yellow... are the major subdivisions of biology *and* culture, belongs to a particular historical period."[33]

François Bernier's *Nouvelle division de la terre par les différentes espèces ou races qui l'habitent* (1664) represents the earliest Enlightenment attempt to classify humanity into races. Bernier proposed "two criteria" for distinguishing five races based on "a Eurocentric aesthetic of 'beauty' or 'handsomeness' and the presence or absence of the accoutrements of 'civilization' as Europeans understood them."[34]

Many other racial classification schemes loosely based on Eurocentric standards were to follow in the eighteenth and nineteenth century. An early and highly influential account was that of Carl Linnaeus in the tenth edition of his *Systema Naturae* (1758) where four human varieties were offered – Americanus (obstinate, merry, regulated by custom); Asiaticus (severe, greedy, ruled by opinions); Africanus (indolent, governed by caprice); and, Europaeus (gentle, inventive, governed by laws).[35] Linnaeus' work was followed through the late eighteenth and nineteenth century by a variety of attempts to classify scientifically 'races' by climate and geographical origins, facial angles, brain size and composition, skull shape, and linguistic origins. Happily for Europeans, these classifications always placed them on top of whatever racial hierarchy was proposed.[36] Still, following Beasley,

> the dominant view in the eighteenth century was of a human unity-across-colours, with the colour differences coming from degeneration: the various human groups had degenerated from the common stock of Adam, probably because of climate and environment. These differences were by no means set in stone... They merely represented poles within one human field – that is, one group shaded

off into the others with no clear breaks between them. Change was easy and fast. Because everyone had Adam and Eve as their common ancestor little more than 6,000 years before...[37]

Near the end of the eighteenth century, human classification schemes began to work from a radically different assumption: that humankind did not share common ancestors and that the supposed differing physical, intellectual and moral endowments of 'races' could be traced to their biologically distinct origins. Nineteenth century racial pseudo-sciences including physiognomy, craniology, phrenology, and comparative philology all developed from this premise. Warnings of European racial decline began to develop as a major and disquieting theme within this line of research. Robert Knox's *The Races of Man* (1850) and Arthur de Gobineau's *Essay on Inequality of the Human Races* (1853-1855) both declared that interbreeding between the races presented a serious danger as it could enfeeble and corrupt western civilization and lead to its eventual collapse.[38] Ferguson has observed that while in the seventeenth and eighteenth centuries some areas of the imperial world had been "a racial melting pot ...by 1901 there had been a worldwide revulsion against 'miscegenation'."[39]

During the nineteenth and early twentieth centuries, Europeans spread their control of the globe's land surface from 35 per cent in 1800, to 67 per cent in 1878, and to 84 per cent by 1914.[40] Race-thinking supplied a needed ideological underpinning for this unique moment in world history. But it was the publication of Charles Darwin's *Origin of the Species* (1859) that was to catapult widely held ideas about race hierarchy into the foreground of late nineteenth and early twentieth century European politics. Darwin's theory of evolution placed natural selection at the centre of an account explaining the variety of life on earth. Changes in species or varieties of life occur spontaneously or accidentally and afterwards more offspring of the best adapted variants survive.

Darwin's theory was not itself racist.[41] Indeed it explicitly ruled out that humans with different skin colors were different species or that some human groups were closer to apes than others. However, the crude outline of Darwin's theory was seized upon as a biological metaphor within European society to account for the existing domestic and international social order. In the evolutionary struggle, only the fittest could survive and so, social Darwinism contended, the international hierarchy imposed militarily on the world's peoples by Europeans was nothing less than biological natural selection in operation. Humanity's evolutionary more advanced races were exercising the "burden" of their superiority over backward races.

During this period, Europe's ongoing conquest of the world was reflected in a deeply rooted, widely pervasive, social Darwinist ideology. As Ferguson observes, "the idea of an ineradicable 'race instinct' became a staple of late nineteenth and early twentieth-century writing."[42] The lesson that was most often taken was that races/nations and their states would expand or decay. The social Darwinist assumptions glorifying military conflict and presaging World War I are clear in this passage from a 1911 book by German General Friedrich von Bernhardi

> War is a biological necessity of the first importance, a regulative element in the life of mankind which cannot be dispensed with, since without it an unhealthy development will follow, which excludes every advancement of the race, and therefore all real civilization. 'War is the father of all things.' The sages of antiquity long before Darwin recognized this... Might is at once the supreme right, and the dispute as to what is right is decided by the arbitrament of war. War gives a biologically just decision, since its decisions rest on the very nature of things...[43]

This kind of logic was widespread in Europe in the early twentieth century. For example, Karl Pearson, the first Galton professor of Eugenics at University College London, wrote in 1912 that "National progress depends on racial fitness and the supreme test of this fitness was war. When wars cease mankind will no longer progress for there will be nothing to check the fertility of inferior stock."[44]

CHALLENGES TO BIOLOGICAL RACE-THINKING AND RACE POLITICS

Deterministic race-thinking, however pervasive and growing in influence, was not the only big idea shaping the late nineteenth and early twentieth century international order. Some very significant strands of both religious and liberal political opinion emphasizing individual equality found themselves in serious dispute with the conclusions and policy prescriptions of racist pseudo-science.

From the outset, many Christians had significant theological difficulties with the division of humanity into biological races. The Old Testament presents Adam and Eve as the sole parents of all mankind – monogenesis. So dividing humanity into higher and lower species – polygenesis – could be considered heretical. For its part, the New Testament proclaims an unambiguous message of human equality and universal access to salvation – "Here there cannot be Greek and Jew, circumcised and uncircumcised, barbarian, Scythian, slave, free man, but Christ is all, and in all."[45]

Of course, it is certainly true that some Christians interpreted scripture and tradition as supporting racism.[46] Overall, however, Kidd records the "negative inhibitory influence" of Christian theology on the totalizing narratives of race 'science' and racist ideologies.

> ...during the Enlightenment, and even at the high noon of nineteenth-century racism, theological imperatives drove the conventional mainstream of science and scholarship to search for mankind's underlying unities. The emphasis of racial investigation was not upon divisions between races, but on race as an accidental, epiphenomal mask concealing the unitary Adamic origins of a single, extended human family... quietly, subtly and indirectly, theological needs drew white Europeans into a benign state of denial, a refusal to accept that human racial differences were anything other than skin deep.[47]

Spearheaded by evangelical Protestant Dissenters, the internationally successful nineteenth century British campaign to end the slave trade is an excellent example of the continuing power of these Christian beliefs in the oneness of man. The campaign's badge designed by Josiah Wedgewood and distributed in thousands, was an image of a manacled black slave on his knees with the motto: "Am I not a man and a brother?" Great Britain would face divine punishment if the evil of slavery was left uncorrected, the campaign contended. Ferguson observes that the anti-slavery campaign was "one of the first great extra-Parliamentary agitations" and represented the birth of pressure group politics.[48] Kaufmann and Pape determine that Dissenters were able to leverage successfully their hold on the balance of power in the British parliament to forward their abolition project even though the financial costs of the campaign to British society were very high – "roughly 1.8 per cent of national income over sixty years from 1808 to 1867."[49]

Even at the pinnacle of the influence of 'race science', the late nineteenth and early twentieth centuries, robust objections rooted in Christian theology were still being voiced. Protestant missions to the non-European world were built not around hierarchical and static notions of race, but around a binary Christian/heathen dichotomy. The Christian/heathen boundary not only *could* be crossed but *should* be crossed (by conversion). Snow records that as social Darwinism gained popular traction, missionaries were forced to react and develop an "anti-racist" discourse opposing 'race science.' These "anti-racist" discourses were fed back into society as a whole through the religious teachings of their denominations. Snow summarizes:

> Scientific racism explained human difference as a hierarchy of inherited, biologically deterministic racial characteristics, a hierarchy which could never be affected or changed by the "sentimental" work of missionaries to educate, enlighten, and convert. It was directly hostile to missionary work per se, and in fact defined itself partially by its rejection of missionary values of duty, mutual aid, charity, and equality of human worth. Without scientific racism,

and its loud derision for missionary practice, premises, and personnel, missionary ideology would probably never have developed an explicitly anti-racist project.[50]

Liberal ideas presented another site of serious challenge to the determinist lessons of racist pseudo-science. Baum argues that liberalism and racism are representative of "two faces of the Enlightenment's legacy that have always been in tension with each other." One seeks to understand nature so as to benefit from its control while the other promotes human freedom. And so, at the same historical moment as Enlightenment natural science was classifying "the earth's peoples into a handful of distinct 'races or species,' Locke famously declared that 'all mankind' was by nature free, 'equal and independent.'"[51]

In the nineteenth century, utilitarian liberals moved away from Locke's natural rights defence of an individual's life, liberty and estate toward a positive law model that demanded government operate on the principle of utility – the promotion of human happiness, intellectual advancement, and moral development. John Stuart Mill, the most widely-read utilitarian of the mid and late nineteenth century, supported European colonialism on the grounds that it was necessary for the progress of 'barbarian' and 'semi-barbarian' societies towards free representative government. Overall, however, Mill gave little weight to biological determinist arguments judging, in his 1848 *Principles of Political Economy*, that "of all the vulgar modes of escaping from the consideration of the effects of social and moral influences on the human mind, the most vulgar is that of attributing the diversities of conduct and character to inherent natural differences."[52] Mill was attacked in the 1860s for his race-denier views by James Hunt, the President of the Anthropological Society of London.[53]

J.S. Mill did not hold out hope that Britain's colonies were likely to progress to independent liberal democracies in the immediate future. But, like the Protestant missionaries of his era, Mill did not believe that biology determined the limits of what was possible. As Levin put it, for Mill hierarchies were fluid. Individuals could strive to become more cultivated and societies could ascend further up the ladder of civilization. The notion of a civilizing mission is open to obvious objections, but it does at least do colonized peoples the honour of assuming that their advancement is possible. It both designates a gulf between ruling and subject peoples yet concedes or at least intimates that, in the long term, that gulf is bridgeable. In principle, then, the future for both individuals and societies was quite open-ended. No peoples were barred from further development, though some might find it easier to attain than others.[54]

Pitts has stressed that while Mill "resisted racial or biological determinism," he nonetheless "tended to describe national characters through a series of dichotomies – advanced-backward, active-passive, industrious-sensuous, sober-excitable – and to assign the more flattering labels predominantly to the English and the Germans, and the latter to the Irish, French, southern Europeans and 'Orientals' (with characters deteriorating as one moved south and east)." Mill also emphasized a "quite crude distinction" between civilized and barbarous peoples as the justification for British colonial rule since "civilized despots were the only hope of nations with no internal spring of progress."[55]

If racism is understood as a political construction justifying unequal power relations between communities in conflict, then the liberalism of J.S. Mill certainly did its part to legitimize the then existing imperial status quo. But while Mill may have agreed in a general way with the shorter term policy goals of the biological racists in maintaining the rule of empire over 'barbarians' and 'semi-barbarians', it needs to be underlined that his liberal analysis left the door wide open for critiques of biological determinism and the development of an anti-racist discourse.

ANGLO-SAXONISM, BRITISH IMPERIALISM, AND RACE-THINKING

Just as post-Confederation Canada cannot be properly understood outside of its specialized resource-producing role in the international economy, so too must we locate Canada within the cultural/ideological realm of British political and military imperialism and understand the centrality of this location to the production of Canadian ethnic/racial relations during that era. In 1897, the British Empire was "the most extensive in world history" controlling around one quarter of the globe's land surface and population.[56]

Canada was by the definition of its founding constitutional document *'British* North America' and its citizens were by choice and rights self-governing British subjects. Prime Minister Sir Charles Tupper, who was a former Nova Scotia premier, a father of Confederation, and Canadian High Commissioner to the United Kingdom (1883-1895), described Canada's status within the British Empire as being "practically independent." In the years following Confederation, he said,

> Canada rose rapidly to a status that had never before been occupied by any British colony or any outside portion of the British Empire. I need not remind you that, so far as government is concerned, Canada is practically independent. I need not remind you that, so far as measures relating to the internal life of Canada are concerned, we have practically the uncontrolled administration of our own affairs... I need not remind the House that under this improved status, foreign affairs touching Canada are to a large extent placed under our control – that arrangements have been made, with the hearty approval and assent of Her Majesty's Government, by which Canada practically negotiates her own treaties, with the advice and assistance and support of the great Empire of which we form a part.[57]

At the same historical moment when Britain was involved in a 'Scramble for Africa' that ended with it holding a roughly one-third share of that continent, Canada was incorporating the vast North-West Territories of the northern half of North America formerly controlled by the Hudson's Bay Company.[58] Canada was a massive presence on the popularly displayed turn-of-the-century world maps displaying the British Empire in pink (or red) and was vital to the sun never being able to set on it. It is understandable why most Canadians of this era would identify themselves with British imperialist ideas.[59] As Canada's first prime minister famously put it in 1891, "a British subject I was born, and a British subject I will die."[60]

So what did late nineteenth and early twentieth century British subjects think about nationality, political culture, and race? The answer is that there can be no one simple answer. As we have already delineated in this chapter, the British in very general terms approached these questions from several directions including their robust evangelical Christian and liberal political traditions alongside a more recent narrative drawn from a biologically-based social Darwinism. As Bell explains, "levels of civilization could be assessed in relation to theology, technological superiority, ascribed racial characteristics, economic success, political institutions, individual moral and intellectual capacity, or (as was typically the case) some combination of these... the Victorians were... far from unanimous in their conceptions of global order; there was no single imperial imaginary."[61]

Central here to the specific British discourse on nationality and race was the very old and commonly held idea that the British held a unique genius for government and this genius found expression in individual political liberty, democratic institutions of government, and honest and effective bureaucratic administration. This genius was often styled as 'Anglo-Saxonism.' Horsman details how the "myth of Anglo-Saxon England" had its origins in the sixteenth century break of the Church of England with the Roman Catholic Church. The seventeenth century struggles between King and Parliament further refined this myth: "parliamentarians found in the Anglo-Saxons a historical base for their arguments: the supposed antiquity of Parliament and of English common law provided a rationale for opposition to royal pretensions."

Until the nineteenth century, Anglo-Saxonism "was in large part non-racial" although it commonly supposed that freedom was brought to England by Germanic tribes. "The love of liberty, a trait of the Germanic peoples had... been transposed by the

Anglo-Saxons in England into a system of free institutions," Horsman says. But by the later eighteenth century, anglo-saxonism began to take on a more racialized form. Still, it was not until the 1840s that biologically-based narratives of Anglo-Saxonism began to take a hold in influential intellectual circles. Anglo-Saxons, it was said, were a branch of the ancient liberty-loving Teutonic race which had been responsible for liberating Europe from the deadening hand of Roman imperial despotism. "By the middle years of the nineteenth century," Horsman claims, "the idea of a superior Anglo-Saxon race regenerating a world of lesser races was firmly ingrained in English thinking."[62]

However, Mandler argues that the development of "biological racism and organic nationalism" was inhibited in Britain as compared to continental Europe during the first half of the nineteenth century: "the ladder of civilisation, rather than the branching tree of peoples and nations, remained the dominant metaphor." In part, this was because of Britain's relative isolation from the French revolutionary wars and the 1848 revolutions. But it was also due to the "determinedly universalistic and monogenetic" views of its liberal and evangelical Christian traditions emphasizing a "civilizational perspective… potentially universal, available to all peoples." Finally, most of the British "intellectual and political establishment" saw England "as the directive centre of a multi-national kingdom and empire, precisely the form that advanced civilisations should take."[63]

Porter's analysis of "early and mid-Victorian" British school texts led him to conclude that a faith in human progress was "far more central" to their understanding of the world than a deterministic biology-based racism.

> Other peoples were categorized in terms of the 'stages of progress' they had reached, rather than as species… Their cultures were frequently plotted against the graph of Britain's own historical development, with native Americans being put on a level with pre-Roman Britons, Africans located in the English 'dark' or 'middle' ages, and Indians and Chinese put somewhere around the sixteenth to eighteenth centuries… Generally the belief was that the tran-

sition though these 'stages' was inevitable, simply the product of 'enlightenment'... It was for this reason that the worst crime non-Europeans could commit was to deliberately cut themselves off from such enlightenment, as the Chinese and Japanese notoriously did. The importance of environment (as opposed to 'race') seemed corroborated by the oft-observed phenomenon that civilizations could 'decline' as well as progress...

Porter insisted on the "non-racist nature of this kind of world view" as it lacked a belief in the "impermeability of ethnic differences." Yes, he admitted, this 'world view' was 'arrogant', 'prejudiced', 'culturist', but the same time "fundamentally liberal and optimistic." This distinction was he says "important to contemporaries" and undermined biological determinism. "It allowed for the possibility – indeed the likelihood, even the inevitability – that all peoples (or nearly all) could, like Britain herself, 'progress.' It at least gave the 'natives' the chance to catch up."[64]

While the influence of biological determinist and social Darwinist race thinking may have been delayed, somewhat muted and even forcefully contested in nineteenth century British political culture, it certainly made its mark in the decades immediately preceding World War I. Ferguson relates how an 1863 public lecture that claimed Africans were a separate species between apes and Europeans by James Hunt (noted above as having attacked J.S. Mill for not employing race analysis) was poorly received and hissed by some in the audience. "Yet," he says, "within a generation such views had become the conventional wisdom."[65] Douglas Lorimer also records how the biological determinist ideas of "Knox, Hunt, and the Anthropological Society of London" met with "public ridicule and rejection by leaders of the scientific community" in the 1850s and 1860s. After 1880, however, scientific racism in Victorian Britain had become more powerful, acceptable, institutionalized and professionalized with "the development of a technical vocabulary and the application of statistical methods."[66]

Lorimer further argues that until the 1860s Victorians tended "to adopt… an ethnocentric rather than a racist stance." This meant that although "alien cultures" were commonly judged inferior by "British standards," the possibility was still admitted that outsiders could in time conform to the "supposedly superior" British way of "civilized" life. But from the 1860s onwards, "a more stridently racist stance" based in biological determinism began to emerge. Foreigners were increasingly placed in "racial categories" and judged

> inferior by reason of their inherited characteristics. Conversely, it was assumed that the English were members of the Anglo-Saxon race, and were superior due to their innate physical, intellectual and emotional make-up. In this new racialist vision, the ethnocentric hope of civilizing the world in conformity with British standards seem to be the naïve fantasy of an aged, sentimental, and now senile generation.[67]

The movement towards biological determinism and racial Anglo-Saxonism can be seen in the British school textbooks of the later nineteenth and early twentieth centuries. Heathorn's review shows that Britain's strengths were portrayed by these texts as being derived from "Anglo-Saxon racial characteristics – love of liberty, courage, patience and reserve, honesty and plain dealing." The conquering Anglo-Saxons had pushed aside the Celts "according to that apparently inevitable law of nature by which the weaker race disappears before the stronger." The Norman Conquest infused another strain of Teutonic blood "and the two races became one nation. It was easy for them to mix, for English and Norman were really brothers in blood. The Norman was a Northman, just as the Saxons and Danes were." Anglo-Saxonism was also employed to explain the expansion and dominance of the British Empire over lesser races. "As the highest up on the racial scale it was the duty and responsibility of the English to rule those 'lower down,'" it was said.[68]

"Greater Britain" was one influential turn of the twentieth century 'big political idea' derived generally from Anglo-Saxonism. Built on an imperial federation of Britain, the 'white dominion' self-governing settler colonies and even, some enthusiasts imagined, the United States, Bell observed that "greater Britain was to be an Anglo-Saxon political space, a racial polity." The colonies of military occupation like India, where three-quarters of British subjects lived, were not included in this vision. India was, Bell concludes "still an imperial possession, still alien" while "the settler colonies were an extension of the British (or more commonly English) nation, constituting an 'empire of liberty' that was to be transmuted into a single postimperial global formation."[69] Burgess succinctly expressed the views of the imperial federation enthusiasts towards India: "Nobody ever seriously contemplated a situation whereby all the English-speaking parts of the empire could be outvoted by Hindus."[70]

Canadian imperialists of this period swam in the same currents that we have seen to be characteristic of British political thinking on nationality, political culture and race. According to Berger, it seemed undeniable to many English Canadians "that the Anglo-Saxon race displayed a special genius for self-government and political organization." Racial explanations were "conventional as well as respectable." But Berger also points to some "confusion" about how race categories were employed. This confusion reproduces the split we have observed in nineteenth century British race thinking between a more-open ended evolutionary understanding of race and political development and the more rigid determinism of biological models of racism.

> it is not clear, for instance, whether they generally believed racial character to be permanently fixed and unchangeable or they really thought that habits and aptitudes could be learned and acquired. Sometimes the phrase 'Anglo-Saxon race' was simply a synonym for a total culture which was itself understood to be the product of history and not only racial instincts; sometimes, race was quite explicitly associated with the biological analogies of Darwinian science. However vague and confused it might be, race was none the less frequently identified with aptitudes for liberty and self-government.[71]

Berger's observation of societal "confusion" over the meaning of 'race' is mirrored in our study of late nineteenth and early twentieth century parliamentarians. On the one hand, we will see that 'race' could refer to biologically-defined communities rooted in a supposedly shared ancestry and, on the other hand, it could refer to sociologically-defined communities sharing a common history, culture, language, and religion. It will become evident to readers of subsequent chapters that the word 'race' was employed somewhat carelessly in Commons debate in the sense that speakers could have in mind one meaning or the other or, sometimes and confusingly, both. Context will prove to be everything in guiding the reader towards a determination of what the speaker intended to say.

OUTLINE OF THE BOOK

We began this chapter with the question of when and how Canada's political character 'transformed' from racist intolerance to accommodative multiculturalism. A recently published university-level textbook, *Racism in Canada*, tells us that racist beliefs were "common" in turn of the century Canada. By the 1930s it is said that "there was already some discomfort with what we would now call racist thinking" but it was only after World War II and the Holocaust that "the notion that there was something abhorrent with theories that categorized human value in terms of race or biology crystallized..."[72] The view of this textbook faithfully reflects the chronology set out in more specialized studies of Canadian society. For example, Backhouse posits that modern racism was a product of the post-Enlightenment "white scientific community" in the service of rationalizing "colonial hierarchies" and reached "something of a pinnacle" during "the first two decades of the twentieth century." Indeed, "the subject of race inferiority was beyond critical reach in the late nineteenth century. Until about the third decade of the present century, most people in the so-called western world, including most social scientists and historians, took for granted the hereditary inferiority of non-white peoples." However, influenced by "a new breed of anthropologists" in the 1930s and in the face of the "horrendous implications" of Nazism, "Western governments ushered in a host of policies that proclaimed an intent to eliminate discrimination on the basis of race" during the late 1940s.[73]

Generalizations concerning the supposed near universality of racism in late nineteenth and early twentieth century Canada characterize much of the existing historical research. Given that the analysis of racially discriminatory state policies focuses on the victimization of minorities, it is not altogether surprising that too little weight might be given to the notion that race-thinking was complicated and contested and a far from settled matter in the minds of the political elite. For example, Buchignani, Indra, and Srivastava in their study of discriminatory legislation against South Asian Canadians forcefully reject the idea that racism was primarily a British Columbia "aberration uncharacteristic of Canada at the time." In fact, they assert, "British Columbia racial stereotypes differed little except in intensity from those in the rest of Canada…" "Liberal sentiment" was demonstrably feeble as it was "never strong enough to force a single significant change in federal policy toward South Asians."[74] Troper, accounting for the administrative barrier constructed against African American immigrants to Canada by the Department of the Interior, offers his view that "although Canadians may self-righteously have prided themselves on their distance from American racial troubles, Canadians proved as racist as their American neighbours."[75]

This chapter suggests that development of race-thinking in British North America is considerably more complex than a one-dimensional sketch that suggests an uncomplicated historical progression from a "common" acceptance of racism to the idea that there was "something abhorrent" in racial theories. Although it was growing in influence in the late nineteenth century Canadian political life, biological determinism never had the field entirely to itself. It was challenged by long-established Christian traditions of human equality based on religious doctrine along with widely-held liberal ideas of civilizational evolution and political development that also supported equality rights. No question that both Christian and liberal perspectives were often circumscribed by the ethnocentric privilege they gave to European culture and support they offered to the imperial rule of Europeans over the rest of the world. Still, their view of the political future was far more open-ended than that of the biological racists. There is no path from biological racism to multiculturalism. On the other hand, late nineteenth and early twentieth century arguments for equality or equal treatment based on liberal political theory or Christian values both undermined the legitimacy of a biologically determinist racism and helped to point in the direction of a more inclusive Canadian polity after World War II.

Following on from this introduction, the remaining chapters of *Blood Must Tell* will survey debates of the Canadian House of Commons during four and a half decades between 1880 and 1925 to report how race-thinking and ethnic identity in this era was articulated and debated on the Commons floor by its members. Although encompassing no more than a subset of opinion in Canadian society as a whole, the Commons nonetheless provides an especially good focus for research on the reflection, formation, representation and contestation of race thinking in Canada during these decades. Its ethnic membership was overwhelmingly drawn from the dominant Anglo-Celtic and French communities and it was filled with lawyers and other educated and articulate men of class privilege. In many instances these elected representatives were voicing popular opinions as expressed through the concerns of their constituents or in newspaper reports and editorials.

Our book's examination of parliamentary debates is first and foremost a study of ideas rather than of public policies or personalities. Common threads in ideas of race and identity are traced across policy fields, across nearly half a century of time, and across 'races' in the sense that relations between Canadians of European origins are explored alongside relations between Canadians of European and non-European origins. As befits a study of political ideas, parliamentary speakers have when necessary been quoted at length in order that the reader can be confident that opinions have been properly interpreted.[76] And, in order to keep our focus on the debate over ideas of race and identity, the partisan, regional and occupational identities of Commons speakers are introduced only when they help to contextualize their statements. The reader should keep in mind that we are surveying a historical period where members were less scripted by their party leadership than is the case today and could, and did, speak more spontaneously on matters of personal conscience.

We should always remember that these parliamentary debates, insofar as they reflected abstract political ideas and principles, were also oriented towards political practice – the 'authoritative allocation of values' – in the form of state policies. Canadians are fortunate to have an extensive literature of case studies, relied on and cited throughout this volume, that examine racially discriminatory policies and administrative practices during this period. But this volume seeks to expand upon what has already been accomplished in this field. What is being attempted here is a record neither of the particulars of these policy decisions nor of how the opinions of individual members might have evolved and changed over their lifetimes. Instead, we seek to frame a wide-angle photograph of the considerable variety of ideas on race and identity that were articulated within the Commons during this era. At the foreground of this photograph are members vigourously and heatedly disagreeing with each other. In subsequent chapters, we will see that it was scarcely possible to stand in the House to make a speech denigrating a 'race,' without someone rising in principled objection to remarks that they considered unBritish, unchristian, illiberal, or just plain prejudiced. Racial determinism was met head-on by those who rejected the lessons of racism thereby setting the political stage for the post-World War II development of contemporary multicultural Canada.

Race-thinking, as noted earlier in this chapter, is grounded in the power relations of the international system. Chapter 2, then, will take up the pattern of thinking concerning the British Empire among Canada's parliamentarians during the 1880-1925 period. How did their understanding of the international politics of this era influence their attitudes on race and identity in Canada? The answer to this question will allow us to trace and give meaning to debates on relations between European 'races' in Canada (Chapter 3), relations between Canadians of European origin and native peoples (Chapter 4), and relations between Canadians of European origin and Canadians of Asian, South Asian and African origins (Chapter 5.) Four general themes will emerge as critical to the debates recorded in Chapters 3, 4, and 5: the British Empire, Christianity and liberalism, racial pseudo-science and biological determinism, and political representation. In pursuing these themes, the reader will be brought to the view that Canadian race-thinking in this era cannot be confined within watertight European, Native, and non-European categories but must instead be understood as whole taking place within and between these 'racial' categories (Chapter 6).

Notes

1. Canada, House of Commons, *Debates*, August 4, 1944. p. 5948.
2. Richard Gwyn, "John A. Macdonald was ahead of his time," *Ottawa Citizen*, August 23, 2012.
3. For example, see "Japanese Internment: British Columbia wages war against Japanese Canadians," CBC Learning, Canada: A People's History. Accessed September 20, 2012. http://www.cbc.ca/history/EPISCONTENTSE1EP14CH3PA3LE.html

4. *Debates*, September 5, 1958. p. 4641.

5. Ibid., April 2, 1984. p. 2623. Could Trudeau have been unaware of the historical record of the internment of Japanese Americans in the United States in the face of a constitutionally-protected Bill of Rights? In 1944, the Supreme Court upheld "the mass incarceration of 120,000 Americans of Japanese ancestry during World War II without charges, notice, trial or due process, and without any evidence of espionage and sabotage by persons of Japanese ancestry." Susan Kiyomi Serrano and Dale Minami, "Korematsu v. United States: A 'Constant Caution' in a Time of Crisis," *Asian Law Journal*, Vol. 10, Issue 1, 2003, pp. 37-38.

6. Ibid., September 22, 1988, pp. 19499-19500. Mulroney went on to marry this apology to the historically revisionist notion that "the Canada of our ancestors" was a "pluralist" and "tolerant" country and that Japanese Canadian internment during World War II "went against the very nature" of the country that "our ancestors worked to build." Six weeks prior to Mulroney's statement, President Ronald Regan signed into U.S. law the Civil Liberties Act of 1988, Restitution for World War II internment of Japanese-Americans and Aleuts. For an analysis of the successful lobbying campaign that convinced Congress to support this legislation see Leslie T. Hatamiya, *Righting a wrong: Japanese Americans and the passage of the Civil Liberties Act of 1988*. Stanford: Stanford University Press, 1993. For an insider's discussion of the Canadian lobbying campaign behind Mulroney's apology, see Roy Miki, *Redress: Inside the Japanese Canadian call for justice*. Vancouver: Raincoast Books, 2004.

7. In his memoirs, John Diefenbaker asserted that he did speak out against the wartime treatment of Japanese Canadians because: "...to take a whole people and to condemn them as wrongdoers because of race was something I could not accept... The course that was taken against Japanese Canadians was wrong. I said it over and over again. It was considered unbelievable that I would take this stand... I was strongly criticized..." John G. Diefenbaker, *One Canada: Memoirs of the Right Honourable John G. Diefenbaker, The Crusading Years 1895-1956*. Toronto: Macmillan of Canada, 1975. In fact, however, there is no record of

Diefenbaker speaking in the 1942 or 1943 Commons concerning this issue. As one study of Diefenbaker concluded "...in truth, he did not utter one word in Parliament in defence of the Japanese at the time of their internment... He would oppose the order given to intern the Japanese, but only retroactively." Robert M. Belliveau, "Mr. Diefenbaker, Parliamentary Democracy, and the Canadian Bill of Rights," M.A. thesis, University of Saskatchewan, 1992.

8. For a discussion of the history, operation, and functions of institutionalized adversarialism in the Canadian House of Commons, see Thomas A. Hockin, *Government in Canada*. Toronto: McGraw-Hill Ryerson, 1976. "A persistent complaint about the adversary process in Canadian politics is that Canadian political parties at the Federal level are not clear ideological enemies, that they do little more than conduct furious arguments about the minor issues which divide them... [but] the adversary activity of opposition parties [in the Commons] helps to ensure that the executive cannot completely dominate the atmosphere in which decisions are made." p. 194.

9. In this instance, opinion in the Commons mirrored opinion in Canadian society. See Ross Lambertson, *Repression and Resistance: Canadian Human Rights Activists, 1930-1960*. Toronto: University of Toronto Press, 2005. "There was also little opposition to the initial violation of Japanese Canadians' civil liberties, when in early 1942 they were treated as potential subversives and forcibly relocated away from the west coast, losing much of their property in the process. While it is today conventional wisdom that the internment policy was an unjustifiable violation of liberal-democratic values, in 1942 virtually all Canadians saw it as a necessary evil, justifiable in terms of national security, a defence against the possibility of anti-Japanese mob violence, and a way of solving the 'Japanese problem' by helping them to disperse and assimilate. Even the CCF, which had long advocated equal rights for Asian Canadians, was unwilling to criticize the policy, and the churches were likewise on the side of the government." p. 102. Pressure from civil society on the B.C. coast was very intense, even, as MP Angus MacInnis judged it at the time, "almost hysterical." Commons, *Debates*, July 2, 1942. pp. 3878-3879. For an excellent account of the explosion

of B.C. public opinion against Japanese-Canadians in early 1942 see Peter Ward, *White Canada Forever: Popular Attitudes and Public Policy Toward Orientals in British Columbia*, Third Edition. Montreal, McGill-Queens University Press, 2002. "The public outcry… reached unprecedented volume… thousands of west coast whites petitioned Ottawa for the immediate evacuation of all Japanese. Individuals, farm organizations, municipal councils, civil defence units, constituency associations, service clubs, patriotic societies, trade unions, citizens' committees, chambers of commerce – even the Vancouver and District Lawn Bowling Association – all demanded the total evacuation of Japanese from coastal areas… Never before had west coast race relations been so seriously strained." p. 151

10. Angus and Grace MacInnis. *Oriental Canadians, outcasts or citizens?* Vancouver: Federationist Publishing Company, 1943. Accessed August 20, 2012. http://content.lib.sfu.ca/cdm/compoundobject/collection/ubc/id/2844/rec/6

11. Commons, *Debates*, July 2, 1942. p. 3878. Other CCF members eloquently articulated the racial equality position of the party in wartime speeches decrying Nazi crimes against the Jews in Europe but had nothing specific to say about the predicament of the Japanese Canadians. For example, Clarence Gillis (Cape Breton) "So far as I am concerned the human race is one family. Where you were born, what is your religion, or your nationality, or the colour of your skin, is an accident of birth; you are not responsible for it. Unless we break down this idea of merely regarding as Canadians those who were born in Canada, I can see very little hope for the future of the world on the basis of the promises which are now being made concerning post-war policies." July 12, 1943. p. 4655 and Stanley Knowles (Winnipeg North Centre) "…we are trying to establish a better world in which we will get rid of racial hatred, prejudice, and antagonism." July 9, 1943.

12. Commons, *Debates*, July 12, 1943. pp. 4680-4681.

13. Ibid., p. 4681. B.C. member A.W. Neill dismissed this anecdote with sarcasm: "…what percentage is one out of 25,937?" p. 4682.

14. Ibid., February 19, 1942. p. 719.

15. Ibid., February 9, 1942. p. 399.

16. Patricia Roy, *The Triumph of Citizenship: The Japanese and Chinese in Canada, 1941-67.* Vancouver: UBC Press, 2007. p. 61. Reviewing many primary sources beyond the parliamentary debates examined here, she concludes that "...a major reason for moving Japanese Canadians from the West Coast was to protect them lest physical violence follow verbal attacks." p. 66 Roy suggests that some contemporary observers saw interning Japanese Canadians as a "version of protective custody." p. 65. This was how Grace MacInnis, a CCF leader in this era of B.C. politics, presented it in an interview in 1973 "...when the war came finally after Pearl Harbor, the climate was such that nobody in the NDP or CCF as it was at that time, was urging that the Japanese be left here. It would have been bloodshed and great, great trouble all around if this had been done. What our people did was to devote themselves ... up until then we had urged complete rights and so on and we weren't going back on that. But the situation of hysteria was so great that I don't think it would have been a good idea at all to insist on them staying there because there would have [been] all hell to pay. So what our people did was to concentrate on trying to get them removed and looked after and cared for as well as they could... It was a choice of which of two evils was the worst." Quoted in Werner Cohn, "Persecution of Japanese Canadians and the Political Left in British Columbia, December 1941 - March 1942," *BC Studies*, no. 68, Winter 1985-86., pp. 3-22. Accessed August 20, 2012. http://www.wernercohn.com/Japanese.html Ward records that in February of 1942 King believed that there was "every possibility of riots" on the west coast. *White Canada Forever*, p. 155.

17. Commons, *Debates*, May 8, 1922, p. 1556. For a study of King's involvement in the post-riot crisis management strategy of the Laurier government see Julie F. Gilmour, *Trouble on Main Street: Mackenzie King, Reason, Race and the 1907 Vancouver Riots*. Toronto: Allen Lane, 2014.

18. Ibid., February 9, 1942. p. 399. King might have also considered the precedent set during the early months of World War I in the establishment of Canadian internment camps for enemy aliens – Germans and Austro-Hungarian Empire nationals – where

humanitarian motives had factored in since many were indigent and unemployable at a time of economic recession. See Desmond Morton, "Sir William Otter and Internment Operations in Canada during the First World War," *Canadian Historical Review*, March 1974. p. 38. C.J. Doherty, Minister of Justice in 1918, told the Commons that the British government had asked that military age men of enemy nationality not be allowed to leave Canada during the war to prevent them from enlisting in opposing armies. The Canadian government had proceeded accordingly to intern those viewed as "hostile" but also significant numbers "under the inspiration of the sentiment of compassion" since they had been discharged from their jobs and "these aliens were starving in some of our cities… we interned these people because we felt that, saying to them, 'you shall not leave the country,' we were not entitled to say, 'you shall starve within the country.'" *Debates*, April 22, 1918, p. 1018. Just as it had in World War I internment, co-operation with wartime allies also figured into World War II decision-making concerning Japanese Canadians. As King told the Commons, "in handling the Japanese problem we shall attempt, in so far as it seems desirable, to maintain a policy that in a sense can be considered as part of a continental policy. The situation in the United States in a great many essentials is the same as our own, and to the extent that it seems desirable we shall endeavour to ensure that our policy takes account of the policies which are being applied south of the border." Ibid., August 4, 1944, p. 5916. For a more complete discussion of wartime coordination, see Roger Daniels, "The Decisions to Relocate the North American Japanese: Another Look," *Pacific Historical Review*, 51 (1982).

19. Commons, *Debates*, February 19, 1942. p. 706.
20. Ibid., June 19, 1942. p. 3485.
21. Ibid., p. 3487.
22. Ibid., pp. 3488-3489.
23. Ibid., August 4, 1944. p. 5948.
24. Ibid., p. 5931.
25. Ibid., p. 5949.

26. My use of this term is inspired by the seminal argument of Hannah Arendt in her "Race-Thinking before Racism," *The Review of Politics*, Vol. 6, No. 1 (Jan., 1944), pp. 36-73. Here she presented race-thinking as a precursor to the development of a full-blown political ideology of racism. "...an ideology differs from a simple opinion in that it claims to possess either the key of history, or the solution of all the 'Riddles of the Universe,' or the intimate knowledge of the hidden universal laws which are supposed to rule nature and man ...every full-fledged ideology has been created, continued and improved as a political weapon and not as a theoretical doctrine," she said. Central to the transformation of race-thinking into racism, she observed, was the effect of "imperialist politics" on the international system. This volume likewise argues that during the period surveyed Canada's political, economic, and cultural location in the international system determined the context for debates over race and identity.

27. See Andreas Osiander, *Before the State: Systemic Political Change in the West from the Greeks to the French Revolution*. Oxford : Oxford University Press, 2007. "only the universal community, christendom, was characterized by a clear distinction between inside and outside, between members and non-members: one was a christian or one was not (to be sure, there was estrangement between the Church of Rome and the Church of Constantinople, but, despite everything, not to the point of denying that the other was christian). Even here, it is worth noting that it was not difficult to become a christian - much less so than it usually is to acquire the citizenship of a 'nation' state... Within christendom no division between particular communities could be total. Politically, no one could be a foreigner within christendom. Outsiders to one's own particular in-group might be disliked, even hated, but could never be considered totally alien. Whoever they were, they remained 'brothers' (or 'sisters') - the traditional christian form of address..." pp. 247-248.

28. See Nicholas Hudson, "'Nation to 'Race': The Origin of Racial Classification in Eighteenth-Century Thought." *Eighteenth-Century Studies*, Vol. 29, No. 3 (Spring, 1996). p. 250 "European explorers certainly imagined themselves as superior to all the peoples they

encountered. But this sense of superiority was founded not on a race hierarchy, but on the belief that Europeans had achieved a level of civilization unknown in other nations. African and American peoples were scorned as 'beastly' (or often as 'rustic') to the extent that they appeared to fall short of European ideas of urbanity and sophistication… And this awareness of "national" differences outweighed anything approaching a modern tendency to identify a particular skin-color or physiognomy with a 'race.'"

29. Eduardo Bonilla-Silva, "Rethinking Racism: Toward a Structural Interpretation," *American Sociological Review*, Vol. 62, No. 3 (Jun., 1997), p. 471.

30. Ian F. Haney Lopez, "The Social Construction of Race" in *Critical Race Theory: the cutting edge*, Second Edition. Eds. R. Delgado and J. Stefancic. Philadelphia: Temple University Press, 2000. p. 168.

31. Audrey Smedley and Brian D. Smedley, "Race as Biology Is Fiction, Racism as a Social Problem Is Real: Anthropological and Historical Perspectives on the Social Construction of Race." *American Psychologist*, January 2005. p. 16.

32. Colin Kidd, *The Forging of Races: Race and Scripture in the Protestant Atlantic World, 1600-2000.* Cambridge: Cambridge University Press, 2006. p. 3. Further, "All theories of race – from the simplest and most obvious to the most sophisticated and contorted – are examples of cultural construction superimposed upon arbitrarily selected features of human variation. All racial taxonomies – whether popular or scientific – are the product not of nature but of the imagination combined with inherited cultural stereotyping as well – to be fair – as the empirical observation of genuine (though superficial, trivial and inconsequential) biological differences." pp. 8-9.

33. Edward Beasley, *The Victorian Reinvention of Race: New Racisms and the Problem of Grouping in the Human Sciences.* New York: Routledge, 2010. p. 9.

34. Bruce Baum, *The Rise and Fall of the Caucasian Race: A Political History of Racial Identity.* New York: New York University Press, 2006. p. 55.

35. John P. Jackson Jr. and Nadine M. Weidman, *Race, Racism, and Science: Social Impact and Interaction.* New Brunswick, N.J.: Rutgers University Press, 2006. p. 12.

36. As Baum, *Rise and Fall of the Caucasian Race,* observes, "Race, in short, is an effect of power… the science itself was thoroughly political, with its guiding assumptions and questions informed by prevailing relations of power in society." p. 8

37. Beasley, *Victorian Reinvention of Race,* p. 10.

38. Mike Hawkins, *Social Darwinism in European and American Thought, 1860-1945: Nature as Model and Nature as Threat.* Cambridge: Cambridge University Press, 1997. pp. 184-185.

39. Niall Ferguson, *The War of the World: Twentieth Century Conflict and the Descent of the West.* London: Penguin Press, 2006. He says, "By this time, the idea that miscegenation implied degeneration, and that criminality was connected to the ratio of native to white blood, had generally been accepted in expatriate circles. Throughout the Empire, there was also a growing (and largely fantastic) obsession with the sexual threat supposedly posed to white women by native men." pp. 19-21.

40. Paul Kennedy, *The Rise and Fall of the Great Powers: Economic Change and Military Conflict from 1500 to 2000.* London: Fontana Press, 1989. p. 192.

41. See Robert C. Bannister, *Social Darwinism: Science and Myth in Anglo-American Social Thought.* Philadelphia: Temple University Press, 1979. Chapter 1. Beasley, *Victorian Reinvention of Race* affirms in Chapter 6 that while the earlier Darwin was animated by anti-racist sentiments, his later work denies racial categories while at the same time relying on them in suggesting that cultural differences can become physical differences.

42. Niall Ferguson, *Empire: The Rise and Demise of the British World Order and the Lessons for Global Power.* New York: Basic Books, 2002. p. 260.

43. Friedrich von Bernhardi, *Germany and the Next War,* excerpted in *Sources of European History Since 1900,* Second Edition. Eds. M. Perry, M. Berg and J. Krukones. Boston: Wadsworth Cengage Learning, 2011. pp. 43-44.

44. Ferguson, *Empire*. p. 261

45. Colossians 3:11, and similarly, "There is neither Jew nor Greek, there is neither slave nor free, there is neither male nor female; for you are all one in Christ Jesus." Galacians 3:28. Such passages were traditionally taught by Christian theologians to stand alongside Jesus Christ's message offering salvation not only to the Jews but to all of humankind as in John 10:16 where Jesus says "And other sheep I have which are not of this fold; them also I must bring, and they will hear My voice; and there will be one flock and one shepherd."

46. As for, example, a frequently employed justification of African blackness and slavery rested on Noah's Biblical curse of his son Ham's children to be servants of servants. For a survey of racist directions taken within Christian thought see Alan Davies, *Infected Christianity: A Study of Modern Racism*. Montreal: McGill-Queen's University Press, 1988.

47. Kidd, *Forging of Races*. p. 26.

48. Ferguson, *Empire*. p. 121.

49. Chaim D. Kaufmann and Robert A. Pape, "Explaining Costly International Moral Action: Britain's Sixty-Year Campaign against the Atlantic Slave Trade," *International Organization*, Autumn 1999. p. 636

50. Jennifer C. Snow. *Protestant Missionaries, Asian Immigrants, and Ideologies of Race in America, 1850–1924*. New York: Routledge, 2007. pp. 25-26. In Canada, George Leslie Mackay, as Presbyterian Moderator and a former missionary to Taiwan, convinced his church's General Assembly in 1894 to pass a motion to work "in conjunction with other churches to endeavor to bring... influence to bear upon the government of Canada" to remove the head tax on Chinese immigrants. "Canada ought to welcome people from all countries to develop her resources; that it is contrary to righteousness, to international comity, and to British practices and treaties to so discriminate," he said. See Michael Stainton, "Relieving human misery: George Leslie Mackay set the tone for progressive missions," *Presbyterian Record*, January 2007.

51. Baum, *Rise and Fall of the Caucasian Race*. p. 60. Jeremy Waldron argues

that Locke's vision of political equality was grounded in Christian notions of equality in his *God, Locke, and Equality: Christian Foundations of John Locke's Political Thought*. Cambridge: Cambridge University Press, 2002. "My aim in this book is not just to establish that Locke held a position on human equality, and that that position was held on theological grounds; I also want to show that this commitment to basic equality is an important working premise of his whole political theory, and that its influence is pervasive in his arguments about property, family, slavery, government, politics and toleration. It is not just a piece of religiously inspired egalitarian rhetoric wheeled out up front as a sort of edifying decoration… Basic equality operates for Locke as a premise and as a constraint." p. 151.

52. Quoted in Katherine Smits, "John Stuart Mill on the Antipodes: Settler Violence against Indigenous Peoples and the Legitimacy of Colonial Rule," *Australian Journal of Politics and History*, Volume 54, Number 1, 2008. p. 8.

53. Georgios Varouxakis, *Mill on Nationality*. New York: Routledge, 2002. pp. 47-48. Varouxakis maintains that "while accepting vaguely that racial origin is one of the factors influencing the formation of national character, Mill went further to establish that racial predisposition in itself could prove nothing and was liable to be modified out of any recognition through the agency of circumstances such as institutions, historical accidents and human effort." p. 43.

54. Michael Levin, *J.S.Mill on Civilization and Barbarism*. New York: Routledge, 2004. pp. 52-53.

55. Jennifer Pitts, *A turn to empire: the rise of imperial liberalism in Britain and France*. Princeton, N.J.: Princeton University Press, 2005. pp. 136, 142, 145

56. Ferguson, *Empire*. p. 240.

57. Commons, *Debates*, March 3, 1896, pp. 2721-2722

58. Dating as far back as the 1950s, one of the oft-repeated bromides of Canadian 'middle power' diplomacy has been that Canada was not itself a colonial power and so is positioned uniquely to bridge divisions

between the former colonial powers and their colonies, the north and south of contemporary global politics. While this polite fiction might be considered true in some technical sense, it nonetheless completely misses the main point concerning Canada's role within an expanding British Empire. See C.P. Champion, "Putting the Empire Back into Canada," *The Dorchester Review*, Vol. 2 No. 1 Spring/Summer 2012. Accessed October 10, 2012http://www.dorchesterreview.ca/2012/10/08/putting-the-empire-back-into-canada

59. In his classic study of Canadian political culture during this period Carl Berger concluded that imperialism was a form of Canadian nationalism and that imperialists were "characterized by a profound attachment to Canada. Far from denigrating Canadian things, imperialists were positively utopian in their expectations and it was exactly this overestimation of Canadian capacities which enabled them to believe that their country would become 'the future centre and dominating portion of the British Empire.'" Carl Berger, *The Sense of Power: Studies in the Ideas of Canadian Imperialism, 1867-1914*. Toronto: University of Toronto Press, 1970. pp. 260-261.

60. Patricia K. Wood, "Defining 'Canadian': Anti-Americanism and Identity in Sir John A. Macdonald's Nationalism," *Journal of Canadian Studies*, Vol. 36, No. 2, Summer 2001, p. 52.

61. Duncan S.A. Bell, "Empire and International Relations in Victorian Political Thought," *The Historical Journal*, Vol. 49, March 2006, p. 283.

62. Reginald Horsman, "Origins of Racial Anglo-Saxonism in Great Britain before 1850," *Journal of the History of Ideas*, Vol. 37, No. 3, July-September, 1976. pp. 388-89, 410.

63. Peter Mandler, "'Race' and 'Nation' in mid-Victorian thought," in *History, Religion and Culture: British Intellectual History 1750-1950*. eds. S. Collini, R. Whatmore, B. Young. Cambridge: Cambridge University Press, 2000. pp. 225, 227, 230, 233.

64. Bernard Porter, *The Absent-Minded Imperialists: Empire, Society, and Culture in Britain*. Oxford: Oxford University Press, 2004. pp. 78-79.

65. Ferguson, *Empire*. pp. 259-260.

66. Douglas Lorimer, "Theoretical Racism in Late-Victorian Anthropology, 1870-1900," *Victorian Studies*, Spring 1988, pp. 428-430.

67. Douglas A. Lorimer, *Colour, Class and the Victorians: English attitudes to the Negro in the mid-nineteenth century*. Leicester, U.K.: Leicester University Press, 1978. p. 16.

68. Stephen J. Heathorn, *For Home, Country and Race: Gender, Class and Englishness in the Elementary School, 1880-1914*. Toronto: University of Toronto Press, 2000. pp. 104, 107, 111.

69. Duncan Bell, *The Idea of Greater Britain: Empire and the Future of World Order, 1860-1900*. Princeton, N.J.: Princeton University Press, 2007. p. 10.

70. Michael Burgess, *The British Tradition of Federalism*. London: Leicester University Press, 1995. p. 57.

71. Berger, *The Sense of Power*, pp. 115-116. For an examination of how anglo-saxonism was reflected in the pages of the 1887 to 1900 Ottawa periodical *Anglo-Saxon*, see Paula Hastings, "'Our Glorious Anglo-Saxon Race Shall Ever Fill Earth's Highest Place': The *Anglo-Saxon* and the Construction of Identity in Late-Nineteenth-Century Canada," in *Canada and the British World: Culture, Migration, Identity*, ed. Phillip Buckner. Vancouver: UBC Press, 2006. pp. 92-110.

72. Vic Satzewich, *Racism in Canada*. Toronto: Oxford University Press, 2011. p. x.

73. Constance Backhouse, *Colour-Coded: A Legal History of Racism in Canada, 1900-1950*. Toronto: Osgoode Society for Canadian Legal History, 1999. pp. 5-7, 10.

74. Norman Buchignani, Doreen M. Indra with Ram Srivastava, *Continuous Journey: A Social History of South Asians in Canada*. Toronto : McClelland and Stewart in association with the Multiculturalism Directorate, Department of the Secretary of State, and the Canadian Government Publishing Centre, Supply and Services Canada, 1985. p. 67.

75. Harold M. Troper, *Only Farmers Need Apply: Official Canadian Government Encouragement of Immigration from the United States, 1896-1911*. Toronto: Griffen House, 1972. p. 122. In the next sentence in

this paragraph, Troper goes on to link J.S. Woodsworth, "a future father of the Canadian social democratic movement," with Canadian racism. Illustrating the dangers of overgeneralization on this subject, Woodsworth appears in Chapter 5 of this volume as a vigourous opponent of racial prejudice and the politics of discrimination during his time as a member of the House of Commons.

76. As noted earlier, this is especially important because of the contrasting meanings given to the word 'race' by late nineteenth and early twentieth century parliamentarians. 'Race' could be given a biological or a sociological location. The only way to determine for certain how it was meant by a speaker is to give careful consideration of the full context in which 'racial' references were being placed. To illustrate, in his important study *"Race," Rights and the Law in the Supreme Court of Canada: Historical Case Studies*. Waterloo: Wilfrid Laurier University Press, 1997, James W. St G. Walker asserted that late nineteenth century Canadians commonly "assumed that 'races' were evolutionary units, fixed in their physical and behavioural characteristics. These units were destined to compete at the group level, for their interests, dictated by biology, were inherently in conflict." Following this supposition, Walker cast Prime Minister Sir Wilfrid Laurier as one among several biologically-determinist parliamentarians who "confessed that 'racial antagonism' was irreconcilable and 'amalgamation' with Asians was 'neither possible nor desirable.'" pp. 29-30. While it is true that parliamentarians of this era often spoke of 'assimilation' or 'amalgamation' in regards to 'races,' as is noted in Chapter 6 of this volume, sometimes these terms were used in relation to biology and miscegenation, but more commonly they would refer to supposedly insurmountable barriers of economics, culture, politics and religion. The only way to be sure how Laurier was using it here is to place Walker's quote in its complete context. Laurier was explaining to the Commons that his government was raising the Chinese head tax to $500 to accommodate "a very strong feeling against Asiatic immigration" in British Columbia. In this respect, Laurier noted that British Columbia was much like California or Australia "…in fact wherever the two races, Caucasian and Mongolian have come into

contact, the same feeling has manifested itself. After giving it full consideration, every one who has looked into the matter must come to the conclusion that this antagonism is based on ethnical considerations, the difference between the two races. It seems impossible to reconcile them, and the conclusion of all who have considered the matter seems to be that the amalgamation of the two is neither possible nor desirable. There are so many differences of character that it is supposed to be impossible to overcome them." Clearly, for Laurier in these remarks, the difference between the 'two races' was sociological, not biological, because "ethnical" refers to "many differences of character." What is playing out in his remarks is not a social Darwinist race war, but the *political accommodation* of British Columbian pressure based in "strong feeling against Asiatic immigration." In fact, Laurier goes on to disassociate himself from the "prejudice" he ascribes to British Columbians by observing that "with regard to Japanese immigration, the same prejudice, I am sorry to say, exists in British Columbia concerning the Japanese as the Chinese. I say I am sorry for it, because for my part I make a distinction between Japan and China. Japan is one of the rising nations of the present day. It has shown itself to be very progressive, it does not seem to me at all doubtful that within a short period Japan will have placed itself in the fore front among the civilized nations of the earth. But whatever may be my feelings in this matter… there can be no dispute that in British Columbia the feeling towards the Japanese is exactly the same as towards the Chinese." So, to summarize Laurier's position here – 1) Asians were racially distinct in a sociological sense, 2) it was "very doubtful" that they would "assimilate" with British Canadians because of having "so many differences of character" but, 3) they were nonetheless capable of rising to "the fore front among the civilized nations of the earth." This is not the stuff of biological determinism or "inherent" race conflict (or race war) especially considering that, as Laurier pointed out later in this speech, by treaty Japan was "an ally of Great Britain" and so Canada had Empire "obligations" not to offend the Japanese government. Commons, *Debates,* March 27, 1903, pp. 598-601.

CHAPTER 2.

DOMINION ANGLO-SAXONISM WITHIN THE INTERNATIONAL SYSTEM

Let it never be forgotten that the price of our liberty, the price of our national existence, the price of the British race being on top is the eternal vigilance of the citizens of the Empire. The doctrine, I say, is borne out by the Scriptures... spoken by our Lord himself. 'I came not to bring peace on earth, but a sword.'[1]
–W.F. COCKSHUTT, 1913.

Anglo-Saxonism, Chapter 1 argued, developed in close relation to the international politics of British imperialism and the expansion of its Empire. In this first substantive chapter of our study of race-thinking in Canada's parliament between 1880 and 1925, it follows that we must set the stage for the coming chapters through considering how Canadian parliamentarians regarded the international system of their day.

Bell and Tepperman have reminded us that "politics makes sense only when we know the political culture, the pattern of thinking and meaning, that participants share... allow[ing] different individuals to come together in political combat and co-operation."[2] This chapter will demonstrate that examined from Canada's vantage point, its Empire identity was seen to be as much spiritual as it was spatial. Politics rather than biological race were typically believed to demarcate its boundaries.

Although subsequent chapters highlight the many differences of Commons members regarding race and identity, this chapter will focus more on points of general agreement about the character of the British Empire and Canada's place within it.

POLITICAL LIBERTY AND MORAL MISSION

Most characteristically, the British Empire was described by parliamentarians as a historically unique project whose overriding purpose was to advance political liberty. R.B. Bennett, who later was to become Prime Minister, observed on the eve of World War I that membership in the Empire with its universal and liberating citizenship was both a privilege and an obligation.

> Wherever the British flag has gone, wherever Englishmen have planted the outposts of Empire, there has followed order, justice, liberty, freedom, equality under the law. That is the great thing, the right to worship God in any way men please, under their own vine and fig tree, and none may say them nay. Whether they be Mahomedans, or Hindoos, Buddhists or Catholics, Protestants or atheists, it matters not, all have equal rights under that great flag, and I say that it is our bounden duty as loyal devoted British subjects to do what we can to sustain that civilization and the Empire that has made it possible.[3]

Nearly two decades earlier, Sir Wilfrid Laurier had also opined that liberty, not race, was the glue holding together the British Empire.

> ...if the day should come – which God forbid – if the day should ever come – which I again say God forbid – when England should have to repel foes, I am quite sure that all British subjects, all over the world, would be only too glad to give to her what help they could – all British subjects all over the world, not only British subjects of her own blood, but British subjects who are not of her own blood, but who have received from her the inestimable blessing of freedom.[4]

For A. Thompson, "the love of self-government" had been

"deeply embedded" in the "breasts" of the Anglo-Saxon "race" from the dawn of recorded time.

> I submit that there is no principle so deeply embedded in the hearts of the Anglo-Saxon as that of responsible and representative government. When you trace the history of this race from the time that history first discovers them on the banks of the Weser and Elbe, in northern Germany, down to the present day, you will find running through it that one bright thread. You will find that wherever they are, on any section of God's footstool, they want the right to elect their own representatives to govern themselves... So long as this race is on this sphere, and wherever you will find a section of this race, you will find in the breasts of the people that love of self-government...[5]

It was "inspiring," Thompson declared, how historic British political principles like "liberty for the individual" and "the eternal principles of freedom, justice and toleration" had motivated the Empire's "various races" and "religious denominations" to converge "upon the home of the Aryan race in Europe" to join the struggle against Germany during World War I.

> Is it not an inspiring sight to see the various races coming from the different countries in ships that plough all the seven seas converging upon the home of the Aryan race in Europe to settle this great question of principles? There must be some underlying reason for this magnificent spectacle of the people of England, of Ireland, of Scotland, of South Africa, of New Zealand, of Australia, of Canada fighting side by side in this war. The Maoris of New Zealand, the Indians of our own country, the natives of India, the Soudanese, all take their part... Why do all religious denominations join with united voices in support of this war? The Mahommedans, the Hindus, the Sikhs, the Parsees, the Buddhists, join with the Presbyterians, the Methodists, the Anglicans, the Baptists, the Roman Catholics, the Greek Catholics, and all other Christian communities... Why is it that this vast concourse of men of so many different races, religions, and climes are going to the front to take part in this struggle and are willing to make, and are making the supreme sacrifice. Why? Because they live under the flag that floats over Parliament Hill. And they have found that wherever that flag waves, there you will find liberty for the individual, security for his life, and

safety for his property; there you will find freedom of thought, freedom of speech, freedom of religion, and freedom of the press... And there you will find a state based on the eternal principles of freedom, justice, and toleration.[6]

Likewise G.E. Foster painted a word portrait of the British Empire's 'world historical' moral mission and Canada's strategic position within it.

> The most sublime figure in all history... is the figure of the old mother empire, the great-hearted mother who has given birth to the young nations that circle the globe, the great-hearted mother that has gone outside of her own kith and kin and has mothered nation after nation, people after people, continent after continent, brought them out of darkness and slavery and set them upon the path of a better civilization. That grand old mother nation, endued with great heart and more than Titanic force to sustain world burdens – behold her course. Watch her in India and see what she has done for its three hundred million people, follow her in Egypt and see what she has done for the physical, the moral and the national betterment of that country, everywhere we know that she has done more in beneficent, scientific, humanitarian, uplifting action than any country in any age of history. What has she done in Africa, what has she done in America, from those early times when her armaments, her soldiers and her navy began to carve out of this North American continent the great heritage which she once enjoyed upon this continent a large portion of which she has given over to us. Today, Great Britain has her armed guards of the Pamirs, and in the passes of the Himalayas, her sentinels on every frontier line, her sailors and flag in every sea, her bodies of living scarlet and khaki here and there dispersed throughout the world and though she has done all that and bears the immense burden today, she has yet to exact the first penny of tribute from any country that she has liberated or any people that she has made free.[7]

Sam Hughes similarly stressed that British liberal political innovations had vindicated the Empire's international supremacy.

> She is at the pinnacle of her greatness. No nation has ever attained a higher position. She is the parent of responsible government, having taught the nations of the earth the rights of man and the proper methods of governing humanity. She has reclaimed nearly one-half

of the world and made savage and waste lands teem with plenty. In the Soudan alone, in the few years anterior to Britain's acquisition of that country, there were upwards of three million natives massacred there in less than ten years – massacred as the result of inter-tribal conflicts among barbaric and semi-barbaric people – but since Britain has acquired the Soudan, the loss of life has been comparatively small and that country today has become productive.[8]

Hughes also suggested that enlightened British colonial policies were at the root of the conflict in the Boer War. Whereas the Empire had abolished slavery, the Boers were trying to reinstitute it.

> We are told... that the Boers trekked from Cape Colony on account of British tyranny. They trekked because Britain freed the slave, because the Wilberforce Act passed in Great Britain had freed the slaves wherever the British flag flew... Consider how the Kaffirs are treated by the Boers. A Kaffir dare not walk upon the sidewalk, but must take to the middle of the road. He could not own an acre of land; he must not carry on a trade in vegetables; until two years ago he could not be married legally. More than that, he had to be attached to some baas and wear a bandage on his arm with his number on it. If he did not wear this bandage, he might be arrested and made a slave of the state.[9]

A failure of British power would spell "disaster" for "the teeming millions of India or the teeming millions of Egypt" according to R.B. Bennett.

> Some smile and say, we will not accept these responsibilities. Why not? They are the responsibilities that belong to this race, this Anglo-Saxon race... Britain did not seek them. Britain did not desire India or Egypt; she had them forced on her. To let go our rule in India would be anarchy. It would be such anarchy as the world has never seen. The teeming millions of India would crush one another. There would be internecine strife, internal warfare, kingdom against kingdom and ruler against ruler. Look at Egypt; the same state of affairs would prevail. Blood would flow in the streets and rivers of that country.[10]

Beyond its moral identity, the British Empire was also given a spatial identity and Canada, with its immense physical extent, was said to play a leading role in creating that identity. In 1896, J. Grant told the Commons that:

> Since the Queen [Victoria] ascended the Throne [in 1837], the "Thin Red Line," which marks the British territorial boundaries has extended very considerably Since 1843, the acquisition of India of Scindh, Punjab and Oudh and Upper Burma as well as the Shan States have added to the Indian Empire fully 275,000 square miles of territory. In the same period the occupation at Aden, the administration of Hong Kong, as well as considerable portions of North Borneo, have given to the Empire an additional 80,000 square miles, in fact a territory fully as large as Great Britain. When the Queen commenced her illustrious rule, England had in South Africa 100,000 square miles; at present she hold sway over 300,000 square miles, in this same region. The North American and Australian colonies cover over 6,500,000 square miles of territory. When the Queen ascended the throne, Canada had about 1,000,000 population. Now we have over 5,000,000 people. During this same period the progress of the Australian colonies has been very marked indeed. In Australia in 1837 – the population was about 175,000 – today the population is fully 4,500,000... Today the British Empire embraces an area of fully 10,000,000 square miles with a population of 350,000,000 of people."[11]

Partnership in this vast Empire was Canada's inheritance; a gift freely given. "The mother country," observed G.H.R. Cockburn, "...gives us protection of its army and navy and diplomatic service free of charge, whose people are ready to shed their blood for us, and who, at an expense of £800,000,000, have acquired their great Colonial Empire and hand it over to us, without demanding one farthing or one fraction for the immense sacrifices they have made."[12]

Like many parliamentarians in this era, J. Charlton employed the possessive pronoun 'we' when linking Canadians, and their proprietorship of half of North America, to the international power of the Empire.

> Now, this maintenance of British supremacy... is a matter in which we colonists in Canada are very directly and intimately interested... Here we have half of the North American continent, just in its infancy. We have room here for 75,000,000 people who can be fed from our own soil. We have in Australia an empire which will support probably 100,000,000 people. We have this magnificent region in South Africa... We have our hands upon every important naval strategic position in the world... its power is ubiquitous. Its sails are found on every sea; and its armies are collected in almost every part of the globe. Its accomplishments have been almost beyond human belief.[13]

H.H. McLean imagined that because of its huge territorial expanse and geostrategic location, Canada was destined to become the leading force in the Empire and so the world.

> Canada will become the greatest English-speaking nation in the world, with the possible exception of the United States. We have room for so many millions of people that we hesitate to fix a limit. England and Scotland could be drowned in one of our great lakes. Allied with Great Britain, we will be the most potent power in the world. Australia must ever be on the fringe of a nation; South Africa is burdened with a black problem and lacks our climate and land.[14]

Similarly, J.W. Edwards looked forward to the day when the Empire's centre of gravity would be located in Canada.

> I dissent from the view that Canada's destiny is independence. I am proud of my British citizenship; I am proud to belong to an empire which comprises one-third of the earth's surface and which contains probably one-fourth of the people on this planet. Eminent philologists... estimate that at the end of 100 years there will be in this world... over 800,000,000 speaking the English tongue, of whom some 80,000,000 will be in the Dominion of Canada... the Anglo-Saxon race is to continue to be the dominant race in this world... I look forward... to the time when Canada will have a larger population than Great Britain, and still be a portion of the British Empire. I look forward to that day when Canada will be the dominating and controlling factor in the affairs of our empire... when the Dominion of Canada [will] be the link that would bind the two great branches of the Anglo-Saxon race together; meaning the Anglo-Saxon race within the confines of the British empire,

> and that other great branch of the race which inhabits the United States... I believe that is the noblest destiny for us to look forward to.[15]

Even after World War I, when many Canadians believed that their country had earned the right to forge its own foreign policy, the view that a newly confident and assertive Canada was destined to lead the Empire resonated strongly. As H.C. Hocken saw it,

> I believe that the highest and best destiny for Canada is to be a part of the British Empire, not only now, but when she has double or triple or ten times her present population... I am of the opinion that here in Canada we will in time by the admixture of the English, Irish, Scottish, French, and other blood develop a race of men that will be just a little superior to the race of the Old Land, and that as a result of our growth, individually and as a nation, we will be able to aid in the development of a higher civilization to a greater degree that even the Mother Country has done. The Canadian breed has shown what it is capable of doing in the war, and the Canadian people in civil life have never give a greater demonstration of their endurance under difficult conditions than they are doing today. So that whether it is in war or in civil life Canadians have the right to hold up their heads as among the most enduring, the most intelligent, and ...the most capable of the nations of the world.[16]

THE PROTECTION OF BRITISH GUNS

The Empire's political reach and sway, it was generally appreciated, was underwritten by its ability when necessary to apply superior military force. Especially key was its naval power. H.B. Ames married succinctly the Empire's moral mission with its underlying realpolitik.

> What is it after all that binds together the Empire? Is it origin, race, language, religion? No, we differ on all these points. It is not that, it is the recognition that the British system of government is the best, the freest and the highest development of government that the world has ever seen. It is the determination that as far as we are concerned we want to see that system continued and maintained, because we believe our best development will go on under it. It is

because we believe there are other races under the flag more backward than ours, struggling towards the light, who need this system of government, to come into the full stature of manhood as we have done. The Empire can only be preserved and maintained by supremacy on the sea.[17]

The navy was the Empire's "police force" according to O.J. Wilcox and "by the very existence of that police force, peace is established, because that force is beneficial not only in what it does, but even to a greater extent in that which it prevents being done."

> ...I would remind hon. gentlemen that the King's subjects number 460,000,000 people, and that 360,000,000 of those subjects are neither of our colour nor our race. Let me remind them of, shall I say, the exquisite delicacy of Imperial diplomacy in the government of many of these colonies forming part of this great Empire, and of the phenomenal degree of fair-mindedness and patriotism exercised governing of 360,000,000 aliens without encroaching more than is necessary upon their individual freedom and their ancient customs, and at the same time establishing and maintaining principles of British justice, and the protection of life, virtue and property.[18]

R.B. Bennett stressed that Britain must be able to "command peace" through its naval power.

> If there is one reason more than another for the peace which we have enjoyed within the British Empire during all these years, it is that we have had a naval force such as no other power has had. Although some people may call Britain a bully we have had behind us a power so strong that we have been able to command peace. We talk about our hundred years of peace; we dream the dream when men shall war no more and swords shall be beaten into ploughshares, but the student of history knows that we depend for peace absolutely upon our ability to strike; and we must be able to strike harder than anybody else if we command peace.[19]

Robert Borden, along with most parliamentarians of this era, believed British naval power was the guarantor of Canada's security.

> A world-wide empire such as ours; an empire which reaches out on every continent and spreads over every ocean can only be maintained by absolute naval supremacy. The moment a naval power arises which can effectively challenge the supremacy of Britain's navy that moment may the British Empire be dismembered and that moment Canada may cease to be among the nations of that great empire... Like Sir John Macdonald, I was born a British subject, I shall remain a British subject, I hope to die a British subject. I trust the day will never come when the British flag will cease to float over this Canada of ours. But as has been eloquently said, Britain staggers under the too vast orb of her fate, and so it behooves us her children to decide how we can best assist the motherland to maintain control of the seas.[20]

Canada, a tempting geostrategic prize, was still in the early stages of consolidating her political hold over the northern part of the continent. Canada, therefore, was vulnerable and required British naval power to protect her, according to H.H. McLean.

> If British power is broken Canada is left defenceless. We should be eight millions of people in possession of the richest half-continent in the world, and with no fleet. If Germany were mistress of the sea, where could she find a better colony than Canada? What would keep the Japanese from landing on the Pacific coast, or how long would it be before the billions of regenerated China would flow into our tempting prairies?... Great Britain must not only have a margin of safety over Germany, but she must have such a decisive command of the sea, that no probable coalition could be brought against her. Great Britain should not be obliged to bear this burden alone; the dominions over the seas and her colonies should assist her.[21]

W.F. Maclean warned the Commons that Canada would have to work together with Britain to "maintain the highest and the strongest sea-power" to protect British Columbia in the coming "struggle for supremacy" between "the yellow and the white races."

> When you look at Asia and see the people there, and read what the highest thinkers are saying today in regard to that Asia problem, you see a great struggle for supremacy between the yellow and the white races, and it depends absolutely on the sea-power whether

that struggle between the white and the yellow race is to take place in Asia, or in our own Pacific province, and in the American Pacific states. To my mind that view of the situation must make us realize how important our position is if we wish to secure our future in the matter of not only developing sea-power ourselves, but joining with the mother country in maintaining the highest and the strongest sea-power for many years to come[22]

Canadians abroad enjoyed the security of British guns, according to W.F. Cockshutt.

the protection of British guns; that is what gives security to the British subject the round world over. Any man travelling in distant lands knows the sense of security imparted by the possession of a passport bearing evidences of the soverignty (sic) of our King, and his guarantee of safe convoy through distant and dangerous lands. I have carried one of these in my pocket in the course of my travels, and I felt it as my only salvation when absolutely alone among men with whose language I was unacquainted, and whose appearance did not indicate their lack of a desire to strike me down at any time. There is no force on the high seas to-day superior to the navy of Great Britain, and that is the sense of security which stands at the back of every Canadian…[23]

Prime Minister Robert Borden offered the Commons some specific examples how the Imperial "sense of security" stood at the backs of individual Canadians overseas.

For forty-five years as a confederation we have enjoyed the protection of the British navy without the cost of a dollar… Has the protection of the flag and the prestige of the Empire meant anything for us during all that period? Hundreds of illustrations are at hand, but let me give just two. During a period of disorder in a distant country, a Canadian was unjustifiably arrested and fifty lashes were laid on his back. Appeal was made to Great Britain, and with what result? A public apology was made to him, and fifty pounds were paid for every lash. In time of dangerous riot and wild terror in a foreign city a Canadian religious community remained unafraid. 'Why did you not fear?' they were asked, and unhesitatingly came the answer, 'The Union Jack floated above us.'[24]

Canada's international trade also sheltered behind British guns, stated J.D. Hazen, Minister of Marine and Fisheries in 1912.

> Canada benefited by the power of the whole British navy distributed over the face of the globe... The protection thus afforded to Canada constituted as it were the insurance on Canadian commerce against foreign attack, and enabled Canadian traders to extend their business all over the world without fear of interruption, and without fear of hostile action on the part of any country.[25]

In what ways was Canada expected to contribute to Britain's military supremacy during the late nineteenth and early twentieth centuries? Some like J.H. Burnham saw the Empire as a shelter against a potentially threatening international system and that Canada should "at all times" be ready to do its part to defend it since this was nothing more than "what we ask the others to do for us."

> We say that we are at all times ready to do what we are asked, and what we ask the others to do for us, or pray what use on earth is it to talk of making laws for the government of our immigration if we had not Great Britain and the other dominions behind us to back us up in these laws? Japan and Hindustan and China would wipe us out in an hour. We presume that the British Empire is behind us, and surely, if we are at all above the ordinary greedy spirit of a child, we will agree that we will reciprocate and say, whatever they may do, we will always stand behind them. That is the spirit of empire...[26]

This line of thinking promoted the contribution of Canadian forces to British military campaigns like the Boer War in South Africa (1899-1902). As Sir Charles Tupper pronounced to the Commons:

> ...take the position of Canada from any standpoint and you cannot find, on the face of the globe... [a] people occupying a prouder, a more advantageous, or a more splendid position. She has the glory of British institutions; she has the security for life and property which is alone to be found under British institutions... As to foreign aggression, every person knows that not a foreign foot can touch the soil of Canada, no finger from any foreign power can

be placed upon a Canadian... Will you show me any people in any country in the world that enjoy these advantages on the terms that Canada enjoys them, with the most absolute, the most perfect... the most complete independence, enjoying everything that complete independence can give us and standing today as part of the British Empire... Under these circumstances where is the man to be found who will say that Canada, in this hour of her great prosperity, will shrink for one single moment from the duty imposed by the grandeur of our position, the strength of our position, will shrink for a single moment from standing by in the hour of her necessity that great empire, that great country, that gives us all this and absolutely for nothing.[27]

In a similar fashion, Frank Oliver held the opinion that an attack on the prestige of the Empire anywhere was an attack on Canada.

I look upon the prestige of the British empire as a question of the most intimate local character, concerning every dependency and every citizen in every dependency throughout the empire. The maintenance of the prestige of Great Britain is just as necessary to the peace and welfare of Canada as it is to the peace and welfare to the county of York in England. So long as Canada is a part of the empire, the safety of Canada depends upon the strength of the empire. Anything that weakens the empire weakens Canada, endangers Canada, and hurts every citizen of Canada. Just as this is the sentiment which prompted our young men to volunteer in thousands to risk their lives on the battlefields of Africa, so it should be the sentiment with which this parliament should approach this question.[28]

But, as Laurier qualified, while all Canadians would defend Great Britain from direct attack, many objected to fighting in the Empire's wars of choice.

...if England at any time were engaged in a struggle for life and death, the moment the bugle was sounded or the fire was lit on the hills, the colonies would rush to the aid of the mother country... There are no two opinions upon that point. But while every Canadian admits that he would be ready to contribute our treasure and our blood, and the resources of Canada at the disposal of this country, for the rescue of England, were she engaged in a life and death struggle, there are many Canadians who are not ready to take part in the secondary wars of England or to contribute to the defence of the empire in any part of it.[29]

Others, like D.D. McKenzie, believed that extending Canada's continental reach was more important for "general advancement and spread of Britishism and British authority" than "the building up of armies and navies."

> We have started preparing the soil, preparing the country to be the home of hundreds of millions of British born and men who come to this country and become British subjects, and in making homes for them under the British flag... ...we were serving the Empire in building the Canadian Pacific railway, in constructing the canal system of Canada, in making the St. Lawrence the great avenue of trade it is today, in building the Transcontinental railway, in developing the great Northwest, in dividing it into provinces and in giving them educational and other facilities.[30]

And so, the suppression of the 1885 Riel Rebellion of natives and 'mixed-race' Métis in the North-West was understood to be part of the larger world-wide project of Empire-building. Sir John A. Macdonald told the Commons that the "claims of the half-breeds are a mere pretext, and the real desire is that the country should sever its connection with the Dominion of Canada, should become independent in some way..."[31] Linking the Rebellion to the contemporaneously famous siege of Gordon at Khartoum, Macdonald claimed Riel had "excited" the natives and "made them believe he was a sort of El Mahdi."[32] Both the government and the opposition were well aware of the international attention given to this uprising on the North American frontier of Empire[33], and Macdonald was able to boast that in putting down the rebels "speedily and gallantly" Canadian forces

> convinced... the mother country, in whose good opinion we take so much pride, that we have as good a militia as their own, that we have men who, untrained as they are, can still listen to the voice of discipline, and will do everything they are called upon to maintain the credit of their country. Their action has raised the credit of Canada, not only among the right-minded thinking men of the

world, but even in the sordid purlieus of the stock exchange. The credit of Canada has risen, because Canada has shown, as a vindicator of herself, that she is worthy of being a nation, and worthy of the credit of the world.[34]

THE DEFENSIVE, PEACEFUL EMPIRE

Notwithstanding the success of the Canadian militia in putting down the Riel Rebellion, Macdonald took care to contextualize it within the often-repeated British argument that their Empire was built on political liberty and peaceful administration, not militarism and war. He applauded the "peace, quiet, and the order" of the Canadian North-West where "from 1870 until 1885 not one single blow, not one single murder, not one single loss of life has taken place" while

> there has been rising after rising in the United States, although they had their whole frontier lined with soldiery, 25,000 men, or nearly so, watching the western frontier and the northern frontier. There they had continued trouble; we heard of Indians being shot down like dogs; we heard of cruelties and outrages committed upon the aborigines.[35]

The moral superiority of British North America's non-violent management of its natives when compared to United States was a familiar trope in this era. Frank Oliver, when he was the minister responsible for Indian Affairs, declared in 1908 that he had "always understood that it was the traditional policy of the United States to make the Indian a citizen of some other world than of this; whereas, it was the policy of Great Britain and it has been the policy of Canada to treat the Indian honestly to the last cent and the last acre."[36] Speaking nearly four decades later than Macdonald, R.J. Manion, destined to become leader of the Conservative Party, told the Commons that

> ...I believe that Canada has been treating her Indians probably a great deal better than the people to the south of us have treated theirs, as is evidenced by the fact that throughout the time we have dealt with our Indians there have been practically no difficulties or

troubles in connection with them, whereas in the United States the authorities have undoubtedly met with many difficulties in the way of guerilla warfare and so forth.[37]

Unlike the Americans, it was said that the British respected their treaties with natives. Laurier spelled out how British "humanity and prudence" was employed to rescue lands "roamed over rather than possessed by savage nations" from remaining forever "barren and unproductive." Treaties guaranteed "fair and adequate compensation" to natives including lands reserved for their exclusive use.

> It has always been the policy of England, ever since she has had establishments in North America, to compensate the Indians for the dispossession of their lands. England, and all other Christian nations who planted colonies on this continent, always felt that it was not contrary to moral law to take possession, and even forcible possession, of territories which were roamed over rather than possessed by savage nations – territories which in their hands must forever have remained barren and unproductive, but which under civilised rule would afford homes and happiness to teeming millions. It has always been held as a doctrine of international law that when such territories were discovered, the discovering nation had paramount authority therein; at the same time it is to the credit of England that she is one of the civilised nations which gave the fullest development to the doctrine that the Indians were not to be ruthlessly thrown back before advancing civilisation without some fair and adequate compensation. That doctrine was based, not so much on principles of abstract justice as on motives of humanity and prudence.[38]

In the view of the Liberal Party, the Riel Rebellion was the logical result of the failure of Macdonald's government to live up to British standards of "humanity and prudence" in its treaty commitments. D.M. Cameron was blisteringly critical of what he described as the "shameful official misconduct" of Canadian officials "...placed over the untamed, uneducated, uncivilised, unchristianised wards of the nation with whom this country was bound to deal honestly and fairly, because Canada induced the

Indians of the North-West to surrender their possessory rights to what is practically an empire for the merest pittance." Natives in the North-West were "robbed, defrauded and swindled, frozen to death and starved to death" by Ottawa and "the solemn covenants entered into with the Indians have been shamefully, openly, persistently and systematically broken by this Government. The confidence which the Indian usually has in the Sovereign of this Dominion, has been shaken. He can no longer rely on the faith of the Crown, and the result has been a rebellion in the North-West Territories..." Rather than preserving the peace through following traditional British practices, Macdonald's government stood accused of repeating U.S. native policy failures – "A policy of fraud; a policy of violated treaties and broken promises has been tried in the neighbouring republic for 100 years, and without success... Nothing but discontent and dissatisfaction and rebellion could be expected from the course pursued by hon. gentlemen opposite."[39]

Turning to affairs in the wider Empire, most parliamentarians in this era would have agreed with G.E. Foster who maintained that

> Britain is not an aggressive nation. I say that without fear of contradiction. Her hostages [colonies] are such that she dare not be aggressive. Her possessions are so great that there is no will or wish to be aggressive. Her great problem is to organize, develop and maintain what she has got. She is a defensive, peaceful nation and must remain so.[40]

Laurier also stressed that "unlike the empires of the past" the British Empire was held together not by "force" but by "the will of the colonists themselves."

> The British empire today is composed of nations; it is an aggregation of nations all bearing allegiance to the same Sovereign, and there is this difference between the British empire of the present day and the empires which have been seen in the past, that whereas the empires of the past rested on force, the British empire so far at

> least as the great colonies are concerned, rests altogether on the will of the colonists themselves...[41]

Although the British Empire eschewed "militarism" and did not want to be "drawn into the conflicts of Europe," Laurier believed that defensive measures might be necessary to protect England and thereby preserve Canada's "civil and religious freedom."

> ...I would deprecate Canada being drawn into the vortex of militarism existing in Europe. The situation of Europe today is on which cannot be characterized as other than madness. Europe is an armed camp. Every nation there is living in a condition of armed peace almost as intolerable as war itself. England is the one nation which has not lost her head, which has resisted militarism as much as she could, which has refused to adopt the conscription and sacrifice her children on the altar of this insatiable moloch. I hope the day shall never come when we will be drawn into the conflicts of Europe. But I have no hesitation in saying that the supremacy of the British empire is absolutely essential... to the civilization of the world... I have no hesitation in saying also that if the day should come when the supremacy of Britain on the high seas will be challenged, it will be the duty of all the daughters of the nation to close around the old mother land and make a rampart about her to ward off any attack... the salvation of England is the salvation of our own country that therein lies the guaranty of civil and religious freedom and everything we value in this life.[42]

While this defensive and relatively pacific viewpoint is perfectly compatible with the idea of an Empire organized around a 'world historical' moral mission in the service of developing political liberty, it is less so with social Darwinistic notions that understood the international order as being the product of biological determinism and race war. Simply put, social Darwinists were left with little to work with when the Empire was described in political rather than biological terms.

Nonetheless, from time to time "jingo warlike ideas"[43], as they were sometimes dismissively characterized, were heard in the Commons. H.H. McLean, supporting the building of a Canadian navy, reasoned that "military races" needed continuously to get "ready to fight" in order to maintain their rank within the realist international system.

> The fallacy that peace and progress are synonymous, that war is retrograde, has lately been in vogue... We find around us nations armed to the teeth, watching an opportunity for dividing among themselves, this, our empire, and it is the preacher of this galling senseless doctrine that may yet open the door for them. Wherever civilization has found its way, there it has been carried by the sword, and nurtured by Christianity. Every nation that has risen, has carved its way up by the sword, and retained its position only by a preparedness with force of arms. When once its weapons have been laid aside, then has been the signal for decadence... The pages of history show the following nations have expired in peace: Portugal, Holland, Sweden, Norway, Greece. Japan, a nation born yesterday, she could to-day, by force of arms, encompass the overthrow of the whole five combined. Thus were these nations betrayed, standing as beacons to guide us, the proud possessor of an empire, an empire entering upon a period of peace adoration which is foreign to the clime of military races. Other nations have recognized that the greatest evil, attendant upon civilization, is the abhorrence of war, and they have, in time, taken the steps necessary to counteract the dislike of fighting, by getting ready to fight.[44]

In 1913, W.F. Cockshutt boasted to the House he was "more or less of a student" of German General Friedrich von Bernhardi (see Chapter 1) and read lengthy quotes from him into Hansard including Bernhardi's maxim that "Might is at once the supreme right and the dispute to what is right is decided by the arbitrament of war."

> ...I admire General von Bernhardi, because he has laid before the people a patriotic mind and a spirit of self-sacrifice that is worthy of every Canadian and every citizen of the British Empire. I only wish that as many men in Canada and as many men in Great Britain were as ready to lay their services on the altar of the country as are willing and ready to do so in the country of Germany. Why should hon. gentlemen opposite brand us as jingoes or men who are unchristian? It is the duty of every one, be he Christian or be he Pagan, to defend his land when it is attacked, and to meet the enemy in the

gate like a man who is not afraid to live and who is not afraid to die.[45]

W. Pugsley was offended by Cockshutt's "warlike remarks" and suggested they were un-British.

> The hon. gentlemen treated the House... to a disquisition upon the beauties and the desirability of war from a national standpoint; and to those of us who long for universal peace, the hon. gentleman's remarks came somewhat as a surprise, because he sought to throw around war, which we were accustomed to regard as having horrible surroundings, a glamour of beauty and pleasantness... I do not think that language of that character is befitting a great representative assembly, such as this is, of one of the most important nations comprising the British Empire. Language of that kind would not be tolerated in the British House of Commons...[46]

Certainly, after the Great War began, there were no more appeals to the authority of General Bernhardi. On the contrary, rather than being cast as a social Darwinistic race war, World War I was universally characterized as a struggle between British ideals of individual political liberty and German ideas of nationalism and militarism. For example, J.W. Edwards contrasted the German Empire's communitarian "national machine" with the historically grounded tradition of individual liberty in "the Anglo-Saxon world" where

> democratic principles have been given expression to in such measures as Magna Carta, the Habeas Corpus Act, the Bill of Rights. But what are the conditions in Germany? In Germany for generations they have taken the opposite course. There the individual has been taught that he must blot himself out as an individual, that he must become or should become a mere military number, and that he has no right to be anything else; that he must become and should become a mere cog in the national machine. The gospel of hate has been preached in that country, in their schools, in their colleges and in their universities, yes – and from their pulpits; and men throughout the German Empire have been taught to regard the war teachings of Bernhardi and the writings and theories of Treitschke as something more worthy of their admiration and adoration than the

gospel of Christ... The world is too small for these two ideals to exist side by side; one or the other must triumph; either democracy as represented by Great Britain and France and Russia will triumph or militarism will triumph.[47]

W.G. Weichel likewise told the Commons that the War was a struggle for political liberty and against social Darwinistic doctrines of militarism. "Liberties that we have prized and that have been handed down from generation to generation will have to give way to a new doctrine that might is right should the teachings of Nietzsche, Treitschke, and Bernhardi prevail; the very existence of the democratic institutions which we have learned to revere and love would be threatened," he said.[48] "The most discreditable thing that could happen to this country or to the Empire or to civilization would be that this war should not prove to be a success in putting down for all time the abominable doctrine that the Huns are preaching today, that they are the elect of God to rule and govern mankind...," W.F. Maclean supposed.[49] Borden was even prepared to read a 'barbaric' Germany out of modern western civilization.

> Germany has practically reverted to paganism in this war. The ideals of the old faith of Thor and Odin dominate her people today more really than the dictates of Christianity. Otherwise no such reversion to barbarism could have been witnessed as that with which she shocked the world's conscience and brought so many of its nations in arms against her. Confronted with such a menace, we dare not stay our hand.[50]

German military writers had been completely wrong, Laurier said, in predicting that the decentralized British Empire's political liberalism would make it unable to prosecute successfully a continental war. In the end, "blood and iron" was not as durable as "freedom" and "the principle of liberty."

> ...the struggle that has been going on in Europe for the last six months is a contest between two principles: the principle of liberty and the principle of dominance... the proof is supplied by the conduct of the dominions, the colonies and the dependencies all over

the world which acknowledge British sovereignty. It is a well-known fact that German publicists and German military writers have prophesied that whenever a continental war should come England would be powerless to take part in it; that the moment the first shot was fired England would be torn by internecine factions; her possessions beyond the seas would sever their connection. We must not be surprised at this conclusion of those who believe that the only rule of government is force. But German publicists have yet to learn that there is a greater force than force, and the British Empire, resting on the basis of freedom is more durable than the German Empire resting upon the basis of blood and iron. If anything could open their eyes it would be the spectacle of British colonists from all over the world taking their places behind England...[51]

It was telling that "the Boer in South Africa, who was our sworn enemy only fifteen years ago, [is] willing today to enter the lists for Great Britain against men of his own blood," J.H. Sinclair observed in 1916. This was because "Britain's colonial policy of the open door, and self-government, has knit the Empire together as no military system ever could have done." Since Britain "trusted" the Boers and "accorded them the right to govern themselves," Sinclair reasoned, liberty proved to be a stronger tie than "blood" since "loyalty is the child of freedom."[52]

ANGLO-SAXONISM IN CANADA-US RELATIONS

This chapter's sketch of the several points of general agreement expressed in the Commons around the big questions of Dominion-Empire geostrategy and foreign policy would not be complete without some discussion of where Canada-US relations fit into the overall picture. Canadians recognized that the United States was their most serious potential security threat. War could come to Canadian territory as a result of bilateral conflicts either between Canada and the United States or Great Britain and the United States. Berger observes that "the image that history had fixed in Canadian minds of a bellicose republic persisted into the late 1890s not only by the inertia of tradition but also because of the resurgence of American expansionism..."[53]

Parliamentarians expected that Canadians would fiercely resist any American invasion of their territory and that Canada's defence would be backed by the full military might of the British Empire. A. McNeil told the House that

> ...if we are assailed, we believe that we shall not prove altogether unworthy of the stock from which we came, and we know that at our back will be all the resources of an Empire whose resources are practically inexhaustible, more especially as regards the number of fighting men that can be, in case of emergency, placed in line. Those who know anything of the Sikh war, those who know anything of the losses that were sustained by the British forces at Chilianwalla, and on many other battlefield of which Lord Gough could tell only too well, and those who know anything of the extraordinary military prowess of the Ghoorkas and the many other tribes of hardy hillmen of India (among the most warlike races in the world), and those who recollect with what promptitude and enthusiasm our eastern troops responded to the call of Lord Beaconsfield when he summoned them to Malta some twenty years ago, will understand to what I refer. In so far as the number of fighting men is concerned, are practically inexhaustible, and we are not altogether destitute of the financial strength which would be necessary to prosecute a great war to its conclusion.[54]

Because he feared triggering a continental arms race, French Canadian nationalist Henri Bourassa objected in 1904 to "jingo" proposals to strengthen Canada's militia with an eye to defence against the U.S.

> It is as a Canadian and a true British subject that I oppose an increased military expenditure in this country. The worst service we can give to the Canadian people and to the British Empire is to launch the country upon a policy of militarism that will lead the American people to reply. If we boast that we are going to organize more regiments and build a navy for this country – that we are going to organize ourselves so as to be able to stand a fight against the United States – can we be surprised if any of the border states of New York, Michigan, Minnesota, or Dakota, shall wish to expend as

much on naval and military organization as we do? Instead of rendering a service to Great Britain by launching on a policy of this kind... we shall be sowing the germs of great embarrassment for Great Britain and the British government.

But E.B. Osler countered with the opinion that the Empire would not be 'embarrassed' to come to Canada's rescue.

> The hon. gentleman [Bourassa] stated that this land is not worth fighting for, that if the United States choose to attack us, we would have to lie down like whipped curs and take our medicine. He said we had no defence, but he omitted to say that we had England at our back... They will defend us as long as we stand by the old flag. They will defend us even if there are men in this country like the hon. member for Labelle... I have no fear that if we get into trouble with any nation, [Britain]... would come to our defence...[55]

Sir Richard Cartwright, who served terms as Minister of Finance and as Minister of Trade and Commerce in Liberal governments, and who was to be appointed in 1898 to the Anglo-American Joint High Commission to resolve diplomatic problems between Canada and the US, saw the continental military situation as a 'mutually assured destruction' standoff – "...if it were possible that our neighbours to the south should carry fire and sword to every town in Canada, it is equally true that the British fleet could lay in ashes every city on the seaboard of the United States."[56] Sir Charles Tupper, who held appointment as Canada's High Commissioner to the United Kingdom from 1883 to 1895, told the Commons how unlikely it was that Britain would be drawn into such a war due to shared commercial interests and sentiments of anglo-saxonism.

> ...from 1868, when I had occasion to deal with an important question relating to Canadian interests with her Majesty's Government, down to the present hour. I have been struck very forcibly with the unwillingness on the part of Her Majesty's Government to allow any circumstance whatever to even threaten a collision with the United States. There is every reason in the world why Great Britain should be most unwilling to have such a collision. While she would

feel perhaps the most terrible event that the civilized world could witness would be armed collision between Great Britain and the United States, apart from the natural feeling, the feeling that they are of our own blood to a large extent, that feeling, accentuated by the closely interwoven commercial relations between Great Britain and the United States, has produced a strong impression upon the minds of the governing parties, and I do not refer to the present Government alone but to whatever party is in power in England.[57]

Speaking from a Canadian perspective, A. McNeil echoed in the Commons that "kinship" made such a war "unnatural."

But, Sir, we do not want war. And we do not expect we are going to have war. And least of all do we want war, and least of all do we expect to have war with our own kith and kin. There has been an extraordinary development of the sentiment of kinship... among the British peoples during the last ten or fifteen years. So that in the Empire today... a war with the United States would be regarded as a horrible and unnatural fratricidal strife.[58]

Likewise, G.E. Casey stressed how the "connection of blood" between Canadians and Americans should temper their diplomatic relations.

By connection of blood, by long tradition, we ought to be the closest friends in the world. But it often happens that those who are the most nearly related by blood... are not always on the very best of terms... I am in great hopes, however, that the present state of irritation existing... may only be of the nature of a lovers' quarrel, or a quarrel between near relatives, which will soon be composed by more serious considerations.[59]

"Largely speaking the same language, largely drawing inspiration from the same sources, and worshipping at the same altars, I believe..." asserted L.H. Davies, "that, after all, blood is thicker than water, and that the man or the nation that precipitates a war and all its horrors between these two great English-speaking nations, would be committing a crime against humanity..." Canada could best lever the Empire's geostrategic position, he continued, by cultivating "the kindliest feelings between us and the great republic lying to the south of us. An alliance between Great Britain and the United States would be the guarantee of the world's peace, no nation and no combination of nations is strong enough to withstand a union between the greatest Empire in the world and the greatest republic in the world."[60]

Anglo-saxonism was also dragged into the frequently contentious issue of managing Canada-US trade relations. For example, Rodolphe Lemieux, Laurier's Postmaster General in 1911, defended the Government's proposed tariff Reciprocity Treaty with the United States against charges that it would lead ultimately to "the fusion of Canada into the United States." On the contrary, he claimed, Reciprocity promoted "Anglo-Saxon solidarity" and was a fitting tribute to the century of peace enjoyed on the Canada-US frontier since the War of 1812.

> ...not only are we against any idea of political union with the United States, but on the contrary, we believe that such agreements as these make for genuine Anglo-Saxon solidarity. The Trent Affair, the Fenian Raid, the Behring sea seizures are things of the past. A firm friendship between the several branches of the Anglo-Saxon race is worth striving for... At the end of this century of peace (the celebration of which will take place in 1912...), this reciprocity agreement will be the crowning event of that century. We believe that it will be a means of serving the empire and Canada; we believe it will prove a link between the mother country and the great republic... We have fairly won our way into the British brotherhood, and we will not hear with patience that any trade arrangement, however favourable, will turn us from the course we have freely chosen for ourselves within the greatest empire that has been.[61]

On the other side of this debate, some stressed that shared British political values were considerably more important than any Anglo-Saxon racial solidarity. Restating traditional arguments stretching back to the United Empire Loyalists that the American republic was "unstable and chaotic,"[62] W.F. Maclean warned the Commons that "today things are so bad" in the United States "that the people are almost on the verge of revolution." Canada-US Reciprocity was a wedge for American "continentalism:" a scheme to annex the whole continent so as "to put down a revolution at home" by diverting "public attention from domestic troubles." The incorporation of Canada was said to be politically essential to "continentalism" so as to protect the Republic's racial balance.

> In the past we know that they were not friendly to us. The people of the United States drove out the United Empire Loyalists, who made this country. They invaded this country more than once, they allowed the Fenians to invade this country and the dream of every American statesman today is the unification of the continent. They have the plan all laid out for taking over Mexico any day, but they say with Mexico in its present condition the people are too yellow for them and they propose to counterbalance them with the white people of Canada and bring the two countries in together. Will anybody deny that such a feeling is existing over there? I have read it time and time again. The republican party of the United States have refused to entertain a proposal to extend their states farther until a Canadian counterbalance of white people is brought about.

Maclean concluded his analysis with a restatement of the British Empire's moral mission in promoting liberty and political development along with Canada's importance to its success.

> The hope of the world is the domination and success of the British system of politics, that system of government which we have inherited from the old land. There is more thought of humanity and progress in the British association of free states like the mother country, Canada and Australia, than in anything else. There is no hope for humanity in the domination of the American republic over the whole of this continent. They are not taking up any of the great questions of today. They are not fighting the battles of humanity, they are not fighting the battle of the heathen or the oppressed in the distant continents of Africa or Asia. The hope of humanity [is] in the British system, and one of the bulwarks of the British system is the maintenance of Canadian nationality on the northern half of this continent.[63]

E.N. Lewis raised the issue of whether the United States could any longer be considered fully Anglo-Saxon as for several decades it had been drifting away from its biological roots in "the sturdy races of northwest and western Europe – Scandinavians, Germans, French, Anglo-Saxons…" Before 1880, Americans

> acquired a national type and characteristics of a strong, sturdy, moral self-reliant people. The height, weight, and chest measurement was steadily rising. Since 1880 these measurements are all decreasing, and the moral, physical and mental average lowering due wholly to the immense immigration of people from inferior races [southern and eastern Europeans], the small birth rate among native citizens and the great birth rate among foreigners.

The result had been "race trouble" and even "race suicide" in the United States because "in immigration heredity is far more important than environment or education." Canada should "profit" from the negative American example because the United States was "founded by men of the same fibre as Canadians and grown up under similar conditions and climate." "Why should we not keep for our own descendants and old country relations this fair heritage of ours and be… a contented people dwelling in a land of milk and honey," he asked, "…the best citizens we have are our own race."[64]

For his part, Prime Minister Laurier stressed the strategic advantages to the British Empire in permanently defusing tensions between Canada and the United States. While he admitted that some in the US still 'harboured' hope that Canada would be annexed, many other Americans were more realistic. Laurier then challenged Canada's "American friends," as well as the Commons, to consider an alternate security vision, a pacific one that would benefit the United States, Canada, Great Britain and the Empire.

> There may be a spectacle perhaps nobler yet than the spectacle of a united continent, a spectacle that would astound the world by its novelty and grandeur, the spectacle of two peoples living side by side along a frontier nearly 4,000 miles long, with not a cannon, with not a gun frowning across it, with not a fortress on either side, with no armament one against the other, but living in harmony, in

mutual confidence, and with no other rivalry than a generous emulation in commerce and the arts of peace. To the Canadian people I would say that if it is possible for us to obtain such relations between this young and growing nation, and the powerful American republic, Canada will have rendered to old England, the mother of nations, nay, to the whole British Empire, a service unequalled in its present effects, and still more in its far-reaching consequences[65]

For J. Charlton, the determining factor in Canada-US relations was the continental community of shared language – "Anglo-Saxon America" – a continent "inhabited by 85,000,000 of people speaking the English tongue... [that] will inevitably exercise a potent, if not controlling, influence upon the affairs to the world." "A matter of transcendent importance" was building good relations between the United States and the British Empire and "the relations existing between Canada and the United States could have a controlling influence" over the global British-American relationship. Charlton was optimistic for the future of Canada-U.S. relations because an industrializing and urbanizing America would require food from Canada's prairie provinces.

> Our vast resources are attracting attention. The period of narrowness and bitterness and ignorance, which characterized certain portions of the public in both of these countries is passing away, and in place of it is coming a broader spirit, a Catholic [sic] spirit, a spirit of toleration, a spirit of mutual conciliation which will bear excellent results in the interests of both countries. New conditions, vast possibilities confront us. We hardly stop to realize their magnitude. When this North-west, where hundreds of thousands are to settle in the near future, with its three hundred millions acres of arable land, of which three millions are now under cultivation, this North-west that can increase its production a hundredfold – when the resources of this country are developed, when its fields wave with harvests, when its surface is covered by farms and towns and cities, then we will see the fruition of the promise we have today... a great nation established on the northern portion of this continent. We will then look back to the past... and wonder at the narrowness and littleness and bitterness displayed by people in the old days before the broad horizon had opened before them.[66]

CONCLUSION

In respect to the international system in this era, "the pattern of thinking and meaning" we discovered among members of the House of Commons contained several shared elements of significance. First, Canada's international identity was most typically grounded within the British Empire. Second, parliamentarians viewed the Empire more as a political and moral community founded on individual liberty than as a spatial or racial project. Third, articulated through a universal and liberating rhetoric, their ideal of Empire citizenship was at least in theory multi-'racial' and multicultural. Fourth, the Empire was seen to depend on overriding military force to defend its political liberalism from militaristic challengers but at the same time it was said that it was neither held together by force nor was it aggressive in its international relations. Fifthly, many argued that Canada's special role in Empire-building was to secure the future of the northern half of the North American continent as British in the face of the jealous appetites of a powerful, but morally, politically and even racially inferior, United States of America. Alternatively, some envisioned the prospect of "Anglo-Saxon solidarity" underpinning a security and economic alliance between the United States, Canada, and rest of the British Empire. In the course of the next three chapters, we will see that debates over the meaning of race and identity in the Dominion rested upon all of these five elements relating to the location of Canada within the international system.

Notes

1. Canada, House of Commons, *Debates*, January 16, 1913, pp. 1641-42.
2. David V. J. Bell and Lorne Tepperman, *The Roots of Disunity: A Look at Canadian Political Culture.* Toronto, McClelland and Stewart, 1979. p. 1.

3. Commons, *Debates*, February 25, 1913, p. 3995.
4. Ibid., February 5, 1896, p. 1216.
5. Ibid., June 7, 1905 p. 7057.
6. Ibid., January 17, 1916, p. 11.
7. Ibid., March 29, 1909, pp. 3491-3492.
8. Ibid., March 18, 1905, pp. 2339-2340.
9. Ibid., March 12, 1901, pp. 1356-1358.
10. Ibid., February 25, 1913, p. 3997.
11. Ibid., February 5, 1896, pp. 1211-1212.
12. Ibid., February 23, 1893 pp. 1173-1174.
13. Ibid., February 13, 1900, p. 377.
14. Ibid., February 7, 1913, p. 2913.
15. Ibid., February 23, 1910, pp. 4106-4107.
16. Ibid., February 19, 1925, p. 316. See Phillip Buckner and R. Douglas Francis, "Introduction" in *Canada and the British World: Culture, Migration, Identity*. They argue that "it is a myth that Canadians emerged from the war alienated from, and disillusioned with, the imperial connection." p. 1.
17. Ibid., December 17, 1912, p. 1304.
18. Ibid., p. 1327.
19. Ibid., February 25, 1913, p. 3996.
20. Ibid., March 29, 1909, p. 3518.
21. Ibid., February 7, 1913. pp. 2912-2913.
22. Ibid., November 22, 1910, p. 101.
23. Ibid., January 16, 1913, p. 1644.
24. Ibid., December 5, 1912, p. 691.
25. Ibid., December 12, 1912, p. 1057.
26. Ibid., March 2, 1914, pp. 1252.
27. Ibid., February 5, 1900, pp. 58-59.

28. Ibid., April 22, 1902, p. 3356.
29. Ibid., February 5, 1900, pp. 64-65.
30. Ibid., February 6, 1913, pp. 2808-2810.
31. Ibid., July 6, 1885, p. 3112.
32. Ibid., March 26, 1885, p. 764.
33. For a review of the Riel Rebellion's international press exposure, see Geoff Read and Todd Webb, "'The Catholic Mahdi of the North West': Louis Riel and the Metis Resistance in Transatlantic and Imperial Context," *Canadian Historical Review*, June 2012. They observe that "the year 1885 was an eventful one in the imperial world. In Germany, the Berlin Conference concluded its work of dividing Africa among the colonial powers; in Indochina, the French faced resistance in South Vietnam and Cambodia, in Afghanistan, Russia and the United Kingdom nearly went to war; in the Sudan, General Gordon's garrison in Khartoum was overrun by the Mahdists... In Canada the expansion of the dominion and settler society also created conflict. As the Canadian Pacific Railroad neared completion, preparing the Canadian West for large-scale European settlement, the Canadian plains, like the Sudanese desert or the jungles of Vietnam, became the site of an anti-colonial revolt." pp. 171-172.
34. Commons, *Debates*, July 6, 1885, p. 3119.
35. Ibid., March 26, 1885, p. 762 and July 6, 1885, p. 3119.
36. Ibid., June 22, 1908, pp. 11053-11054.
37. Ibid., April 24, 1923, p. 2153.
38. Ibid., April 20, 1886, pp. 809-810.
39. Ibid., April 15, 1886, pp. 719, 721, 725.
40. Ibid., December 18, 1912, p. 1397.
41. Ibid., March 13, 1905, p. 2393.
42. Ibid., March 29, 1909, pp. 3511-3512.
43. Ibid., January 14, 1913, p. 1436.
44. Ibid., February 17, 1910. p. 3810.

45. Ibid., January 16, 1913, pp. 1641-1643.
46. Ibid., p. 1654.
47. Ibid., January 29, 1917, p. 205. Heinrich von Treitschke was "the most popular historian of the [German] Imperial period" who argued that "the power of the state was mercury to measure the cultural level of the nation" and "brought the language of nation together with the vocabulary of race." Helmut Walser Smith, *The Continuities of German History: Nation, Religion, and Race across the Long Nineteenth Century.* Cambridge: Cambridge University Press, 2008. pp. 170, 173.
48. Ibid., February 8, 1915, p. 9.
49. Ibid., January 25, 1917, p.135.
50. Ibid., April 19, 1918, p. 939.
51. Ibid., February 8, 1915, pp. 16-17.
52. Ibid., January 31, 1916, p. 415.
53. Berger, *The Sense of Power*, p. 168.
54. Commons, *Debates*, February 5, 1896, pp. 1188-1189.
55. Ibid., July 11, 1904, pp. 6447, 6451-6452.
56. Ibid., February 5, 1896, p. 1206.
57. Ibid., July 22, 1899, pp. 8158-8159. For a study of turn of the century Canadian Anglo-Saxonism, see Edward P. Kohn, *This kindred people: Canadian-American relations and the Anglo-Saxon idea, 1895-1903.* Montreal: McGill-Queen's University Press, 2004.
58. Ibid., February 5, 1896, pp. 1188-1189.
59. Ibid., pp. 1208-1209.
60. Ibid., pp. 1192-1193.
61. Ibid., February 21, 1911, pp. 4038-4039.
62. See the discussion of this in Berger, *The Sense of Power*, pp. 155-162.
63. Commons, *Debates*, February 22, 1911, pp. 4068-4070.
64. Ibid., November 16, 1909, pp. 91-92. Lewis advocated legislation "prohibiting all immigration from Europe south of 44 degrees North latitude and East of 20 East longitude, and from Turkey in Asia." See

also similar remarks by H.H. Miller, December 14, 1909, pp. 1526-1527.

65. Ibid., March 7, 1911, p. 4771.
66. Ibid., April 21, 1903, pp. 1662, 1671-1674.

CHAPTER 3.

DOMINION ANGLO-SAXONISM AND CANADIANS OF EUROPEAN ORIGIN

There are English Canadians – and legions of them – who are English before being Canadians and who, unsuspectingly, are ready to sacrifice the interests, even the future, of the colony to those of their mother country. I do not wish to blame them, for their blood is up, and blood will tell. But neither can they blame my fellow-people for being Canadians before being British, and even for being French Canadians before being only Canadians. In this case also, blood must tell. Yes, without suspecting it, the racial instinct is at work...[1]
–PAUL ARTHUR SÉGUIN, 1917.

What did it mean to be a British subject in late nineteenth and early twentieth century Canada? As we learned in Chapter 2, British subjecthood was commonly understood to confer membership within the world's most powerful Empire. Along with its moral mission to promote individual liberty and free political institutions, the British Empire also embraced, albeit ambivalently, a vision of individual citizen equality that transcended religion, language, colour, and race.

Lowry has importantly argued that following the conquest of New France in 1763, the British North American colonies became the "prototype Dominion" pioneering not only political autonomy in the institutions of "advanced responsible government" (late 1840s) but also the notion of multicultural political citizenship where "French Canadians might be British subjects without becoming English in religion and law." Following the Quebec Act of 1774 and the Constitution Act of 1791, French and Irish Roman Catholics could claim political equality with British protestants under the Crown. In his analysis of the British Empire of the nineteenth and early twentieth centuries, Lowry placed emphasis on the Crown's role as a "personal symbol" enabling an "adoptive nationalism" that could transcend religion, language, and national origins.

> the personal character of the monarchy... avoided the controversies of what it meant to be a Canadian, Australian or New Zealander, in a way that a republican form of government would not have been able to do... The monarchy could be imagined selectively by various groups of imperial subjects. Thus, for example, the Orangemen of Ontario could emphasise the Crown's Protestant character, while, simultaneously, French Canadians and Irish Catholics could stress the monarch's protective concern for their language rights and religion. Notwithstanding the constitutional requirement to uphold the Crown's Protestant character in the metropole, the secret of the monarchy's imperial success was its ability to juggle conflicting and contradictory allegiances across the empire.[2]

Sir Wilfrid Laurier forcefully expressed to the Commons his understanding of the innovative nature of British subjecthood in Canada where individual liberty and political equality was the birthright of "different races... of equal rank."

> If there is any country in the world it is this country of ours, Canada, where we can proclaim this principle, that wherever men of different races, but races of equal rank, are found to live together under the same government, the only policy which can give adequate justice to all, which can give satisfaction to all, which can ensure harmony, is a policy of equal rights and equal justice, a policy which will give to every citizen, without any questions of birth or origin, the same rights, the same liberties, the same privileges, the same aspirations. This is the policy which we have adopted in this

country, and I think we can fairly claim with some pride, that it has proved eminently successful.³

Laurier believed that the Canadian model could be a solution to the Boer War: "a confederation of the Dutch states and the English states, after the pattern of our Canadian confederation" would allow for "the work of civilization and freedom" in southern Africa to proceed.⁴ While Laurier's position reflected conventional wisdom in the Commons during this era on the multicultural character of Canada's democratic institutions, this chapter will record important disagreements on who made up the races of "equal rank" as well as whether these races were sociologically or biologically defined.

FRENCH CANADIANS AS BRITISH SUBJECTS

Not surprisingly given their minority group status, French Canadian parliamentarians often took the lead in defining British subjecthood as an identity constructed around political loyalty rather than being based in any other anchor such as language, religion, or biological ancestry. This identity was most often framed as a group claim based in history, rather than a liberal claim grounded on an abstract concept of individual rights. It was said that not only had French Canadians been among the leading political architects of British North America, but the actions of French Canada had proved absolutely critical to its survival and success.

As C. Marcil told the Commons,

> It is the pride of England, and it is the pride especially of the British Empire, that the greatness of the Empire is to be found in its 450,000,000 subjects of whom 45,000,000 or less are of British stock, the remaining 400,000,000 being composed of all nationalities, all creeds, of all languages. To say that in Canada a man must be of British stock to be a loyal supporter of the Crown and of the flag, is to exhibit a most deplorable ignorance of our history. Canada would never have existed as it exists today but for the subjects of the King who speak the French language... when rebellion did break

out on this continent it broke out among the English-speaking subjects of His Majesty the King. The temptation for the French subjects of His Majesty the King on the banks of the St. Laurence to have followed the new star spangled banner was great; but it stands today to their credit that... it was his French subjects of the province of Quebec who in 1774 saved Canada to the British Crown.[5]

French Canadians had pushed back the American military twice (1775 and 1812) and had led the struggle for the democratic institutions of responsible government, J. Tassé reminded the House.

> ...if our people had emigrated in a body to the States; if they had accepted the place open to them at any time in the American Union; if they had obeyed the pressing appeal of Washington and Lafayette at a critical and decisive period of our history; if they had not repelled the American invader on the memorable day of Chateauguay, under the command of De Salaberry, the British flag would have long since crossed the seas. Moreover, if our forefathers had not been the first and most persevering to fight in our Legislative Assemblies for the securing of responsible government, Canada would not, perhaps, be even yet in the enjoyment of the greatest amount of liberty of which any race can boast of on this continent.[6]

While the loyalty of French Canadians to the Crown had ensured the survival of the British Empire in North America, the British Empire in turn had guaranteed them political liberty along with the preservation of their language and Roman Catholic religion. L.J. Gauthier reasoned that

> The Frenchmen of Quebec... know that the British Crown has granted them the free use of their language, the free exercise of their religion and every liberty of self-government. Every time their rights have been brought into discussion those rights have been protected by the British Crown. And do you think for a moment the Frenchmen of Quebec would be stupid enough to cast away the power that has protected them for a century and a half? – to be flooded, if they were annexed to the United States, or to be flooded by the [English-speaking] majority of this country...[7]

A.A.C. Larivière noted that other British subjects living in the islands of Jersey, Guernsey, and St. Lucia enjoyed a legal right to use French as their official language. Accordingly, French Canadians had not been given an "unprecedented concession... but... a right which belongs to subjects in other colonies of the Empire" and, in fact, were just as loyal as Anglo-Celtic British subjects.

> The gravest insult that can be offered to us... is that men should wish our enemies to believe that because we do not use the English language habitually we are not loyal subjects of Her Majesty. They attack us on this line when taxing us with disloyalty. Well, when we see what our ancestors did when the time had come to defend the frontier, can it not be fairly said that they showed themselves quite as loyal if not more loyal than our fellow subjects of British origin? Can it be that people have forgotten the celebrated battles which we fought against our powerful neighbours the Americans? And if Canada still remains a British possession, to whom does England owe its retention if not to the French – but still loyal – population of the Province of Quebec.[8]

Sir Hector Langevin explained to the House that questioning the loyalty of French Canadians to the Crown was beyond the pale.

> I must add that we are not more loyal than are the other races in this Dominion. In fact, we are all loyal, and the idea even of attacking at this day our loyalty has passed away. We are now on the same footing, and we intend to remain on the same footing which the other races in this country occupy; and we do not intend that they shall imagine that our position as British subjects, as far as our loyalty to the Crown of England is concerned, differs in any particular from theirs. We admire their loyalty – we admire their position, but for ourselves we do not intend to be attacked or belittled.

THE CONFEDERATION COMPACT

In the decades immediately following Confederation, French Canadian parliamentarians typically viewed federalism as a project which institutionalized the political, cultural and religious rights of French-speakers. The poisonous struggle over 'representation by population' in the United Canadas was replaced by a federal structure, where, as Silver observes, "the French Canadians were to take possession of a province of their own – a province with an enormous degree of autonomy. In fact, *separation* (from Upper Canada) and *independence* (of Quebec within its jurisdictions) were the main themes of Bleu propaganda."[9]

Sir Charles Tupper, a father of Confederation, told the Commons in 1896 that in the negotiations for union among the British North American provinces "no consideration... had greater significance or greater importance in the minds of all the delegates present on that occasion than that this measure afforded the means of removing that antagonism of race and religion which had been found to act so fatally in reference to the interests of Canada." Urgent action was necessary as questions of "race and religion" had made "good government" impossible.

> so great had the conflict become, so closely balanced were the parties representing, as it were, Upper and Lower Canada, which, to a certain extent, were divided into hostile camps, that good government had become impossible. The commerce of the country was in a deplorable condition; the financial condition of Canada was anything but such as would afford gratification to any person interested in the welfare of the country; and the credit had sunk so low, that 6 per cent debentures were only saleable at a ruinous discount.[10]

Sir Hector Langevin, another father of Confederation, affirmed to the House that he "agree[d] entirely" with Tupper's account – "We could not proceed with the work of the country, and the country was suffering. The question then was, not only a question of race, or a question of religion, but it was a question of our very existence." Confederation, he explained, was a treaty or compact between provinces: "We have in the Confederation Act a compact, and it was so considered when the Bill was before Parliament in England. They regarded it as a treaty between us, the different provinces, and that such a treaty was to be accepted by Parliament as it stood and passed."[11]

Elsewhere Langevin described confederation as a multicultural venture: "when in 1864, the question came up of making a larger union, you did not see the French race standing up on the one side and not keeping pace with the progress of the country. On the contrary, the French race went hand in hand with the English, the Scotch, the Irish, and the Germans, and the other races of this country – all went together to secure the [federal] institutions which we enjoy today."[12] J. Tassé similarly presented Canada from a French Canadian perspective as "diverse" and its multi-ethnic composition as an asset to her future development.

> Although speaking a language different from that of the majority let me state that we are Canadians before all. As such, we are ready to follow our destiny at all risks and hazards, firmly believing that, under the safeguards of our Constitution and of our well balanced system of parties, justice and liberty shall be always the lot of the subject of Queen Victoria in this country. As such, we are prepared to welcome, to give a helping hand to the emigrants from all climes, from all latitudes, who are in search of bread, space and freedom – as such, we are prepared to welcome the emigrants from all countries, either from the Icelandic shores, from the steppes of Russia, from picturesque Switzerland, from the over-crowded districts of Germany and Great Britain – that nursery of nations – as such, we are prepared to assist the British Government in giving to the Irish people the land which they could not possess in their own country, the peace which they could not find, and the Home Rule for which they are agitating. In fact, our Dominion is broad enough to make a landlord of every Irish peasant. That diversity of races far from being detrimental, will be most desirable, most advantageous. Although at times it may give rise to a considerable amount of friction, it will produce a laudable spirit of emulation. Each would naturally strive for the highest prize. As far as we are concerned, we have learned a great deal in our contact with other nationalities. The great empire to which we belong, the great nation to the south of us, have all be made rich, progressive and powerful by a variety of races – so shall it be with us. We shall combine the energy, the industry and various qualities of all those races, and we shall make of them a great Canadian nationality.[13]

Toleration and a "spirit of justice" underlay Confederation and Canada help to spread these 'advanced' policies throughout "all quarters and all portions of the Empire," said Tupper. Because

Britain has "the destinies and the welfare of multitudes of races and creeds; governing India, Africa, America...", then

> Toleration is the very secret of success, and the secret of the greatness of the Empire; and toleration increases as the years go by. A few years ago it would have been impossible for the Lord Chief Justice to be a Roman Catholic and to sit as Lord Chief Justice in the United Kingdom. He is there today by virtue, not only of the growth of that spirit of toleration, but by the very experience that England has had in empire governing. A member of the late Government in England, one of the most distinguished members of the Liberal Administration, was a Roman Catholic, and before that he was Governor General of the Empire of India. All this indicates plainly and unmistakably to us, that the fathers of confederation were wise in their generation. We, in Canada, have led even public opinion in England, in regard to reforms and advancements...[14]

LANGUAGE, BLOOD AND DUALITY

In the later years of the nineteenth century, however, a significantly different interpretation of confederation emerged. Confederation, it was said, was a compact between two races – French and English – each having equality and guaranteed political rights in all provinces. Henri Bourassa became the leading exponent of this position within the Commons and the country as a whole. Silver has argued that this 'novel' theory of confederation could be articulated only after French Quebecers "discovered" and became concerned about "French-Catholic minorities" in other provinces "only *after* they had tried to help the Métis, only *after* the Riel affair, the racial agitation of the late 1880s and the controversies of the 1890s – only *after* all this that the bilingual theory of Confederation could emerge. Only then could a Henri Bourassa appear on the scene."[15]

Bourassa told the Commons that the BNA Act was "the mere outcome of the compact entered into by the two great groups of the Canadian nation..."; a "compact loyally gone into in 1867 between English and French speaking Canadians," and a product of "two allies whose rights [were] equal by virtue of the constitution." Even if the written provisions of the BNA Act did not make this compact explicit, the principles and doctrines of the agreement between "the two elements" that made up the "Canadian nation" were nonetheless clear.

> ...beside and above the written law, there is a constitutional doctrine... growing out of the very principles embodied in the constitution. The Act of 1867 provided at the outset solely for the organization of the provinces then constitutional. Even before entering confederation, these provinces enjoyed self-government: they had their parliament, their official tongue, their rules of parliamentary procedure. The idea did not occur to the fathers of confederation to alter that condition of things: but in establishing the Dominion parliament, they did so on a basis in harmony with the rights and traditions of the two elements which make up the Canadian nation...[16]

In the midst of World War I, Gustave Boyer reiterated the English-French compact theory of Confederation in service of his views about wartime conscription.

> In 1867, a solemn compact was made by the two nations, English and French. That contract stipulated to each its privileges and its obligations. Nothing is more sacred than the pledged word and more official than the magna charta [sic] of Confederation. Why does one of the contracting parties in this memorable document now wish, in defiance of honour and of solemn promise, pass over and consider the Confederation Act, which guarantees the equality of the French race in this country, 'as a mere scrap of paper.' Is it that we are here living in Germany? Should the sons of those who have signed and approved the Act of 1867 be less honourable and less conciliating than their fathers? The latter have made a compact, which their sons should in honour respect, and in so doing, peace and harmony would be restored in this country. And then the two great races inhabiting it, uniting their common efforts, would in mutual love and respect, work out their destinies[17]

Silver's analysis of the conflicts leading to the articulation of a 'two nations' theory of Canadian political development is correct in so far as it goes. But there is more to the story. French-English conflict in this period was also increasingly influenced by the rising tide of late nineteenth century pseudo-scientific race-thinking that we reviewed in Chapter 1. These racialist ideas presented challenges to the prevailing political orthodoxy stressing equal political, linguistic, and religious rights for all British subjects. They also turned away from the founders' idea of Confederation as a multilayer compact of provinces and ethnic groups. Within this compact, Quebec was constituted as a somewhat autonomous French-Catholic jurisdiction with protected constitutional rights for its English and Protestant minority. Adherents of the older, more liberal, political consensus did not go away quietly, indeed they struggled vociferously against the new strains of determinist race-thinking. This struggle is reflected both in the remaining text of this chapter and in the chapters to follow.

Racial pseudo-science forcefully emerged in 1890 in a debate about language policy in the North-West. D. McCarthy introduced a motion in the Commons opposing the use of French in its territorial assembly based on his understanding of the linguistic racial theories of Edward Augustus Freeman. An Oxford University historian, Freeman had championed the nineteenth century pseudo-science of philology attributing human progress to a superior (but imagined) Aryan language family while denouncing Jews, "the Turk", and "the Negro" as inferior races. C.J.W. Parker observes that "the basis of his racial thought was philological; he would have nothing to do with measuring skulls or any other physiological evidence, despite the growth of such during his life."[18] In Freeman's narrative, the Teutons – including the Anglo-Saxons and the Normans – were an especially vigourous branch of the Aryans with a genius for the institutions of democratic government. Particularly significant for those who sought to apply Freeman's racial theories to Canada was his conviction that "mankind instinctively takes language as the badge of nationality."[19]

"There is no more important matter in the formation of the character of a people than the language that they speak,"

McCarthy opined, "and, after all is said and done, I think it will be found that nations and races are distinguished and are distinctive more by reason of the language that they speak than by the blood which is common to or supposed to be common to them all." Therefore, in order to build up a vigourous Canadian race, it would be best if English was adopted as the national language rather than having dual languages. "If, in truth and fact it is in the interests of this Dominion, that there should be one race, one nationality, and one national life, it is the duty of all of us to strive to bring about that result," he claimed. If, after the conquest of Quebec, French Canadians had been "induced" to adopt English, they could have been completely assimilated into the English race and the "cleavage of race" that was debilitating Canada would have been prevented.

> instead of encouraging them in the use of their language, had a policy been pursued of inducing them – not by any harsh means at all, not by any aggravating measures – to speak the English tongue, I want to know whether today, instead of the difference, the cleavage of race, which we see going on, and which is becoming more and more pronounced, and which is calculated to rend this Dominion in twain, if some stop is not put to it – I would like to know whether we would see the spectacle that we see today. I think it is perfectly plain that we would not see it. I think that no injustice would have been done, and that in one generation, or in two at most, my hon. friends that now represent the Province of Quebec, or their ancestors, would have been speaking English, and would have been English in fact, English in sentiment, just as much as those who have gone to the other side of the line… have now become assimilated and form part of the American people, not merely in name but in truth and in fact.[20]

Speaking in the same debate, J. Charlton, like McCarthy, did not claim English biological racial superiority over French Canadians. "It is not a question as to which is the leading race, as to which has the best lineage, as to which has the best blood," he said. Divisions between the French and English were judged sociological rather than biological and therefore French Canadians, although backward, were 'assimilable.' To be sure, Charlton found the "medievalism" of the French Canadian "race" "a little behind the times." "We do not deny that we would like to see them get rid of their system of tithes, *fabrique* assessments and the other antiquated abuses under which they labor... I shall feel sorry that the spirit of backwardness continues, and shall feel glad that something else should take its place," he said.

Promising to "share equally and fully" the considerable political liberties and accomplishments of Canada and even to treat French Canadians "as brothers," he nevertheless made it clear that "we want to make this an English nation, we wish to have English institutions from ocean to ocean, we wish the North-West with its future 30 or 40 million to be a Saxon North-West" through "gradual assimilation of the races... gradual homogeneity." For now, in the North-West "we merely propose that in a new country, where there are comparatively no inhabitants at all, that the English language shall be used as the official language in place of two languages."

But the end game was advancing racial Anglo-Saxonism. "Our avowed purpose," Charlton declared. "[is] to make this a Saxon state. The avowed purpose of the Anglo-Saxon is to make the Anglo-Saxon race the greatest race on the earth, and the hope of the Anglo-Saxon is that the day will come, and come before many decades have elapsed, when the English language will be the common means of intercommunication between all the races of the world, and the English race will be the dominant race of the world, so that the Anglo-Saxon will fulfil the destiny which God has evidently designed he shall fulfil in this world." The Anglo-Saxon has been placed in the ascendency in North American and

> he intends that this whole continent shall have freedom and free institutions; he intends that it shall have religious tolerance; he intends that the history of the race on this continent shall be marked by the most wonderful material development of this or any other age; he intends to build up a great power on this conti-

nent; and he has done it. Already the second power in the world is the Republic to the south of us; the greatest of Britain's colonies is the one in which we live; and the power of these two countries is increasing in a ration which almost dazzles the imagination. The Anglo-Saxon may be somewhat aggressive, but his purpose is nevertheless a beneficent one, and he intends – it is his fixed determination – that assimilation and homogeneity shall be the characteristics of every part of the land over which he bears sway. That is his fixed intention… [and] he expects to occupy this continent, from the Arctic Ocean to the Isthmus of Panama, there is no doubt.[21]

Another contributor to this debate, A. McNeil, stressed the benefit of intermarriage and assimilation to both the English and French in Canada. The "notorious cause" of the Austrian Empire's "weakness," he stated, was that it lacked a "distinctive nationality" because it was made up of "a bundle of distinct peoples." Anglo-Saxons, in contrast, drew strength from being a composite race that had amalgamated the best qualities of several strong strains. "If the Celts, and Anglo-Saxons, and Normans had not mingled in England and formed one race, but lived as separate races in England today, does anyone suppose that England would occupy the place among the nations of the world which she does occupy?" And so, in Canada,

> if our races were amalgamated, we should be stronger than we are at the present moment. We all know that our French Canadian friends have many qualities characteristic of their race, great and good qualities, which are not characteristic of the race to which we belong; and I think we may say, on the other hand, that we have good qualities characteristic of our race which are not so highly developed in theirs; and I think we may fairly conclude that if there were a blending of the races, that blending would be beneficial to both; but in any case it cannot be doubted that it would add to the solidarity of the Dominion. Then… this perpetuation of different languages has a tendency to keep races apart and to preserve and maintain race distinctions…[22]

The line of race-thinking exposed by McCarthy's motion on the North-West was repudiated by the establishment of both parties in the Commons as they reaffirmed the orthodoxy of the communal equality of British subjecthood in Canada in passionate terms. Edward Blake, former Liberal leader, dismissed the idea that "the Anglo-Saxon" is "destined by fate" "to swallow" up French Canadians. "I say: No, a thousand times, no; …I intend for my part to defend them just as warmly as if I were one of themselves; and I should regard myself as dishonored and disgraced if I were now to yield to the forces which press me to any other course." Blake told the House that the historic success of French Canadians in establishing their rights as British subjects was "a victory for humanity" and challenged "those engaged in this agitation" for assimilation to

> put themselves in the French Canadian's place. You may selfishly wish that he had agreed to be suppressed; you may have a profound conviction of the incomparable superiority of your tongue, your laws, your creed; you may earnestly desire for all men the inestimable boons of British birth, of English speech, of Protestant religion. But still… cannot you put yourself in his place? And can you not, must you not, admire the courage, the fidelity, and the determination with which, at great odds, he fought in all fields – in the legislature, before the people… for what to him was as dear as what you call your birthright is to you? Fought, aye, and conquered too! Cannot you recognize that his was after all a victory for humanity? …[which] gave an opening for the exhibition of still higher and deeper and broader feelings of justice and liberality and tolerance than are permitted to a wholly homogeneous people?[23]

Then sitting Prime Minister Sir John A. Macdonald called the arguments of those who supported McCarthy's motion "foolish and wicked" and stressed there was "no paramount race in this country" only equal British subjects.

> I have no accord with the desire expressed in some quarters that by any mode whatever there should be an attempt made to oppress the one language or render it inferior to the other; I believe it would be impossible if it were tried, and it would be foolish and wicked if it were possible. The statement that has been made so often that this is a conquered country is *a propos de rien*. Whether it was conquered of

ceded, we have a constitution now under which all British subjects are in a position of absolute equality, having equal rights of every kind – of language, of religion, of property and of person. There is no paramount race in this country; we are all British subjects, and those who are not English are none the less British subjects on that account.[24]

But Laurier, the Opposition Leader, upped the ante denouncing McCarthy's "movement" as "anti-Canadian" and "anti-British." Canada was composed of "the most heterogeneous elements" and creating racial conflict was "a national crime."

> Any policy which appeals to a class, to a creed, to a race, or which does not appeal to the better instincts to be found in all classes, in all creeds, and in all races, is stamped with the stamp of inferiority. The French Canadian who appeals to his fellow-countrymen to stand by themselves, aloof from the rest of this continent; the English Canadian who... appeals to his fellow-countrymen on grounds affecting them alone may, perhaps, win the applause of those whom they may be addressing, but impartial history will pronounce their work as vicious in conception as it is mischievous and wicked in its tendency. We are here a nation, composed of the most heterogeneous elements – Protestants and Catholics, English, French, German, Irish, Scotch, every one, let it be remembered, with his traditions, with his prejudices. In each of these conflicting antagonistic elements, however, there is a common spot of patriotism, and the only true policy is that which reaches that common patriotism and makes it vibrate in all, towards a common end and common aspirations. I may be asked: What, then, is to be the future of Canada? The future of Canada is this: that it must be British.[25]

Several backbenchers like Alonzo Wright also spoke out in defence of the ideal of a liberal, tolerant British Empire and against what he judged to be the politically dangerous assimilationist agenda of Anglo-Saxon race-thinking.

> We have a form of government which is free to the fullest extent, and every man has the absolute right of freedom of conscience and worship. All that is wanted to build up this national edifice is a little common sense – a little sense of justice, a little of that spirit of compromise, which is of the very essence of the British system, and

then the work may be said to be accomplished. I must confess that I have been very much astonished at the course which has been taken by the hon. member who introduced this Bill, and his friends who advocate Imperial Federation. They profess to endeavor to bring about the union of the British Empire; they profess to unite instead of dividing us, but what does this course of action mean? Instead of peace and harmony, they bring us the faggot and the sword; instead of the spirit of compromise, which… is of the essence of the British system, and gives it its magnificent power throughout the world, they bring us dissension and disorder.[26]

Beginning in the 1890s some French Canadian members of the Commons increasingly began to explain the federation in dualistic terms – language, religion and race – in place of the older idea of a compact between several provinces or ethnic groups. Following the conceptual path of racial Tuetonism the two 'races' were sometimes said to be biologically intertwined and therefore equivalent. For example, Henri Bourassa sought legitimacy for his arguments by claiming that French and Anglo-Celtic Canadians shared elements of a common British genetic, cultural and political heritage through their Norman ancestors.

> The principles upon which I have based this proposition are not new; they were born with the British nation itself; they were brought by the Saxon pirates from the dark forests of Tuetonia to the Celtic island of the north; they were laid down as the cornerstone of the British constitution by a section of that robust Norman race of which the French Canadians are to-day, perhaps, the most direct and thorough offsprings.[27]

Some Anglophones appreciated this point, here the same idea was expressed by G.E. Casey

> … of the great strains of blood in Canada, although first in colonization, is that race with which we are so proud to be associated, our cousins from France. I say our cousins from France, because, in the course of centuries, what with the Norman conquest of England, the interchange of settlement between the two countries, the mixture that has taken place in Canada, we cannot affect to consider our fellow-citizens of the French race otherwise than as relatives at

the present time. I claim that there is no such thing, or should be no such thing as a racial problem, or a racial difference, between the people of Canada.[28]

Precisely because there was no unbridgeable 'racial difference,' some believed that the "ultra-Protestants" on one side of the duality had been plotting since the Plains of Abraham to assimilate French Canadians. H. Jeannotte described the historical failure of this "chimerical dream."

> That is not precisely a new thing. That is the system of politics inaugurated by the conquerors the morning after the cession of Canada, although the French Canadians were then only six thousand... This style of politics has not been always affirmed brutally as it was under the Military government, but it has never varied. All of which, however, has not hindered the French race and Catholicity from growing and propagating... the French Canadians... are today two millions in Canada, all as French as on the first day of the English domination... Such is the result of persecution whether open or concealed. If our enemies imagine that they can at last accomplish what so many others before them have failed in, they are very naïve. Let them understand, Mr. Speaker, that the French Canadians will remain as they are. The fusion of races in this country is a chimerical dream: there is not a sensible man who can reasonably entertain the idea of it.

To preserve the social and political peace, it was necessary Canada's "two races" be left alone to develop separately while their citizens mutually enjoyed equal political rights as British subjects.

> There is only one means of making peace reign between the races, and that is to leave upon the beautiful soil of our Dominion the two races to develop and grow side by side in full liberty guaranteed by the laws which do not prevent any person from exercising his rights and the duty of well-doing. It is not indispensable to speak only English and to be Protestant in order to be a loyal subject of Her Britannic Majesty, and to be a good citizen.[29]

IMMIGRATION

We began this chapter with reference to Laurier's assertion that British subjecthood in Canada meant that individual liberty and political equality was the birthright of "different races... of equal rank." Which were considered among these "equal rank" races? Around the turn of the twentieth century, one can discern at least two lists delivered in Commons debates: one we have previously seen in the speeches of Laurier and others to be more expansive; English, French, Welsh, Scottish, Irish, along with Germans, and the other was a more exclusive English-French list. This question was to take on increasing significance as Canada sought immigrants to develop her newly opened North-West.

Henri Bourassa argued for maintaining Canada as a select club restricted to its two founding "races."

> This country was settled and founded by the French and conquered by the English. After the feuds of many years these races have agreed together to found a vast Canadian nation. But sir, it never was in the minds of the founders of this nation... [that] we ought to change a providential condition of our partly French and partly English country to make it a land of refuge for the scum of all nations... The idea of the founders of this nation was that the double current of our national and mental activity should go on, that the British civilization and the French civilization should be maintained in this country, and that we should not give the better half of our continent to people who have nothing in common with us – nothing in common with us in history, nothing in common with us in blood, nothing in common with us in education or economics... before twenty years are over at the present rate of movement, they will be the masters of the country and the two races that have formed the Canadian people will be swamped by these 'intruders'... Because the fathers of confederation decided, and decided wisely, that this should be a dual country – French in its origin, British by assimilation, taking from both races and both civilizations its best moral, social and political characteristics – I claim that the equilibrium between the two should be maintained and that it is in the interest of all British citizens in Canada that a French speaking population should be developed.

In future years, the Canadian parliament will be controlled by "foreigners who came to this country to make money, who will try to control this parliament so as to make money... who will be quite content to see British institutions disappear from our midst," Bourassa warned.[30] Similar "scum" arguments were made by Armand Lavergne who told the Commons that in order to satisfy land speculators with an interest in the North-West, Canada was accepting "a mongrel population, a population that comes in by flocks."

> there are only two classes of desirable immigrants that we need in this country; those are immigrants that come from the British isles and those that come from France or Belgium. They are easily assimilated; they are already under the same laws and civilization that we enjoy in this country.... The French immigrant would compare more than favourably with the Polish Jews, the Prussians, the Galicians and the Doukhobors... The motto of the Immigration Department seems to have been: The Doukhobors rather than the French... the scum of continental Europe... If this goes on, in twenty years, there will be no such thing as the Canadian ideal... The best proof of what I say is the fact that for the first time last year we had in Montreal... a socialist parade with the red flag of anarchy at its head, and possibly this year, if the police do not interfere, we shall have a repetition of that procession. In a few years the Jewish population of Montreal has increased from 8,000 to 40,000.[31]

Some Anglo-Celtic members also favoured immigrants from France or Belgium over those from eastern and southern Europe. T.S. Sproule, for example, warned that Canada's "indiscriminate" immigration policy was encouraging the entry of hundreds of thousands of "the riff raff of every country of the world."

> It is one of the greatest dangers that confront us. We are importing the undesirable elements of Europe and continental countries – people who know nothing about our institutions, who are not in any way to the manor born, who are alien to the conditions of Canadian and American life, who are imbued with instincts and natures which have not in themselves any tendency to elevate humanity but rather to lower it in every particular... We do not inquire whether they are physically, mentally or educationally

suited to the country. Their elevation in the scale of morality or civilization appears to be a matter of indifference. We ask nothing of these important factors, but we say that the government are entitled to our thanks because two or three thousand of these Galicians or Doukhobors or Finns or Russian Jews or Poles or Mexicans have come to settle in Canada. Canada to-day is the dumping ground for the refuse of every country in the world. And the time will come... when the social problems of life will press as heavily on us as they are doing to-day on the people in European and continental countries...

Sproule listed those "races" he favoured as immigrants giving prominent place to the "French."

...we desire to get as many as we can of Irish, English, Scotch, German and French. All of these are welcome because they make good and desirable immigrants... I do not apprehend any danger from people of the races that I have named, but I do apprehend danger from those coming from European continental countries where the degeneracy of human life is greater than in the others... We welcome people coming from England, from Ireland, Scotland, Germany or France, because we know what they are. They belong to the races to which we belong, they are men who will tend to the elevation of our population and to the progress of our country. They are accustomed to our institutions, they are suitable to our climate...[32]

Similarly, J.D. Reid maintained that "nobody can doubt that our own young English Canadians and French Canadians are better suited to settle and develop our Northwest than any foreigners can possibly be."[33] And, E.G. Prior questioned

...why cannot we have more of the French people in this country instead of bringing in these Galicians and Doukhobors... we would be glad to see some of those French colonists amongst us, rather than many who are coming at present. The aim should be to people Canada with those who have the courage and the wish to build up the British Empire and perpetuate British institutions.[34]

Despite some calls to restrict immigration to 'two races,' a more open attitude generally dominated debates.[35] While holding out Anglo-Celtic and French Canadians as the model for British subjects in Canada, most seemed prepared to welcome other European groups judged to be sociologically assimilable. Tolerance was a British value. Laurier put it in a nutshell. "I am not prepared," he said, "to favour the immigration of these Mongolian races which do not assimilate with us, but as to the Caucasian races and European races – not all of them, but all those who readily assimilate with us – it is our duty to open our doors to them and follow the example of the mother country in that respect."[36] R.G. Macpherson got to the heart of the matter. "The white man", he observed, "may not be just exactly the kind of man that you would like to invite into your parlour; he may not talk the language or understand it, but his boys and girls are going to school, they are given education along the required lines and they are singing 'God save the King' and 'Rule Britannia' within six months after they come here."[37]

W.M. Ross deplored the speeches decrying eastern European immigration as "very narrow in their ideas" and stressed the determinant role played by the common bonds of Christian European civilization.

> The Irishman, the Englishman, the Scotchman and the Frenchman will come to us for generations yet just as well as these people from the continent of Europe. These people from the continent come to Halifax, well clad and pay their way to the great North-West. Will these hon. gentlemen turn them back again as we do the Chinese? I say no, let them come and work out their living and their destinies in this country. I am sorry to hear intelligent men preach such doctrines as we have had to listen to to-night. These people to whom they allude come from the midst of civilization and bring with them the civilization and the characteristic of their native countries, and we should deal with them in a broad-minded and Christian spirit and not treat them as outcasts and publicans.[38]

W. McIntyre, one of the first members elected from an Alberta constituency, forcefully contested Henri Bourassa's assertion that eastern Europeans were "foreigners" who would overwhelm Canada's two founding "races" in Canada's political institutions.

> Does not the hon. gentleman know that every man who comes into Canada and proves upon a homestead must take the oath of allegiance! and I claim that no man who has taken the oath of allegiance should be termed a foreigner. What difference does it make whether the accent which he used comes from the highlands of Scotland, or of sunny France or from Galicia. If he is a good citizen, if he be an honest and industrious man, contributing to the wealth of the country, he should have the sentimental protection of not being called a foreigner... I claim... that when a man takes the oath of allegiance and becomes a citizen of this country it ill becomes another citizen to stand up and call him a foreigner.

McIntyre went on to critique the two "founding races" theory of Canada and countered with more open-ended vision of Canadian nationality.

> ...the time was when this country was divided into French and English colonies... They drew to themselves their particular race and their particular co-religionists. They tried for 150 years, yes, more, the French on the one hand and the British on the other, to build up a country, but what was the result? The great minds came from these colonies and they formulated the theory that if we were to ever become a great country we must bury our racial differences and also our religious differences. They formulated that wonderful piece of legislation known as the Confederation Act which gave liberty of conscience and liberty of race, so to speak, to every nationality that should seek our shores. That was the condition, that was the law that made this Canada as Canadian as possible. [39]

Bourassa's position on the exclusive charter of the two founding "races" was also vigorously attacked as intolerant by Rodolphe Lemieux, then Postmaster General, who held that

> ...no human law can prevent the thousands of Hungarians, of Germans, of Danes, of Norwegians, of Russians, of Poles, from leaving their own country and coming to the western world to breathe the free air of America... I appeal to the liberalism of... [Mr. Bourassa]; will he prevent this foreigner who after all, is a unit in the brotherhood of man, from seeking a home among his brothers... will my hon. friend exclude these downtrodden people, who, after a few years in this country, contribute to its progress and prosperity and

become law abiding citizens? As a Canadian and as a Liberal, I say that Canada should open her doors to all desirable emigrants, and I trust that our country may be known, as Great Britain is known, to be the land of the free, and the happy home of refugees from oppression. [40]

Still, immigrants from eastern and southern Europe were claimed by some members to be subhuman. E.G. Prior told the Commons that "...the Galicians live under circumstances that, I think, can hardly be found to exist even among the Chinese. Their manners... are very little removed from the habits of animals... The Chinese... are bad enough... but I do not think that they are one bit worse than the Galicians."[41] This speech earned Prior an immediate rebuke from Laurier who characterized it as "an appeal to some of the worst passions that may be in our population."[42] And, Clifford Sifton, who was responsible for administering immigration policy as Minister of the Interior, also weighed in on this question.

> ...I do not care what language a man speaks, or what religion he professes, if he is honest and law-abiding, if he will go on the land and make a living for himself and family, he is a desirable settler for the Dominion of Canada; and the people of Canada will never succeed in populating Manitoba and the North-west until we act practically upon that idea... Our experience of these people [Galicians] teaches us that they are industrious, careful and law-abiding, and their strongest desire is to assimilate with Canadians.[43]

Experience was, indeed, an important teacher on questions of race. Members, based on their 'knowledge by acquaintance,' regularly confronted chauvinistic generalizations through offering personal anecdotes. As immigration from outside of Anglo-Celtic, French, Germans and other northern European groups expanded in the early twentieth century, more personal testimony was heard. For example, R.B. Bennett confessed that, influenced by Commons debates, he held "considerable prejudice" against Galicians until he travelled to the Northwest and actually saw with his own eyes what "good settlers" they were making.

> So far as the immigration to the Northwest Territories is concerned, none of us denies that a large body of the immigrants from foreign countries are very desirable settlers indeed – Icelanders, Norwegians, Swedes, Danes, Mennonites, Germans, and many other nationalities which I might enumerate. For my part, I am bound to say that when I visited the Northwest some eighteen months ago I was agreeably disappointed in what I heard and saw of the Galician settlers. I went there with considerable prejudice against them... [from] listening to the hon. member for Alberta (Mr. Oliver) in this House. That was the source of my information. I had listened to that hon. gentlemen making three or four speeches in which he had decried these people very thoroughly. For that reason I went to the Northwest with a prejudice against them, but I came back with that prejudice entirely removed, because I found that the Galicians were making good settlers. Their children were going out to work, their girls were going into service and intermarrying with English settlers, and in the second or third generations they will probably hardly be distinguished from the ordinary English settlers.[44]

In a similar fashion, A.A. Wright defended the ability of Polish immigrants to become excellent British subjects in Canada.

> Something has been said with reference to the Polanders. I wish to say that thirty years ago a large party of Polanders came to Renfrew. They were very poor, so poor that the women went out to the fields to glean after the harvesters and gather berries to earn their subsistence, while the men worked on the farms. What has been the result? A large number of those immigrants who came originally never learned our language except in an imperfect way, but their sons and daughters did learn our language. They went out to work, and their descendants have become today some of the best farmers in Renfrew. They have become comparatively wealthy, and what is more, they have made some of the best citizens that we have. When war broke out in South Africa it was the sons of these men... who volunteered and fought on the battlefields of Africa in support of our honour and our integrity... I have a Polander in my employ who has worked for me for seventeen years, and I have never had a better man, and I do not think I ever shall. As a matter of fact, the only way in which we can now distinguish the children of these Polanders from our own people is that perhaps they are better looking,

better dressed, more thrifty and make better citizens than our own people do.⁴⁵

Jewish Canadians likewise had their supporters in the Commons. A.C. Macdonell judged that

> ...there are no more law abiding citizens of His Majesty in this country than are our Hebrew fellow subjects. They enjoy perfect security under our British constitution, they enjoy equal rights with their Christian fellow subjects and in their turn they respect the law which protects them, and evidence their desire to uphold the constitution. They are a charitable race... They are a people who maintain their own poor; they make that a practice of their religion. We see no Jews in the public charitable institutions of the country, and I am happy to say very few of them in the prisons and penitentiaries."

Laurier seconded Macdonell's assessment observing that "our fellow citizens of the Hebrew race... are industrious, they are peaceful, they are frugal, they are respectable citizens of Canada in every sense of the word."⁴⁶

When C.B. Heyd spoke out against "Italians or any of that class of immigrants that come from southern Europe" saying "...we can never assimilate an Italian labourer and make a farmer out of him... the fewer of that class you bring into this country to compete in the labour markets of the cities and towns of Canada, the better for Canada," he was directly contradicted by M. Avery:

> It is said that the Italians are no good. I say they are good workmen if they are properly trained, and I take notice that now, when the Canadian people have any large contracts in building sewers and building railways, &c., in swampy ground, the Italians are the only class who can be got to go into the soil and take out the wet soil and throw it on the bank to grade the roads. If these people were taken care of and educated, we could make good citizens out of them.⁴⁷

"Syrians and Italians" brought to Canada through the United States looking for contract labour were defended by T.W. Scott, soon to become Saskatchewan's first premier, who decried on liberal grounds the rise in senseless talk about the alien and the foreigner. It is no disgrace to be an alien and a foreigner... We had not formerly the same idea about the alien and foreigner that has grown up in recent years. What is the reason that Canada, with its six million people where there are room and resources sufficient to sustain a population of sixty millions, we have come to regard the term alien and foreigner as a term of opprobrium, disability and disgrace? Is it not because of the criticism that has been made in season and out of season by hon. gentlemen opposite and their newspaper press against a certain class of aliens and foreigners who in the last seven or eight years have been coming in some numbers into this country? I refer to the Galicians and the Doukhobors.[48]

CALL OF THE BLOOD: WORLD WAR I AND "ENEMY ALIENS"

In the late nineteenth century, German Canadians were frequently listed along with English, French and Irish, as being among Canada's charter groups. In Langevin's account of Confederation, it will be remembered, Germans were among the "races" that had come together to create Canada. Similarly, Laurier listed Germans among the "heterogeneous elements" that made up Canada. German Canadian Hugo Kranz represented the riding of Waterloo North in the Commons between 1878 and 1887 and lobbied in the Commons for a Senate seat for Ontario's many German Canadians. He asked "whether the Government have considered the fact that each senator for Ontario represents, on an average 80,000 souls, according to the last census, and that there were then over 200,000 Germans in that province? If so, is it their intention to grant one or more representatives in the Senate to the German minority in Ontario?" Avoiding any specific commitment, Macdonald nonetheless replied that "the Government is full aware of the value and the number of Germans settled in Ontario."[49]

When World War I began, W.G. Weichel, another German Canadian representing Waterloo North, told the Commons that while German Canadians were "proud of the race from which they spring; proud of the progress that country has made in science, in art, in music, in literature, in philosophy, in chemistry," they opposed Prussian militarism. They had "left their old fatherland... to escape military domination" and were "just as eager and anxious as you are for the obliteration of this curse which has been weighing so heavily on Europe for so many years." Weichel said that for Anglo-Celtic Canadians "the call... of the blood" explained their desire to join the fight against Germany, but for French and German Canadians it was gratitude for the liberty enjoyed by British subjects.

> ...it is easy to understand why Canadians of British breed answer the call. The French-Canadian today is a natural participant in the present conflict, and besides is grateful for liberty of religion and customs under British rule. But, Sir, is there not a fuller meaning in this spectacle of men going from the German communities of Waterloo, Huron, Bruce and Perth. For them the call is not of the blood; it is duty that calls, and gratitude to the mother country for the many blessings they have enjoyed for so many years in this the land of their adoption. Shoulder to shoulder with all other Canadians, no matter of what nationality they may be, they will do their duty, realizing to the fullest extent that this is a fight for liberty and for future existence – and, let us hope, for the eradication of militarism from the world.[50]

The idealistic and optimistic attachment of Weichel to the idea of a universal British subjecthood based in political liberty was tested by the 'prejudiced' treatment of German Canadians by many of their Anglo-Celtic brethren as the war dragged on. In 1917, Weichel again addressed the Commons noting that he was "the only one of the 221 members in this House whose parentage is German... I represent a constituency, sir, where the greater majority of the people are of German ancestry..."

> Let me say a few words with regard to discrimination along race lines. If there is in this House one man who knows something about racial prejudice, that man is myself. I never knew what racial prejudice meant until August, 1914. From that time on, I have known what it is to have insult and ridicule and everything else that makes life unenviable heaped upon one. When I hear the hon. Gentlemen

from the province of Quebec speaking about racial prejudice, I came to the conclusion that the prejudice against my race must be of a different brand from that against theirs. Discrimination along the lines of religion, of birthplace, of race, of language, is un-British and absolutely wrong. We must not forget that this is a cosmopolitan country. For years, you have let the bars down and have invited hundreds and thousands of people from foreign lands to settle in the Dominion of Canada. These people came here and made a home for themselves. Speaking for my own people, I know that through thrift and industry they have succeeded nobly.[51]

Widespread in society at large, and a factor in interning several thousand German and Austrian Empire nationals for at least part of the war[52], anti-German Canadian sentiment was also in evidence in the Commons. For example, P.A. Séguin asked:

Has the government done all in their power to help win the war? Why then, even at this very late date, are Germans, and Germans and still more Germans to be found in all the departments of the Civil Service? There are Germans in the Department of Agriculture, even amongst the chief clerks. There are Germans at the Observatory, in the Department of Militia, in the Department of Mines, everywhere. For the last three years the public have been wondering at this state of affairs and to all our questions the Government have been satisfied with making the same answer: "These Germans are good Germans." Good Germans, indeed, for they never miss an opportunity to help their country... this government keeps them with a most paternal solicitude in the fat jobs they enjoy to the detriment of the real Canadians...[53]

H.S. Clements saw "no reason why every alien enemy in the Dominion should not be conscripted and placed at work doing something for the State, instead of being allowed to run at large as disloyal aliens and pro-Germans are now doing to the disadvantage of Canada."

...I say it is galling indeed to the fathers, mothers and daughters of those who so gallantly responded to the colours, to see these seditious elements surrounding them at every point on that [northern B.C.] coast, watching and waiting like a hawk watches a bird, to take advantage of the positions that these gallant men filled before they left for the front, waiting to swoop down upon every fishing or other privilege that they enjoyed. On several occasions, I have brought these matters to the attention of the Government, and have referred to these seditious elements who are always skating as close as possible to the thin ice so as to avoid arrest. Finally, some one would plead that he was a naturalized Canadian, it may be an Austrian living in our country as a naturalized citizen. The officials have told me that, under these conditions, it was impossible to deal with such individuals owing to their being naturalized. Well, Sir, if we have not the machinery to deal with them, it is high time that the Government instituted some machinery. There are thousands upon thousands in this country who should be dealt with with an iron hand.[54]

H.C. Hocken complained that "the electors in every riding in the city of Toronto are hedged around by a foreign population which is contributing nothing to the conduct of the war, and which is living in ease, comfort and luxury. Some of them, indeed, are laughing at their English-speaking neighbours who have been forced to do their duty."[55] Petitions by national organizations such as the Great War Veterans' Association and "large mass meetings" "to bring the enemy alien under some control" were reported to the Commons by R.C. Cooper

> Some of our industries in British Columbia, notably the railways and the mines, are practically controlled by enemy aliens of Austrian or German origin. These men have absolute liberty, and they earn anywhere from $4 to $10 or $12 a day. What do they contribute to the country? How do they help the country carry on this war, which was saddled upon us by their own people? Absolutely nothing... Today the ranks of labour are full of enemy aliens. I venture to say that at least one-third of the total membership of the labour unions in Canada consists of enemy aliens or aliens of neutral countries.[56]

But anti-"enemy-alien" remarks were not the only ones to be heard. There were also supportive 'knowledge by acquaintance' testimonials. R.J. Ball appealed for restraint:

In western Canada we have a great many German people. Many

of these people are in my own riding. They find themselves in a very difficult position at the present time. Many of them have their brothers and friends fighting in the war against Britain. These people are endeavouring to be, and I believe are, loyal to the Crown under which they live. We can understand their difficulty. They are deserving of our sympathy, and we ought to be careful not to estrange such German citizens at this time. In my own riding they are an industrious, law-abiding, thrifty and loyal people.[57]

Representing his Manitoba constituents, F.L. Davis told members that they should stop fixating on "enemy aliens" as the eastern and central Europeans of his riding were in "truth" doing their part to contribute to the war effort. Such men should be treated as "brothers" and fellow Canadians rather than aliens.

…what is the idea which each member has in his mind with regard to the enemy alien? How many men has he acquaintance with who would come within that class? In Manitoba we have had many Austrians who are called alien enemies, offering for enlistment. A few we have accepted and some we have rejected. I know men of Polish, Hungarian and Galician birth who have given their lives for Great Britain in the battlefields of Western France… we must not for a moment think of treating our aliens as enemies. 'Enemy alien' is a concept which has not a truth in it. These men have expatriated themselves for the purpose of becoming Canadian citizens; many of them have changed their names to Anglicized forms in order that they might be able to enlist. If we treat such men as men and brothers, it will make Canadians of them; if we treat them in any other fashion, we will make of them an alien element in Canada – and that, above all things, God forbid.[58]

Under the Wartime Elections Act of 1917, "enemy alien" British subjects, including German Canadians and Austrian Empire Canadians like the Galicians, who had been naturalized less than fifteen years and did not a relative serving in the military, were stripped of their right to vote. Racial instinct was employed by the Borden Government to explain and defend this legislation. For then Secretary of State Arthur Meighen it was "human nature" for "blood" to determine that "the German and Austrian in Canada" were potentially disloyal.

> Does anyone suggest that such a man [immigrant] would look upon the issue of that struggle as would his neighbours of the blood of his adopted land? Does anyone suggest he would be animated by the same desire for the triumph of the army of his adopted country, as would those next door to him, who were of the blood of that adopted land. Human nature is human nature in us all, and is human nature in the German and Austrian in Canada.[59]

R.B. Bennett leaned on the authority of an unnamed "great historian" to establish that "blood" is the prime determinant of human behaviour.

> ...we in this country are at war and those who know, great historians and philosophers, have told us that the tie of blood is the strongest of all. A great historian... said: "I put the motives of men thus, in order of their strength: (1) Blood, that is race or nationality. (2) Patriotism or love of land and country. (3) Interest of the means by which man lives in trade and commerce. (4) Religion, which is the life and refectory of his soul but as a motive uncertain and incalculable in its influence, and (5) Politics, including all constitutional questions which are merely the means or instruments for attaining these ends." So that blood ranks first in the motives influencing the minds of men.

Bennett claimed to have talked to some German and Austrian Empire Canadians "and they tell me that the tie of blood is strong among them... that they will do nothing wrong, but will try and behave themselves – but the call, the insistent call of the blood is ever upon them. And these men should never be permitted to say whether or not or soldiers in the trenches are to be reinforced by their fellow-Canadians."[60]

The idea that blood fixes political instincts was rejected by those opposed to this legislation. They argued that an individual's political choices and political socialization were far more important. J.A. Currie directly challenged Bennett's attempt

> to justify the action of the Government by saying that these men should not be trusted, because, according to some authority, the name of which he did not give, blood is the most potent incentive of the actions of men. I am not sure that I agree with his philosophy.

> Blood is certainly a powerful tie; we all admit that. But there is a tie still more powerful, and that is the tie of home; the associations connected with home are more potent than the ties of blood. When a man leaves his country to settle elsewhere, though the land of his ancestors may be dear to him, the land of his children is still dearer. When a man leaves a country he does so because he is not satisfied with the conditions that he leaves behind him... He leaves, he comes to Canada; he is welcomed; he comes upon invitation; he is given all the privileges enjoyed by other citizens; he is entitled to become an owner of property and to have the franchise. Suddenly we tell him: We cannot trust you anymore.[61]

Similarly, Laurier stressed that German and Austrian Empire immigrants chose to make Canada their real "home" and placed their "hearts" there. "I do not admit the doctrine that when a man leaves Europe – whatever may be the part of Europe whence he comes – and comes to this country, when he swears allegiance to His Majesty the King, when he becomes a citizen of Canada, when he builds a home for himself and for his family, I am not prepared to believe that if a conflict arises between the land of that man's birth and the land of his adoption, that he will go back upon the country to which he has sworn allegiance," Laurier declared.[62] Blaming "the German people" as a whole or "our fellow-subjects of German origin" made less sense than blaming the "government of Germany" for Germany's war "crimes."

> It seems to me that this man ought to be treated as a British subject. His heart must be somewhere, and his heart would probably be where his home is. I would say this to my hon. friend from Calgary: there is far more to be gained by trusting people than by distrusting them. And if I object to this legislation, it is not so much for its present effect, as the effect it will have in the future. We are striving to make Canada, young nation as we are, a great and powerful nation. We have long realized that to do that by ourselves would be a long and painful task. We have opened our door to the whole world, and have sent our agents everywhere. I have here a pamphlet in the German language urging Germans and Austrians to settle in Canada: we offer them everything we have. Many of these people have come to our country; they have settled here and behaved well, and we cannot break faith with them. The Germans have committed crimes

in this war that have no parallel in the last fifteen hundred years, but the blame is to be attached not too much to the German people as to the government of Germany. For my part I have not lost faith in the German people... I have faith in the German people; I have faith in our fellow-subjects of German origin in this country.[63]

Another line of attack on the supposed "blood" disloyalty of Canadians of German or Austrian Empire origins was to insist that disenfranchising them was unconstitutional because all British subjects in Canada had the right to vote. But Meighen undercut this argument by reminding the House that while this might be true in principle, it was not true in practice, and that in British Columbia and Saskatchewan Asian Canadians had always been denied the right to vote.

> The rights of British subjects here are rights given under the law of Canada. The law of Canada must be dictated by the needs of the hour, for the safety of Canada. Does the hon. Member say that in British Columbia there has been a breach of faith because for years past, if not since the birth of that province, they have refused the franchise to British subjects naturalized by the very same certificate, the Japanese and men of alien birth? Is it a breach of faith that those two provinces have done this for years? There is not a shadow of a breach of faith.[64]

In a similar vein, critics tried to shame the government by suggesting that denying the franchise was discriminatory and therefore unBritish through comparison to the behaviour of less civilized jurisdictions. G.E. McCraney, representing Saskatoon, and "elected by a considerable number of Mennonites, Galicians, Doukhobors, Ruthenians, Hungarians, Norwegians, Slovaks – possibly as cosmopolitan a rural population as there is in western Canada," asked rhetorically if he could really be expected to vote "to disfranchise the very people by whose authority I was sent here, and whose authority I respect?"

> We are going to say to those people now being disfranchised: 'We shall put you in the same position as are the negroes of the southern portion of the United States.' And when our people in western

> Canada are put by the Conservative party in the position of the negroes in the South, and are disfranchised in this way, I think they will remember it for many years to come.[65]

While Galician Canadians were cast as southern "negroes," Borden's Government was said to be trying to "out-Prussian the Prussians." R. Lemieux opined that

> just because Germany is putting herself without the pale of civilization, Canada, being a civilized country, should not imitate Germany. We have, unfortunately, in Canada some people who are bound to out-Prussian the Prussians. The War-time Elections Act, passed by Parliament last year, was a Prussian act, nothing more and nothing less… the Government disfranchised the Galicians who, although they came from Austria, were far from sympathetic with the Central Empires. The Galicians should not have been deprived of their right to exercise the franchise as they came to Canada, they, the victims of the Austrians in Europe, solely to enjoy here the freedom which they had been denied for centuries under the Austrian flag. That is what I meant a moment ago when I qualified the War-time Elections Act as being nothing else but a Hunnish and Kaiser-like measure.[66]

CALL OF THE BLOOD: WORLD WAR I AND THE QUEBECOIS

World War I was an especially low point in relations between French and Anglo-Celtic Canadians.[67] The comparatively low enlistment rates of French Quebecers in the military was at the heart of the conflict – a conflict that was frequently described by parliamentarians as being racial in character. By 1917, tensions were so high that C.A. Wilson told the Commons that "some of the honourable members are asking themselves if we are not on the verge of a civil war."[68]

Communal divisions over this question had been rehearsed a decade and a half before during the Boer War. [69] On the one side, English-speaking Canadian imperialists had very strongly believed it was their duty to support Great Britain's war effort and more than seven thousand answered the call to fight in

South Africa. As G.E. Foster explained, "within these last years there has been growing up in every dependency of Great Britain, and in the old country as well, the belief that the future of these countries was intimately bound up with the unity of the empire. And, Sir, if there is one thing that thrills in the blood of the Canadian volunteer today it is the subtle symbolism of the flag of the empire. It is not the Maple Leaf, it is not the Australian flag, it is not the flag of the Cape Colony, but it is the flag of that grand old empire which he feels symbolizes the progress of his race as a whole, which symbolizes the permanency and extension of liberty civil and religious."[70]

On the other side, French Canadian opinion was very decidedly against Canada's participation in the South African campaign. Henri Bourassa, representing the views of Quebec's soon-to-be formed *Ligue nationaliste*, gave three reasons to the Commons for his opposition. First, he said he was "anti-Imperialistic, but strongly attached to British institutions..." By this he meant that as a liberal, he could love British liberty and democracy, while still opposing the Empire's illiberal military adventures along with "...99 per cent of the French Canadians [who] detest this war, as the whole civilized world does, as nearly one-half, if not more of the United Kingdom does. They think that it could have been averted by arbitration; they believe that the political difficulties in the Transvaal did not justify it; they are convinced that Mr. Rhodes's [sic] rapacity, and that Mr. Chamberlain's arrogant and brutal refusal to arbitrate, were the real causes which precipitated the conflict; they wished that it should be stopped."[71] Bourassa argued that Canada needed to avoid the temptation to become dragged into imperial wars listing thirty-two British colonial wars in the second half of the 19th century: "...we are on the eve of a general conflagration in Europe and, if England wants to keep her colonies and her possessions all over the world, there will be at least as many wars in the next fifty years as there have been in the last fifty."[72]

Secondly, Bourassa said that he was anti-militarist. "I am in favour of a policy which will induce the youth of this country to go on the farm, to go and work peacefully at intellectual or manual work," he said. "Are we going now to start a policy... to take the flower of our youth, descendants of the two great races that have settled this country, and send them... to Africa, Oceanica or Asia. I am opposed to that policy."[73] Finally, and perhaps most significantly, Bourassa declared that Canada's sole military role in the Empire was self-defence: "Canada is not bound and should not be called to any other military action than the defence of her territory."[74] When necessary, French Canadians had capably defended Canada's territory and had in this way paid their military dues to the Empire. Indeed, according to this line of thinking, if it was not for the defence of Canada mounted by French Canadians at key historical moments, British North America would have disappeared.

Bourassa's anti-militarism was attacked in the House by S.E. Gourley who claimed it would put Canadians on a level with the "despised and despicable Chinese" who, not being a "military people," were unable to defend themselves from more powerful adversaries.

> I want to see every man in Canada prepared; if war comes we wish to be on top. What was Japan fifteen or twenty years ago, before they became a military people? Unheard of, almost, and despised when heard of. Today, if they win out in this [Russo-Japanese] war, they will occupy the proudest position among the nations of earth because they are a military people, a people trained in the defence of their country against all odds. I do not want war, but if war is thrust upon us I want this country to win glory in the way that Japan is winning it in her fight with Russia. But sir, if men like the hon. member for Labelle (Mr. Bourassa) were to have their way we would be like the poor Chinese, the object of contempt the world over. They abhor militarism and the hon. member for Labelle (Mr. Bourassa) and those gentlemen who think as he does would have us pursue a course which in a few years would reduce us to the state of the despised and despicable Chinese, and we would be properly despised as they are.[75]

It was commonly suggested that Quebec public opinion on the Great War had been "led astray by the false doctrine that has been drummed into and preached to the people" by Bourassa and the nationalistes.[76] And, tellingly, it was in Gourley's social Darwinistic world of international racial struggle that many English-Canadian imperialists cast the failure of French Quebecers to volunteer for the military. This line of attack was especially intense in Ontario and was reflected indirectly through the accounts given by parliamentarians. As R. Lemieux reported, elements of the English press "branded... [Quebec] as a province of shrinkers, of slackers, of cowards!"[77] The Orange Order was identified by F.N. McCrea as fuelling this campaign: "the war had hardly commenced before Ontario was hurling insult at them about being slackers. Ontario appears to be very much interested in Quebec, and it spends a lot of time and energy abusing the people of Quebec for not recruiting."[78] G. Boyer deplored how a policy question had been represented as an issue of race. "The conscription issue has been completely set aside by some hon. Members on the other side of the House, who saw fit to base their arguments upon racial grounds. Truly, one might be led to believe that conscription is not a military question but rather a racial issue," he observed.[79] The conscription issue had allowed for the release of "pent up" feelings in Ontario against French Quebecers pronounced J. Bureau.

> Reasons have been given why conscription was imposed; but the way the leaves move generally indicates the way in which the wind blows. I find the reasons so far given are an imputation upon the province in which I live. Although the subject is grave, the expressions of these gentlemen concerning it are evidently a vent for feelings that must have been pent up for a long time. The Solicitor General (Mr. Meighen) in the course of his speech the other day told us: We of English-speaking Canada have the kindest feelings towards our French compatriots. Thinking of the Toronto Orange Sentinel, of the Toronto News, of the Kingston and Hamilton papers, I said to myself: These men are great verbal acrobats, because if the sentiments expressed by these papers towards the province of Quebec are kindly sentiments, I do not understand English.[80]

Outside the House, some Ontario members were telling their constituents that Quebecers would rather fight Ontarians than Germans. In this exchange, W. Pugsley, a New Brunswick MP, began by citing Borden's praise of the valour of "the 22nd French Canadian regiment which did splendid work in every engagement in which it participated."

> Mr. Pugsley: ...This statement ought to be remembered by those newspaper men who write those savage articles about Quebec and who speak about civil war and about its being a very good thing if our soldiers, while passing through Quebec on their way to fight the Germans, would have a little fight with the French Canadians. It ought to be a rebuke to hon. Members like the hon. Member for South Perth (Mr. Steele), who, at a meeting of the Liberal-Conservative Convention held the other night at Mitchell, in his constituency, is reported in the Montreal Star to have said that the people of Quebec did not want to engage in this war; that they would sooner fight the people of Ontario than fight the Germans.
> Mr. Steele: I should have excepted the 8,000 who have enlisted from the province of Quebec.
> Mr. Pugsley: The hon. Member, I am sorry to say, admits the truth of the report made of the speech delivered by him on that occasion. It is language like that, coming from responsible members of this House; it is writings like that appearing in newspapers in Ontario, which incite racial passions and prejudices in Quebec. That is a course which should be frowned down by every hon. Member who loves his country and who wishes to see his fellow countrymen of all races live in peace and unity.[81]

The relatively low enlistment rates of Quebecers were said by some members to be what made conscription necessary. According to J. Arthurs, "...if the province of Quebec had done its duty, this Bill would have been entirely unnecessary, and the required 500,000 men would have been raised."[82] And, the recruitment failure in Quebec was held to be especially difficult to understand since French Canadians would be fighting side by side with their European French kin to protect their racial homeland, France. D. Sutherland observed that

> The people of Quebec are one of the finest races in Europe. They

have reason to be proud of their ancestry: old France fighting doggedly for her life, is an inspiration today for all the world. I say that this war is doubly their cause, even more than it is the cause of those of English birth, in view of the position of their motherland; and I have always said that the man who forgets the land from which his ancestors come, whatever that land may be, is a poor specimen of humanity.[83]

Similarly, J. Morris assured the Commons that he knew "deep down in the heart of every French Canadian there is a love of his mother country. How could any descendent of the noble French race deny his allegiance to or his love for his mother country. The love of country comes next to the love of God..."[84]

Even more puzzling was the fact that the French were long recognized as a "military people" in the social Darwinistic sense. G.E. Foster declared that bravery was "inherent in the French blood."

> I am not a Frenchman and I have no French blood in my veins, but there is not an atom of prejudice in me against French blood and the French race. There is admiration for their splendid qualities, literary and artistic, in the line of progress and enlightenment, and in the line of warfare and deeds of prowess as well... Who has held the long lines at Verdun? – the French peasant transmuted from his thrifty, lovable home-keeping atmosphere into an actor in the very hell of war where he has held on with tenacity, a heroism, that puts most peoples and nations to the blush. It is inherent in the French blood that they are brave and that they listen to, and act sympathetically with, great ideals and great principles...[85]

"It is worthy of note that many years ago Atilla, the leader of the Huns, who had set out to overrun Europe, was turned back on the plains of France," said J. Morris. "Future history will record that in this war the Hun of this day met defeat on the plains of France. That will be another glorious page in France's history."[86] J.A. Currie, who had served in the early years of the Great War as a Colonel, linked the bravery of the French Canadians in his unit to the Gauls of Roman times.

> I have had the pleasure of having a number of French Canadians serve under me in this war. I have seen them in action and in peace, and every one that I have yet had acquaintance with in this war have belied the slurs that have been cast upon French Canadians by the hon. Gentlemen opposite. Never on any occasion have I seen one of those men falter in the face of the most deadly peril. Never have I seen them anything but happy under the most terrible conditions of mud and climate. They never fail; they are brave fighters. Can you tell me that men of that calibre are cowards and are going to refuse their country if they are conscripted? That is unbelievable to me, and it is an insult to those people. According to Julius Caesar, when the call went forth for the Gaelic race, from which those men have sprung, to gather to the war, the last man who arrived on the scene was killed by his comrades for being late. Do you mean to tell me that people derived from that race are not capable of doing their duty and going to the war just the same as we are? It is an insult to them to say otherwise.[87]

According to Laurier, some explained the seeming reluctance of French Quebecers to fight in Europe as evidence that their blood had "degenerated."

> It has often been wondered why the people of Quebec have not volunteered in larger numbers. It has been asked: Has their blood degenerated? It is sufficient to say that those French Canadians who have enlisted have given answer to that question upon the battlefields of France and Flanders, where they have performed their duty in such manner as to win the applause of all their comrades in arms, and of all the Canadian people. The fact that the men of Quebec have not enlisted in larger numbers does not mean that they have degenerated.

Laurier met a biological interpretation with a sociological refutation. Enlistments, he said, "proceeded negatively in proportion to the length of time that the men have been in the country": that is, "the English-born are at the top of the list, the Canadian-born speaking the English language come next, and the Canadian-born of French origin are at the bottom of the list." "While there is not an English-speaking family in Canada which cannot claim relatives in Great Britain," Laurier continued, "I am sure that not one man in the province of Quebec has any relatives" in France.[88]

Laurier was rehearsing here a variation on a theme that we have seen to be common to French Canadian political thought in this era: that the defence of the homeland against foreign aggression was the sole military call that made any sense. C. Marcil explained this position to the Commons:

> The hon. Member for Brantford (Mr. Cockshutt) spoke about the French race not having degenerated on the battle fields of Europe. France has shown that she still remains the first nation of continental Europe: she has shown that she still has in her veins and in her very heart the force that has at all times placed her at the head of Europe. She has repelled the Hun at Verdun after a fight which is the admiration of the world... It is merely a repetition of what they did eight centuries ago at Poitiers when Charles Martel repelled the Saracens and Mohammedans who were over-running Europe. The member for Brantford says: I hope that the French people in the province of Quebec will be as good as the French are on the other side of the Atlantic. The French on the other side of the Atlantic are defending their homesteads and all that is sacred to them. Place the French of the province of Quebec in a similar position. The invader has invaded the province of Quebec on two occasions... but for the activity of the French population in 1776 and in 1812 there would perhaps be no British flag today in North America to defend. The province of Quebec is ready and willing and prepared at any time to do its share, and it has done its share.[89]

"...The French Canadian's first thought is for Canada. The English Canadian's first thought, however, is for England," suggested P.J.A. Cardin. "I do not want to reproach him with it; but it seems to me that he has no right either... to accuse us of being too strongly attached to our land and institutions and preferring above all Canada, the land where our ancestors were born and died and on whose soil we intend to die ourselves."[90] The racial instinct of self-preservation explained why French Canadians were "unwilling to weaken ourselves" by taking casualties in the War, opined P.A. Séguin.

> Shall I be rightly understood when I say that the instinct of preservation, the strongest sentiment that exists, is leading the French Canadians in spite of themselves? There are English Canadians – and legions of them – who are English before being Canadians and who, unsuspectingly, are ready to sacrifice the interests, even the future, of the colony to those of their mother country. I do not wish to blame them, for their blood is up, and blood will tell. But neither can they blame my fellow-people for being Canadians before being British, and even for being French Canadians before being only Canadians. In this case also, blood must tell. Yes, without suspecting it, the racial instinct is at work among us French Canadians. Instinctively, we feel that it would be dangerous for us to weaken ourselves beyond measure, because we know that for the struggle to come, we can rely only on our own forces. Foreign immigration benefits only the English element in this country: Irishmen, Swedes, Scotchmen, Americans, Germans, Norwegians, Finlanders, Austrians, Greeks, Bulgarians, Turks or Doukhobors, all, in a hundred years hence, will have dissolved themselves in the English element, having its character, its language, its manners and its ideal. No one, except a few Frenchmen or Belgians, will have joined the French Canadian race. We must, I repeat it, depend only on our own resources. Now, instinct does not reason in face of a danger.[91]

Some parliamentarians claimed racial taunts and mistreatment by Anglo-Celtic Canadians were at the bottom of the failure of many French Quebecers to enlist. J. Bureau complained that

> They will come and call us the white-livered brigade, the cold-feet association, the slacker band. Do they think we are going to follow their footsteps? Who is the man who is foolish enough to go and enroll when he knows he will have a greater fight with the men who are commanding him than he will have with the Prussian when he meets him? ...Let me tell my hon. Friends on the other side that the Canadian of Quebec is not afraid of the Prussian. He is more afraid of the man who lives alongside of him, from whom he receives no sympathy, but in whom he feels there is hatred in his heart against the French.[92]

If French Canadians were met with greater respect, heroic

"French blood" would answer the call to duty, according to H. Boulay.

> Let the people of Ontario stop their campaign against our faith and our traditions. But above all, and first of all, erase from the statutes of all provinces in the Dominion all provisions forbidding the teaching of French. If a new campaign of voluntary enlistment is entered upon, with the proper men to carry it out, I am sure that the French blood that flows in our veins, the same blood that flows in the veins of the heroic Frenchmen overseas, will cause our people to do their duty to the utmost limit.[93]

Calls for greater restraint and tolerance in dealing with the divisive issue of conscription came from all sides. Seeking to "blot out these religious and racial differences," Médéric Martin evoked the universal message of Christian brotherhood.

> ...let us discontinue these ill-boding struggles, let us shake hands, let us blot out these religious and racial differences; we are all Canadians; French or English, we are all Canadians. Will our Ontario brethren at last understand? I hope so. As for us, we are familiar with such maxims, our religion teaches it, we know that we should live as brothers in this world.[94]

Above all, parliament should act as a brake on racial conflict and runaway public opinion, it was said. C.J. Doherty, then Minister of Justice, chided other members observing that "things have been said from one point of view and from the other that, frankly, I do not think it could have been pleasant for any Canadian to hear."

> We are of different races in this country, but we are all Canadians. I have suggested that we forget for a moment that we are of different races. I do not want to suggest that it is desirable that we should drive from our memories the history of our progenitors. I firmly believe that there is no greater or more overpowering influence that directs the actions of men than the race feeling, and no call which men respond to more readily than that of the blood. It works for great and good results. I am not here, therefore, to suggest to anybody that it is his duty to forget those from whom he descends, or

to repudiate the race to which he belongs. But there is a time and a place for everything. Here, today, when we are dealing with a question, a right or wrong decision on which will carry with it consequences that none of us can foresee – consequences that will have to be borne, not by ourselves alone, but by our children and our children's children for many generations – am I not right in saying that it is incumbent upon us to concentrate our minds upon the one fact that we are all Canadians, and that this is a question of what is the duty of Canadians to Canada here and now.[95]

Laurier reminded the House that Canada's mission was defined by "diversity towards unity... the unity of all the races that compose the British Empire."

> ...we should always remember that all human flesh cannot be put in the same mould... if the British Empire is to live... it must be in accordance with the idea of unity in diversity, and diversity towards unity. If these words of wisdom... were to be remembered throughout Canada, whether it be Ontario, or Quebec, or any of the other provinces, the bickerings and suspicions which too often prevail between race and race would be forgotten... we are of diverse races, but we are all British subjects; we want to remain British subjects and to preserve the unity of all the races that compose the British Empire. But if we are to attain that end we must respect one another.[96]

Not everyone listened to these appeals to smother racial "bickerings and suspicions." Because French Quebecers had "not enlisted as we had expected they would do," H.S. Clements told the Commons he could see

> no reason why 20,000 – yes – 75,000 French Canadians... should not be conscripted, taken to British Columbia and placed in their natural element, the lumberwoods. Whether this be done under the Military Service Act or not, I mean to suggest that their work should be done under military supervision.... If 75,000 French Canadians in the province of Quebec were conscripted, taken into the province of British Columbia and kept there for six months or a year, I believe that when they returned to Quebec they would make better citizens and would educate the balance of that province.[97]

Not surprisingly, this proposal came under immediate ridicule as being so unBritish as to be Prussian. Understanding it as a call to assimilate French Canadians, R. Lemieux upbraided Clements by reiterating the long-standing Canadian definition of British subjecthood as an identity constructed around political loyalty rather than one based in any other anchor such as language, religion, or biological ancestry.

> My hon. friend repeats the old stock phrase of our Milner jingoes in Canada, that the time has come to have one flag, one king, one language, and one Empire. Well, I do not object to having one flag – the British flag. We have it today, and cannot replace it, and I would not if I could, nor would any French Canadian. We pray in our churches every Sunday for our good lord the King of Great Britain and of the Dominions Overseas, in the words *'Domine salvum fac regem.'* One Empire? We cannot have two empires… One language? There would be no British Empire if it had not been built on a broader basis than that. Sir, the British Empire is the mother of many languages and of many races… The type of Empire of one language is the German Empire, and the methods advocated by my hon. friend this afternoon are the very methods pursued by the Germans in Posen, where at Posen the young Poles were deprived of their national schools, where the lands of the farmers were taken and the farmers deported, as my hon. friend would have the French Canadians deported from Quebec and where all were forced under the lash of the school master to speak and to pray in the German language. In conclusion, I will not say, Mr. Speaker, that there are strangers in the House, but after having heard the language used by some hon. members this afternoon I will say that there are Prussians in the House.[98]

CONSTRUCTING CANADIANS

The many bitter quarrels over citizen rights and duties catalyzed by World War I highlighted the limits to and the contradictions of the Canadian model of British subjecthood. It is easy to find evidence that many parliamentarians were determined to turn a new page and put an end to 'racial strife' after the end of the Great War. For example Saskatchewan MP G.E. McCraney blamed Ontario and Quebec for 'formenting' racial divisions in the rest of Canada. "I am glad that we live 1,500 miles away from both of those provinces. Ontario and Quebec have fattened on their religious differences and racial strifes," he said, "we did not want a racial question entering into our politics in western Canada. We have troubles enough out there, and we settle them."[99] C.A. Wilson decried the "campaign of fanaticism and ignorance" stirring "unhuman" passions.

> As to the insults, insinuations and slanders which have been offered in this House, they are the results of a campaign of fanaticism and ignorance carried on in Ontario and other English provinces and Quebec. Let us be frank about it; we have been abused so much by the Nationalists of Quebec and by their counterparts in Ontario and elsewhere, that we have become accustomed to it. At times, left to ourselves, we might have enjoyed the spectacle of a regular scrap between the two camps of our opponents if it had not been so sad, so unhuman, so depressing. This measure has created a state of excitement amongst the people, and has given rise to all kinds of passions, religious, racial and political...[100]

The harrowing wartime experience of fighting a common foe together in Europe could open a path to overcoming Canada's "racial strife" and uniting the country in the postwar era suggested N.W. Rowell, President of the Privy Council.

> How can we achieve Canadian unity? We can achieve it just as our English and French Canadians achieve it at the front – by marching together to a great objective, seeking to serve and to sacrifice together, and if, under this resolution, the sons of Ontario and Quebec to forth to fight for the homes and liberty of Canada, and they fight and die together on the fields of France and Flanders and mingle their blood in a common grave, the men who return to Canada will put an end to racial strife in this country; they will stand together for a united Canada.[101]

W.G. Weichel also held out hope that the war experience would open the doors to a "united country" that would transcend "the cleavage between the races." "Both sides" of the Anglo-Celtic – French Canadian divide were to blame for creating Canada's "racial bitterness" and it was necessary to realize that Canada was now a "cosmopolitan country." His hope was that "out of it all will come a new people, who, after passing through this ordeal cleansed and purified, will appreciate more than ever British institutions as we have them today. Freedom and justice for all who live in these broad lands will be guaranteed anew, and democracy will have for them a newer and broader meaning than in the past."[102]

More open-minded attitudes along with developing a clearer understanding of how to 'Canadianize' immigrants was necessary in the post-war period, H.P. Whidden argued, because there has been "no national educational conception adequate for the assimilation of foreigners brought into the country."

> We cannot handle the alien problem in a paternal fashion, nor by a policy of drift. We cannot handle it by looking down on the foreigner in our land. There is in our Anglo-Saxon temperament just a little tendency to mean something when we say 'Hun' and 'Dago' and 'Sheeney'; but we are eliminating that, and the men on the battlefields across the sea are compelling us to eliminate it more and more from our thought and spirit. It is not by looking down on them and considering them as an inferior race that the problem will be solved. In our policy toward them fair play should predominate, and we should handle them... not only with regard to conditions created by the war at home, but keeping in view the reconstruction period and the generations that are coming long after this terrible war has become a matter of history.[103]

Michael Steele advocated filling this gap with a comprehensive federal educational programme "to fit and prepare all immigrants of alien origin for assuming the duties and responsibilities of Canadian citizenship."

> All our immigrants who are engaged in industrial life in this country, especially Europeans, should be compelled to observe our laws of health and of society, for otherwise our social organism will suffer. The illiterate, no-English foreigner provides a fertile field for anarchy, Bolshevism, and the many other "isms" and manias that are cursing the world today, and from which no one suffers more

than the same common labourer of foreign birth. Just in proportion as we remove his illiteracy and teach him to read and speak the English language, and teach him proper methods of living, do we increase his value as a national asset, and increase his value to himself and his family. Men who cannot speak our language are generally condemned to the hardest kind of labour and the lowest wages, and they will generally be found in the lowest ranks of our industrial life.[104]

A pervasive desire for postwar improvements in 'interracial' relations did not mean that there was any consensus on how to achieve it. While some wished to restrict the flow of immigrants and "Canadianize" those who were not of British or French origin, others urged a greater spirit of toleration and international brotherhood to meet the reality that Canada had become a multi-ethnic country.

Meighen, the Minister of the Interior in 1920, and so responsible for immigration policy, explained to the Commons that in earlier decades the rapid peopling of the western provinces was necessitated by the imperative of economic development. However, World War I revealed the flaws in this strategy as British born were found to be in the minority and immigrants from "countries who were the enemies of the British Empire was large and constituted... much over half of the non-Anglo-Saxon population." "Had the population all been Canadian or all British born," military enlistments would have been greater. "That was only in the nature of things: that is the only result one can expect, having regard to considerations of sympathy and blood," he supposed. His solution was to accept fewer immigrants and make greater efforts to assimilate, Canadianize, those already here.

> That Canadianization of the immigrants in Canada is a necessity, all of us frankly and enthusiastically admit. We would all subscribe to the doctrine, too, that no matter what the country's effort may be, no matter what means it may adopt or what propaganda it may carry on, no matter what money it may spend, to Canadianize an immigration of that character, it can only absorb and take care of a certain number, proportionate to the already Canadianized popula-

tion, year by year... We are all ready to admit now that in past years the doors have been opened too wide."[105]

National disunity would result if the "hordes of foreigners" that might be expected to come to Canada, were not Canadianized through "proper instruction," declared H.C. Hocken. The object of this policy should be "to build up in this country the most virile race that can be found in any part of the globe."

> The Canadianizing of the people of Canada is perhaps one of the most important things that this Government has to do. It is fundamental that in a new country like this that the people should understand our institutions; that they should learn our standards of living and understand something of the fabric of our society. If we allow those who have come to us to go on as we have been allowing them to drift in the past, without proper instruction as to our institutions or the character and duties of our citizenship, and if we add to them other hordes of foreigners who may come to this land in the years that are approaching, we shall have no ground whatever to anticipate that we shall have anything like a unified country in this Dominion.[106]

E.J. McMurray reminded the Commons of the dismal fate of "conglomerate and polyglot nations" not built from "one stock and woven together into a national fabricate."

> Canada is a young nation, and compared with other nations is merely in its infancy. The nations that succeed are those that have been built up slowly of one homogenous people. The nations that have stood the test of the late war in Europe have been those that were composed of one stock, French, British and German. Those nations have stood the test, but the conglomerate and polyglot nations of Europe, such as Austria, composed of all sorts of elements, dwindled and smashed before the force of the war. It will take us hundreds and hundreds of years to develop our natural resources. It will take us a far longer time to build up a distinctly Canadian type which must come in the process of time, and that type must be absolutely homogeneous. Without that it cannot survive. A rock washed by the waves, of the ocean, if it is not composed of one element, sooner or later will disintegrate. And so it is with

the nations; if a nation is not built of one stock and woven together into a national fabricate, it will sooner or later crumble.[107]

British Columbia members were rarely shy about taking opportunities to speak in favour of excluding Asians from Canada. And so F.B. Stacey, representing Fraser Valley, asked members when considering "the Canadianization of the immigrant, his contribution to the national welfare, and the necessity of his becoming a part and parcel of our Canadian life," to prevent any further "immigration of the Oriental" into British Columbia so as to maintain the province "for a white Canadian citizenship… so that we in the far West may be able to make some provincial contribution to the Canadianization of our entire citizenship."[108]

All of this was a little much in the opinion of A.R. McMaster who directly challenged Meighen's statement that everyone agreed that in the past Canada's immigration doors had been "opened too wide." Indeed, on the whole, he said, the immigrants that Meighen took exception to had proved "good citizens and have done a great deal… to build up the Canadian nation." Meighen's argument was rooted in a conceit of "blood" and was irrelevant to understanding the country's current realities.

> We people of English, Scotch or Irish blood and of the English tongue have no necessity to voice the Scottish mother's prayer that the Lord would give her children a good conceit of themselves. We have that without any divine aid. We are accustomed to regard ourselves [Canada] as an English-speaking, Anglo-Saxon nation. We are nothing of the sort. I suppose English is the native tongue of barely a little more than half our population, and the rest of the population is composed of people whose tongues are almost as numerous as those spoken at the building of the Tower of Babel.

A better way forward, McMaster supposed, was to take inspiration from "the inate goodness of humanity" and to find more effective ways of integrating immigrants into national life.

> I know that in the city in which I live during the past fifteen years numbers of these people have come from Central Europe, — largely

Hebrews from Roumania, Russia and Poland, — and I am afraid that we have not been as careful as we should have been to see that they lived in as healthful physical surroundings as were essential to their proper development. But we have done something to educate them, and some of our schools in Montreal are almost entirely attended by the boys and girls of these newcomers. And, Mr. Speaker, it makes one's belief in the inate goodness of humanity – in spite of the remarks made by the Minister of the Interior [Meighen] who has just taken his seat –to see how these people quickly respond to education. An old college friend of mine, a principal of one of our city schools, assured me that in these families one saw a remarkable difference from the eldest child to the youngest who attended school, and that in the course of one short half a generation the improvement was most strongly marked."[109]

Another Montrealer, S.W. Jacobs, advocated an "open door policy" on immigration. "So long as we can assure ourselves that the people brought into this country are law-abiding citizens, healthy, and able to take part in the work of developing the country, that is all we require." Such a policy would not only be good for the immigrants and their children but would make Canada stronger.

> the Government is making a serious mistake when it presumes to legislate to keep out people from different countries simply because their habits before they come here are not quite the same as ours. We ought to encourage them in every possible way, not only for their own sakes, but for the sake of ourselves... It is part of our duty to teach these people our laws and customs in order that they may become good Canadian citizens. We may not be very successful with the parents, but through our public schools we can reach the children, and the second generation will develop into citizens as good as many of those who belong to the so-called better class. I have only to cite a case in the history of my own race. You will remember when the Israelites left Egypt they escaped from slavery and they wandered for forty years in the wilderness. Not one of those who left Egypt was permitted to enter the Holy Land, but their children did, and the Bible tells us these made good. The same thing applies in the present day.[110]

D.L. Redman also supported a non-discriminatory immigration

policy stating that he was in full "agree[ment] with other hon. Members that we should not adopt in our immigration policy the principle of hostility to any nation or race. History records that eventually our enemies may become our friends... I do not think it is the policy of this country, and I hope it never will be, to exclude people from Canada on account of their religion; we should never act on that principle."[111] "Generosity" towards Jewish immigrants and citizens was strongly advocated by R. Lemieux.

> In the county of Gaspé there are large numbers of Jewish citizens; there are also many Jews in Maisonneuve. Many of these people came from enemy countries, but they are loyal citizens and it would be a great pity to debar them from British citizenship. If there is one thing that is to the credit of Great Britain and of British races generally, it is their generosity towards the Jewish race; in England, we have had the best examples of that generosity in comparatively recent times. One of the great Prime Ministers of England, Disraeli, belonged to the great Jewish race; the great Chief Justice, Mr. Isaac, Lord Reading, also belongs to that race... We have a large Jewish population in Canada which has come, in large numbers, from enemy countries; yet nobody would contend that they harbour any bad feelings toward our King, our Government, our constitution or our institutions. Under these circumstances, I ask my hon. Friend to consider particularly the case of the Jews... During the war Great Britain and her Allies, especially France, have taken up the question of restoring Palestine to the Jewish race... The Government ought to be very careful not to antagonize the Jews and ought to see that they get the justice to which they are entitled."[112]

But a liberal approach stressing "the inate goodness of humanity" or an "open door policy" on immigration provoked rebuttal. H.P. Whidden, a former Baptist minister and Professor of Biblical Literature, drew a stern line between the theory of "church policy" and the practical state policies necessary to create "a united Canada or an intelligent Canadian people."

> We should be slow to make statements, at least without considering all phases of the question, such as were made yesterday in regard to letting down the bars and making Canada an asylum, a place of

refuge, for all who desire to come here. That may be a good church policy; it is not the way to build a nation. It may be desirable that missionaries of one kind and another shall have the spirit which was suggested by the words of the hon. Member (Mr. Jacobs) who spoke yesterday... But certainly, the preaching of that gospel in this country at the present time and the creation of machinery which would make it possible for that gospel to be accepted, will not give us a united Canada or an intelligent Canadian people. It will give us a group of Canadian states – Balkan states if you please – throughout the West. Canada should... so regulate and, if necessary, restrict immigration that only so many of each race of people shall be admitted as can be wholesomely Canadianized.[113]

The leader of the Progressive Party, Robert Forke, opposed "indiscriminate immigration" preferring settlers "of the right sort" from northwestern Europe who could "make good citizens."

...I do not want to see a policy of indiscriminate immigration adopted. Do you know that in the three western prairie provinces the Anglo-Saxon people – and you might include with them those of the French race – are in the minority? Whatever the future of those provinces may be, the population is not going to be of Anglo-Saxon or of French descent; it is going to be something we know no what, and we want to be careful how we start out with foreign stock. I am not at all afraid, but we have at the present time just about enough to absorb of that description in our western prairie provinces. By all means, let us have immigration – immigration of the right sort. Get me young men, young women also, healthy and willing to work, coming from Great Britain, Scandinavia, France. I would not be afraid of Germans either at this time. They are all right; they will make good citizens in time. I will take all the immigration of that kind we can possibly get.[114]

The "sentimental monogenist – the man who says 'Are we not all brothers in this world?' and who points out that the great war was fought for liberty and mankind, and urges, therefore, that no country should shut its doors against any race," was ridiculed by H.B. Cronyn because "of course, if he be logical, he must allow the entry of the natives of Asia and Africa as well as those of

Europe, and while there are advocates who are prepared to go to that logical length, I fancy that a few of them will be found in this country." Rather than open doors, he advocated "selective immigration" only from limited regions of Europe and shared with the Commons the lessons he had learned from contemporary race science.

> Those hon members who have at all been attracted by the recent discoveries in anthropology will know that the distinct trend of present scientific opinion is to the effect that Europe contains three main races which have nothing to do with national boundaries, languages, or religions, but come out of the womb of time, and the characteristics of which have been fixed, according to some scientific writers, by millions of years of growth. These three races of Europe are known by the names, Nordics, Alpines, and Mediterraneans.

Because the "Mediterraneans" were supposed to be not up the higher standards of the "Nordics" and "Alpines," he proposed restricting the entry of "Mediterraneans" "at the present time." "Now it is well known that if you introduce in the body of man or beast an inordinate quantify of food, particularly of a new and strange variety, digestive disturbances arise and toxins are produced," he continued. "And so with the body politic. If you introduce a large mass of strange people who cannot be assimilated, poisoness currents are set up..."[115]

In fact, Cronyn's approach paralleled the regulations of Canada's immigration policy in the postwar era where, as Kelley and Trebilcock record, "...by 1926 there was essentially a four-tiered immigration-admissions system" with top preference to British and American citizens, second preference to northern European countries, restricted admittance "from the non-preferred countries of eastern and southern Europe," and virtual exclusion for Asians or Africans.[116]

CONCLUSION

Chapter 3 has focused on parliamentary race-thinking in late nineteenth and early twentieth century Canada as it related to those of European origins. Canada is shown to be the Empire pioneer of the notion of British subjects of various 'races' or identities sharing a multicultural citizenship based in political equality rights. Partnership between French and Irish Roman Catholics along with English, Scottish and German citizens creates the Confederation compact but this compact is greatly stressed by the rise of pseudo-scientific linguistic and biologically determinist ideas in the later nineteenth century. Large-scale immigration of eastern and southern Europeans at the beginning of the twentieth century creates new communal tensions as does the World War I cataclysm in the international system. Following the War, there is for the first time some attempt to define a Canadian citizenship outside of the traditional equality discourse of British subjecthood described in Chapter 2. Calls for an "open-door" immigration policy were met with derision and the lessons of "scientific" racism. The stage is set for our next chapter's exploration of the Commons debates surrounding the exclusion of Canada's native peoples from the political rights enjoyed by their fellow British subjects.

Notes

1. Canada, House of Commons, *Debates*, June 27, 1917. pp. 2768-2769.
2. Donal Lowry, "The crown, empire loyalism and the assimilation of non-British white subjects in the British world: An argument against 'ethnic determinism,'" *The Journal of Imperial and Commonwealth History*, 31:2, 2003. pp. 99, 102-103, 115-116. Lowry observed that "imperial historians have understandably sought in the Quebec Act the remoter origins of the multiracial Empire and Commonwealth." But in sharp contrast to Lowry's rejection of "ethnic determinism," Kymlicka has emphasized instead the socially confining rigidities of Canada's point of origin as a three-nation "federation" of "English, French, and

Aboriginals." Aboriginal communities and the Québécois were involuntarily incorporated into the federation: "Indian homelands were overrun by French settlers, who were then conquered by the English." "Prior to the 1960s," he said, "Anglo-conformity" along with an "uneasy tolerance" between "French and English" characterized Canada and "...some groups were denied entry if they were seen as unassimilable... Assimilation was seen as essential for political stability, and was further rationalized through ethnocentric denigration of other cultures." Only in the 1970s, "under pressure from immigrant groups" was this model abandoned in favour of a "more tolerant and pluralistic" multicultural policy that "allows and indeed encourages immigrants to maintain various aspects of their ethnic heritage." And so, Kymlicka affirmed, rather than political multiculturalism evolving out of the Quebec Act and Confederation, a clear break from the historical past was required: contemporary "immigrant multiculturalism is best understood as a repudiation of earlier policies of assimilation and exclusion." Will Kymlicka, *Multicultural Citizenship: A Liberal Theory of Minority Rights*. Oxford: Oxford University Press, 1996, Chapter 2, and "Marketing Canadian pluralism in the international arena," *International Journal*, Autumn 2004, p. 837.

3. Commons, *Debates*, July 31, 1899, p. 8993.

4. Ibid., February 5, 1900, p. 70.

5. Ibid., January 24, 1917, p. 120.

6. Ibid., April 30, 1883, p. 893. Allan Greer has concluded that the political agitation surrounding the 1837-1838 Rebellions, alluded to here by Tassé did, in fact, pave "the way for a major transformation of imperial rule" as the British colonial regime in the Canadas was "reconstituted" into "an arrangement known as responsible government" in his "1837-38: Rebellion Reconsidered," *Canadian Historical Review*, Volume 76, Number 1, 1995, pp. 16-17. For a description of the British constitutional conventions of representative and responsible government and a discussion of their "export," first to the British North American colonies, and then to New Zealand and the Australian colonies, see Alan J. Ward, "Exporting the British Constitution:

Responsible Government in New Zealand, Canada, Australia and Ireland," *Journal of Commonwealth and Comparative Politics*, March 1987, pp. 3-11.

7. Commons, *Debates*, January 17, 1913, pp. 1717-1718.
8. Ibid., January 22, 1890, pp. 51, 53.
9. A.I. Silver, *The French-Canadian Idea of Confederation, 1864-1900*. Toronto: University of Toronto Press, 1982. p. 41.
10. Commons, *Debates*, March 3, 1896, p. 2720-2721.
11. Ibid., March 5, 1896, pp. 2918-2919, 2923.
12. Ibid., April 30, 1883, pp. 894-895.
13. Ibid., p. 894.
14. Ibid., March 17, 1896, p. 3709.
15. Silver, *The French-Canadian Idea of Confederation*, p. 192.
16. Commons, *Debates*, July 5, 1905, pp. 8847, 8849-8850. Ramsey Cook has identified Henri Bourassa as "the father of the doctrine of the cultural compact of Confederation" which contended that "Canada was established through an agreement of two founding peoples, the Francophones and the Anglophones." For Cook's comprehensive review of the origins of the "two founding peoples" theory, see Chapter 5, "Compact of Cultures," in his *Provincial Autonomy, Minority Rights and the Compact Theory, 1867-1921*, Canada, Studies of the Royal Commission on Bilingualism and Biculturalism, Vol. 4. Ottawa: Queen's Printer, 1969.
17. Commons, *Debates*, July 3, 1917, p. 2943.
18. C.J.W. Parker, "The Failure of Liberal Racialism: The Racial Ideas of E. A. Freeman," *The Historical Journal*, 24, 4 (1981). p. 826.
19. Edward Augustus Freeman, "Race and Language," in *Essays: English and American*, Harvard Classics, Vol. 28. New York: P.F. Collier & Son Company, 1909–14. Accessed October 15, 2012. http://www.bartleby.com/28/10.html
20. Commons, *Debates*, January 22, 1890, pp. 41, 45, 48. For a fuller examination of the career and ideas of McCarthy, see J.R. Miller, "'As a

Politician He is a Great Engima': The Social and Political Ideas of D'Alton McCarthy," *Canadian Historical Review*, December 1977.

21. Ibid., February 14, 1890, pp. 660-661, 663, 667, 670.

22. Ibid., pp. 690-692.

23. Ibid., pp. 682-683.

24. Ibid., February 17, 1890, p. 746.

25. Ibid., pp. 738-739.

26. Ibid., p. 762. Alonzo Wright was an Ottawa Valley lumber baron known widely amongst his contemporaries as "King of the Gatineau."

27. Ibid., March 12, 1901, p. 1292,

28. Ibid., February 5, 1896, p. 1207.

29. Ibid., March 10, 1896, pp. 3227-3228.

30. Ibid., April 9, 1907, pp. 6182-6186. Bourassa went out of his way to attack some of Canada's overseas immigration agents, the "Hamburg Jew or Liverpool Jew," who, he charged, unpatriotically sent "undesirable immigrants" so as to secure a $2.50 commission from the Canadian government. p. 6179. This was not the first time Bourassa had revealed his feelings concerning Jews or Jewish Canadians to the Commons. In 1906, he disparaged a resolution presented to the Commons deploring the anti-Jewish pogroms then current in Russia suggesting that it had been introduced by an MP who was seeking the "Jewish vote" in his Toronto constituency. Bourassa elaborated: "...the sentiment of hatred against the Jews, not only in Russia but in other countries, does not come from racial or religious feeling but from the fact that the Jew does not assimilate himself to the country in which he is living, except to that extent that will enable him to profit by the citizenship of the country... In Russia especially, they... have lived and enriched themselves to an enormous extent by extorting from the poor people not only their money but the blood of their life... The Russian peasants had been sucked for centuries by the Jewish usurers, it is no surprise now that they are acting terribly in their dealings with them. I think it would be most ridiculous of this parliament to adopt a resolution, inspired, I am afraid, by local conditions of an electoral

character, passing judgment on a problem which has been trying the spirit not only of Russian statesmen but the statesmen of many countries for years, for centuries, a problem which consists in trying to bring the Jewish people to adopt themselves to the social conditions of the country and not merely to use these social conditions for their own benefit." March 15, 1906, pp. 232-233.

31. Ibid., April 9, 1907, pp. 6146, 6150-6151, 6155. Like Henri Bourassa, Lavergne was associated with the Ligue nationaliste.

32. Ibid., July 14, 1903, pp. 6591-6592, 6594.

33. Ibid., April 15, 1907, pp. 6707-6708.

34. Ibid., July 7, 1899, p. 6837.

35. The potency of liberal ideas in determining the outcome of these debates is discounted in some important studies of this period's immigration policy. Casting this as an national economic development issue or a political dispute between organized labour protecting its livelihood and business needing access to cheap foreign workers, the wider debate over empire and race recorded in this chapter is bypassed. For example, Ninette Kelley and Michael J. Trebilcock in their *The Making of the Mosaic: A History of Canadian Immigration Policy*. Toronto: University of Toronto Press, 1998 conclude that "the building of railways... was an essential precursor to prairie settlement. To the extent that foreign labour was needed for railway construction work, the government was willing to override the vehement objections of trade unions, nationalist organizations, immigration officials, and even members of its own party, and permit the entry of workers from what were generally regarded as 'inferior races,'" p. 117 and Donald Avery, in his *Dangerous Foreigners: European Immigrant Workers and Labour Radicalism in Canada, 1896-1932*. Toronto: McClelland and Stewart, 1979 says that the railway companies were "the outstanding spokesmen for an open door policy" while "organized labour for economic reasons, and... nativist elements for social and cultural reasons" took the other side. Sensitive to the power of the associated railway, mining and lumbering interests, the federal government "on balance came down on the side of the railway companies." p. 28

36. Commons, *Debates*, July 7, 1899, p. 6850.
37. Ibid., April 8, 1908, p. 6445.
38. Ibid., July 14, 1903, pp. 6576-77.
39. Ibid., April 9, 1907, pp. 6190, 6192.
40. Ibid., p. 6194.
41. Ibid., July 7, 1899, p. 6841-6842.
42. Ibid., p. 6844.
43. Ibid., p. 6859.
44. Ibid., May 31, 1904, p. 3869.
45. Ibid., pp. 3863-3864.
46. Ibid., March 15, 1906, p. 228. For liberal developmentalists like Laurier, assimilation to British subjecthood was above all else political and economic rather than religious, cultural, or biological. And so, as this statement underlines, Canadian Jews were to be counted amongst his "races of equal rank" who could claim "equal rights and equal justice."
47. Ibid., p. 3860, 3863.
48. Ibid., August 5, 1904, pp. 8619-8620.
49. Ibid., May 31, 1886, p. 1661.
50. Ibid., February 8, 1915, p. 9.
51. Ibid., June 28, 1917, pp. 2801, 2804.
52. See Morton, "Otter and Internment Operations," especially pp. 32-38. See also Kelley and Trebilcock, *The Making of the Mosaic*, pp. 169-172.
53. Commons, *Debates*, June 27, 1917, p. 2767.
54. Ibid., April 22, 1918, pp. 974, 976.
55. Ibid., p. 994.
56. Ibid., pp. 977-978.
57. Ibid., March 12, 1915, p. 958.
58. Ibid., April 22, 1918, pp. 991, 993-994.
59. Ibid., September 10, 1917, p. 5585.

60. Ibid., pp. 5617-5618.
61. Ibid., September 14, 1917, p. 5851.
62. Ibid., September 10, 1917, p. 5573
63. Ibid., September 14, 1917, pp. 5852-5853.
64. Ibid., September 10, 1917, p. 5584.
65. Ibid., September 8, 1917, p. 5564.
66. Ibid., April 22, 1918, p. 980.
67. See J.L. Granatstein and J.M. Hitsman, *Broken Promises: A History of Conscription in Canada*. Toronto: Oxford University Press, 1977. Chapters 1-4. Granatstein and Hitsman believe that the 1917 election campaign of the Union Government under Borden "founded on the Military Service Act and the War Time Elections Act, deliberately set out to create an English-Canadian nationalism, separate from and opposed to both French Canada and naturalized Canadians. No other conclusion can be drawn from this election campaign, one of the few in Canadian history deliberately conducted on racist grounds." p. 78.
68. Commons, *Debates*, July 3, 1917, p. 2930.
69. For an overview of public opinion on both sides of the divide see Carman Miller, *Painting the Map Red: Canada and the South African War 1899-1902*. Montreal: McGill-Queens Press, 1993. Chapter 1.
70. Commons, *Debates*, February 6, 1900, p. 111.
71. Ibid., March 12, 1901, pp. 1309, 1319. For a discussion of the founding ideas of the Ligue nationaliste, see Yvan Lamonde, *Histoire sociale des idées au Québec*, v.2 1896-1929. St. Laurent, Quebec: Éditions Fides, 2004, Ch. 1.
72. Commons, *Debates*, February 13, 1900, p. 411.
73. Ibid., p. 395.
74. Ibid., March 12, 1901, p. 1291.
75. Ibid., July 11, 1904, pp. 6439-6440.
76. Ibid., July 4, 1917, pp. 2980-2981. (J. Morris)
77. Ibid., June 19, 1917, p. 2474.

78. Ibid., July 5, 1917, p. 3039.
79. Ibid., July 3, 1917, p. 2931.
80. Ibid., June 26, 1917, p. 2697.
81. Ibid., June 25, 1917, p. 2648.
82. Ibid., June 26, 1917, p. 2656.
83. Ibid., pp. 2687-2688.
84. Ibid., July 4, 1917, p. 2980.
85. Ibid., June 18, 1917, p. 2409.
86. Ibid., July 4, 1917, p. 2980.
87. Ibid., July 3, 1917, pp. 2913-2914.
88. Ibid., June 18, 1917, p. 2399.
89. Ibid., January 24, 1917, p. 114.
90. Ibid., July 5, 1917, p. 3062.
91. Ibid., June 27, 1917, pp. 2768-2769.
92. Ibid., June 26, 1917, pp. 2699, 2701
93. Ibid., June 27, 1917, p. 2765.
94. Ibid., June 28, 1917, p. 2821.
95. Ibid., July 5, 1917, pp. 3017-3018.
96. Ibid., June 18, 1917, pp. 2402-2403.
97. Ibid., April 22, 1918, p. 976.
98. Ibid., p. 981.
99. Ibid., September 8, 1917, p. 5564.
100. Ibid., July 3, 1917, p. 2930.
101. Ibid., April 19, 1918, p. 953. In 1937, Rowell was appointed Chair of the Royal Commission on Dominion-Provincial Relations (Rowell-Sirois Commission) which issued its highly influential report in 1940.
102. Ibid., June 28, 1917, p. 2805.
103. Ibid., April 22, 1918, pp. 1003-1004.
104. Ibid., March 29, 1920, pp. 812, 815.

105. Ibid., p. 832.
106. Ibid., p. 821.
107. Ibid., May 8, 1922, p. 1527.
108. Ibid., March 29, 1920, pp. 825-826.
109. Ibid., pp. 833-834.
110. Ibid., April 29, 1919, p. 1882. Known for his support of "all minorities," Samuel William Jacobs was "for many years the only Jew in the House of Commons." See Rabbi Wilfred Shuchat, *The Gate of Heaven: The Story of Congregation Shaar Hashomayim of Montreal, 1846-1996.* Montreal: McGill-Queen's University Press, 2000. pp. 112-115.
111. Ibid., April 30, 1919, p. 1922.
112. Ibid., June 27, 1919, p. 4132.
113. Ibid., April 30, 1919, pp. 1923-1924.
114. Ibid., March 4, 1924, p.59.
115. Ibid., May 1, 1919, pp. 1966-1967.
116. Kelley and Trebilcock, *The Making of the Mosaic*, p. 189.

CHAPTER 4.

DOMINION ANGLO-SAXONISM AND CANADIANS OF NON-EUROPEAN ORIGIN: NATIVE PEOPLES

> ...we are Indians in name only; we are self-supporting, industrious, etc. Our people of Caughnawaga are well known practically in every part of the civilized world, and still we are not recognized as citizens. The basis and scope of our Indian Act is wrong, and injurious to us, because it interferes with our enjoyments of natural and inherent rights. We have no voice whatever in legislation. We are often opposed to it and suffer from its effect... Justice is intended to provide for every man in this country whether his skin be white, red or any other colour.[1]
> –LETTER TO THE HOUSE OF COMMONS FROM MOHAWK CHIEF F. MCD. JACOBS, 1914.

Sir Wilfred Laurier's 1899 declaration that "equal rights and equal justice" was guaranteed to "races of equal rank" in Canada opened Chapter 3. While most members of the House of Commons would likely have agreed with Laurier's declaration in the abstract, nonetheless, as we witnessed, defining relations in Canada's real political world between British subjects of differing European origins was hotly contested. Race-thinking influenced both the direction of these political debates and the content of the public policies that flowed out of them. However, these controversies were typically grounded in the idea that the Canadian polity was best defined by individual liberty and democratic governance rather than being determined by language, religion, or 'blood'. And so, French Canadians could appeal to their protected status as loyal British subjects to shield against anglicising forces while German and Galician Canadians could criticize discriminatory legislation as Prussian-inspired and unBritish.

Through their association with the Empire, native Canadians and Canadians of African, Asian, and South Asian descent likewise shared a claim on the "equal rights and equal justice" that in rhetorical principle attended British subjecthood. But there were at least two major catches. The first of these related to their perceived (or actual) position as subjugated peoples. Racism, as we learned in Chapter 1, is a political construction that develops over time as an ideological justification for the domination of one group by another. So, almost by definition, they were often presumed to be either members of developmentally backward, "barbarous" peoples or, alternatively and more deterministically, descended from a biologically inferior stock locked in a 'survival of the fittest' struggle with the Anglo-Saxon race.

Non-white British subjects wishing to make claims for "equal rights and equal justice" faced another significant catch insofar as the legal foundation for such claims was insubstantial. As Gorman observes, Great Britain had an unwritten, rather than a written constitution, and this meant that citizen rights of Empire subjects were nowhere spelled out in statute form. Accordingly, the "unofficial, rhetorical, and localized nature of citizenship gave rise to great discrepancies among imperial subjects in rights, benefits, and duties."[2] In Canada, some written documents were important in defining equality rights. As we learned in Chapter 3, French Canadians relied on the Quebec Act of 1774 and the Constitution Act of 1791 to justify their claims to full British subjecthood notwithstanding their differences in language, religion, and law.

JUS SOLI AND THE VOTE

The most important quasi-constitutional document of the eighteenth century relating to Canadian natives, The Royal Proclamation of 1763, was focused on property rights.[3] There was no intention there to incorporate natives as subjects within the colonial polity. Still, in the late nineteenth century, the language of British subject equality rights framed the thinking both of those who wished to extend political rights and those who wanted to deny them to native Canadians. "Indians are sons of the soil; they are Canadians and British subjects," Sir John A. Macdonald told the Commons in 1885, "and therefore, if they have the property qualification, I think they ought to be treated as other British subjects" and be able to vote in elections.[4] Here, Macdonald was following "the principle of *jus soli*, born of the soil of the place" which "dictated that anyone born on British soil was a natural-born British subject..."[5]

In rebuttal, Sidney Arthur Fisher began by agreeing in principle that qualified British subjects "whatever their color" should enjoy voting rights: "The suffrage is a right which anyone, of whatever color, should equally possess, provided the basis on which they claim the suffrage is the same for all. It is one of the privileges of British subjects, whatever their color, to rank on the same level with other British subjects, provided they possess the same property and qualifications."

But the key for Fisher was his belief that the social and economic development of most of Canada's native peoples was so seriously deficient that they were disqualified from the franchise. Natives were judged to be semi-civilized, uncivilized, or even barbarians. "No one could object," he opined, to "many of the Indians in the Eastern Provinces" getting the franchise as they were an "intelligent and fairly well educated and industrious people" with sufficient wealth to meet the property qualification. But even in the east, most Indians living on reserves "do not deserve the right of voting" as they had not taken advantage of the "opportunities" given by the government through "every reasonable facility for becoming a civilised and agricultural population. It has supplied them with implements, seed and agricultural instructors." Eastern Indians, he judged, had overall made little progress preferring to engage in "boating, fishing and hunting" and only "avail[ing] themselves of a very slight extent of the schools provided for them."

The Indians of Manitoba and the North-West had not even achieved the "semi-civilisation of the Indians of the eastern Provinces" – "they still have in them the savage and ferocious dispositions of ordinary barbarians... ready, on the slightest pretext, to return to their ancient habits of rapine, pillage and murder..." Overall, natives were said to be *"in forma paperis"* obtaining "pecuniary assistance to enable [them] to live." Because of the then existing property requirement to vote, many white men in Canada were denied the franchise and, therefore, Fisher concluded, "before semi-civilized or uncivilised Indians are enfranchised, every white man of full age, and being a resident, should have the right to vote."[6]

Fisher's comments here are well within the mainstream of late nineteenth century liberal thinking. John Stuart Mill, it will be remembered from Chapter 1, supported European colonialism because he believed it necessary for the progress of 'barbarian' and 'semi-barbarian' societies towards free representative government. Fisher argued that no "color" barrier to full British subjecthood for native Canadians should exist, but that it was necessary for them to achieve a standard of "civilised" life in order to enjoy full citizenship. Some natives had already met this standard, Fisher said, and other natives could join them if they took advantage of the educational and vocational training offered by the state. In brief, the issue was one of social development rather than of biological determinism.

Macdonald confirmed to the Commons that Canada's model of native relations as set out in the in the Indian Act was animated by a liberal, social developmental intent.

Of course, there are restrictions in the Indian Act, because the purpose of that Act was by slow degrees – but as speedy degrees as possible, as speedily as the old prejudices and habits of the Indians would justify it – they should be freed from these trammels. As quickly as the prejudices of the Indians themselves will allow, the whole effort of legislation respecting them has been to free them from those trammels, and to enable them to go forward and become independent British subjects as if they were white men.[7]

While many MP's might have agreed with the general theory here, Macdonald's implementation of it was key. With the building of the transcontinental railway during the 1880s, Canada was in the process of absorbing the vast native territories of the North-West. Not only was Macdonald Prime Minister for much of this decade, but he also acted as his own Minister of the Interior and Superintendent-General of Indian Affairs. Accordingly, his assumptions regarding natives influenced policy choices for many decades after he had left the political scene.

MACDONALD AND THE FRAMING OF NATIVE POLICIES

Macdonald's views were a curious marriage of biological determinism and liberal social developmentalism. On the deterministic side, Macdonald often pictured in graphic terms the gulf he supposed to exist between Native and white civilization. "The Indian nature, savage and wild, is a very uncertain quantity," he claimed, "and if you look at the history of the various wars and insurrections that have arisen in the United States, and the constant outbreaks of savagery that have occurred, you will find that in some cases there is no reason assignable or appreciable by the white mind for them."[8] Violent instincts drove Indian behaviour and this explained outbursts like the Riel Rebellion.

…but still we have had the Indians; and then in these half-breeds, enticed by white men, the savage instinct was awakened; the desire of plunder – aye, and, perhaps, the desire of scalping – the savage idea of a warlike glory… was aroused in them, and forgetting all the gifts that had been given to them, forgetting all that the Government, the white people and the Parliament of Canada had been doing for them, in trying to rescue them from barbarity; forgetting that we had given them reserves... they rose against us. Why, Sir, we are not responsible for that; we cannot change the barbarian, the savage, into a civilised man... I have not hesitated to tell this House, again and again, that we could not always hope to maintain peace with the Indians; that the savage was still a savage, and that until he ceased to be a savage, we were always in danger of a collision, in danger of war, in danger of an outbreak. I am only surprised that we have been able so long to maintain peace – that from 1870 until 1885 not one single blow, not one single murder, not one single loss of life has taken place.[9]

"...Indians are Indians," Macdonald opined, "and we must submit to frequent disappointments in the way of civilizing them."[10] Some native communities had more potential than others: he held that "the Indians of British Columbia are of quite a different race from those in the North-West and in the east. There is a good deal of Mongol blood in them, and they are more industrious and self-reliant than the Indians further east..."[11] Still, "the general rule," Macdonald believed, "is that you cannot make the Indian a white man. An Indian once said to myself (sic): 'We are the wild animals; you cannot make an ox of the deer.' You cannot make an agriculturalist of the Indian. All we can hope for is to wean them, by slow degrees, from their nomadic habits, which have almost become an instinct, and by slow degrees absorb them or settle them on the land."

Education could help some Indians to overcome the "general rule," but not all, and not quickly. "We have seen individuals of this race succeed, by means of education, but the exception proves the rule," he claimed.[12] Macdonald told the Commons that "I think we must, by slow degrees, educate generation after generation, until the nature of the animal, almost, is changed by the nature of the surroundings."[13] When asked how many generations it would take for natives to abandon their "nomadic... habits" and "get an aptitude for the cultivation of the soil," Macdonald confessed that he did not know; "I am not sufficiently Darwinian to tell that," he said.[14]

Early childhood education was key to "civilise an Indian," Macdonald stated in 1880, and he was looking for a "more scientific" system that would isolate native children from their 'savage' parents.

> It is quite true that to civilise an Indian you must commence with the child. I hope that we shall have a system by which the children may, be as it were, withdrawn from the parents as much as possible and brought under the influence of civilised Indians. But that cannot be done in a day... I hope that hereafter, when we have more leisure, we may be able to devise a more scientific mode of Government for our Indian wards in the North-West.[15]

By 1883, Macdonald had found his answer in the native residential school movement in the United States operated by Christian missionary organizations.

> Secular education is a good thing among white men, but among Indians the first object is to make them better men, and, if possible, good Christian men by applying proper moral restraints, and appealing to the instinct for worship which is to be found in all nations, whether civilized or uncivilized. A vote will be asked for in the Supplementary Estimates for 1883-84, for a larger description of schools. When the school is on the reserve the child lives with its parents, who are savages; he is surrounded by savages, and though he may learn to read and write his habits, and training and mode of thought are Indian. He is simply a savage who can read and write. It has been strongly pressed on myself, as head of the Department, that the Indian children should be withdrawn as much as possible from the parental influence, and the only way to do that would be to put them in central training industrial schools where they will acquire the habits and modes of thought of white men; so that, after keeping them a number of years away from parental influence until their education is finished, they will be able to go back to their band with the habits of mind, the education, and the industry which they have learned at these schools. That is the system which is largely adopted in the United States.[16]

Just four years later, this scheme of social engineering was advanced far enough to provide for the creation of women's schools so that intermarriage between 'reclaimed' natives could produce a new generation of "educated and industrious children."

> In the North-West, where we have several industrial schools, we have found, on the recommendation of all the heads of those schools, and of the different religious denominations who have taken charge of them, that it is hopeless to expect to reclaim a young man, even if he is taken to an industrial school and educated, if he goes back afterwards to his tribe and marries an Indian who is uneducated. We have, therefore, established at Qu'Appelle a women's school and we have another at Battleford... and it is hoped, by educating Indian women and Indian men in those industrial schools, that both will be drawn from the domestic influences of their tribes, and will intermarry, so that we shall have a valuable class of educated and industrious children.[17]

Disputes "between races as opposite as the Indian and the white man" were to be expected[18], Macdonald believed, and so, until they were 'civilized' natives needed to be confined to reserves for the protection of both parties. This was especially the case in the recently opened North-West where coercive force was necessary to restrain the free movement of natives.

> Under the Indian treaties certain reserves were set apart for the Indians. It has been only by slow degrees that the Indians were got – they have not all been got there yet – to confine themselves to their reserves... It has, however, been accomplished by a series of mingled coaxings and threats... But still there must be a continual, hourly pressure upon the Indians to hold them upon their reserves... The duty of the [North-West Mounted] police is, therefore, a continuous one, and an increasing one, and the increase in the number of white settlers adds to the difficulty... Settlers, as a rule, take a hostile position against the Indians, just as it has been the experience of the United States all along the western frontier. The duty of the police is not only to protect the white man against the Indian but the Indian against the white man... Recent events have shown that the force is overworked; that they are obliged to watch every reserve, in order to keep the Indians on the reserves. They are apt to get away; they are unwilling to endure restraint, and this can be prevented if there is a good agent on the reserve, and a sufficient force at hand to let them know pretty well that if they will

not listen to reason they will be forced to carry out what they have agreed to do.[19]

Providing food to the reserves was tricky because, according to Macdonald, natives were by nature idle and not inclined to be agriculturally self-sufficient. "So long as they know they can rely, or believe they can rely, on any source whatever for their food, they make no efforts to support themselves. We have to guard against that, and the only way to guard against it is by being rigid, even stingy, in the distribution of food and require absolute proof of starvation before distributing it." Nonetheless, the complete withdrawal of food supplies from natives was not a politically viable option: "Public sentiment would not allow it, and no Government would be worthy of their position, if they allowed the Indians to starve as long as we have the means to feed them."[20] All the same, drastically cutting rations was employed as a means to keep natives on reserves.

> We could not allow them to starve, and we placed them on quarter rations only; but still, while Indians can get anything to support life, they will not move... These things must and will happen, and all we can do is to use the most patient perseverance. It is no use to get angry with Indians. They are idlers by nature and uncivilized. If they eat the cattle you must give them a good scolding and not shoot them down because they shot down the cattle and ate them. You must coax them to go on the reserves and do better next year. It is only by slow and patient coaxing and firmness at the same time along that you can manage the Indians...[21]

In summary, Macdonald told the Commons that the policy of all Canadian governments toward natives was to respect their rights as British subjects and to offer "as Christians" the necessary assistance over "the course of ages" to develop their level of civilization to the standard of "the general population."

> To observe good faith towards the Indians, to treat them kindly, and to treat them firmly. If there has been a fault at all... it is that we have been rather over indulgent to the Indians. But what can we do? We cannot, as Christians, and as men with hearts in our

bosoms, allow the vagabond Indian, the pauper Indian, to die before us... The reserves they now hold are given them by treaty. They are their property; we cannot deprive them of those reserves without another treaty.... We are going to pursue the same policy that has been pursued upon these questions so successfully under the auspices of the British Government, and which has been continued ever since, of giving them a portion of the country... There is only one way – patience, patience, patience. We see what patience has done in the older Provinces. Look at the Province of Ontario. The Indian is still an Indian. His color is the same, but he is law-abiding, he is a peaceful man... In the course of ages – it is a slow process – they will be absorbed in the country. You must treat them, and our children, and our grand-children, and our great grand-children, must treat them in the same way, until, in the course of ages, they are absorbed in the general population.[22]

ALTERNATIVE POLICY PATHS?

If Macdonald had not been in a position to drive Indian policy during the 1880s, it is possible that Canada's relations with natives might have turned in a different direction. Some Liberals were impatient with the policy failures of previous decades. David Mills, who had served as Minister of the Interior 1876-1878 in Alexander Mackenzie's cabinet, told the Commons in 1880 that when Macdonald "proposed that we should occupy a long series of ages – on the principle of development, I suppose – in the elevation of the Indians, on the ground that it was absolutely necessary, I did not agree with him." He recommended instead "legislation of a much more radical character" and noted that when he "was at the head of the Department of the Interior, having given a good deal of attention to this subject, I came to the conclusion that important changes in the law were necessary, and had we remained in power, it was the intention of the late Administration to submit a measure to Parliament on this subject."

The "radical defect" at the heart of the problem, Mills believed, was the system of collective property ownership that had been imposed on natives under the reserve system. Natives were not biologically inferior to whites but were instead policy victims of a kind of pre-Stalinist forced collectivization.

> There was one thing that impressed itself very strongly upon my mind, and that was the mischievous effects that flow from allowing the Indians, on the various reservations in the old Provinces, to hold their property in common. In these cases they have all sunk, and necessarily so, to the level of the most indolent; and I fancy that, if the white population of any district was dealt with in the same way, if the consciousness of separate and independent property holdings was taken away, you would, in great measure, reduce them to the same barbarous condition in which the Indians are found at this moment.

The paternalistic attitudes and policies that had failed in the eastern provinces, Mills objected, were now to be employed again in the west: "...we are going in the same groove in which we have long been moving, and are rapidly reducing the Indians of the North-West and of British Columbia to the same condition of helplessness and dependence in which the Indians are in the older Provinces," he said.[23]

With 3000 natives in his riding from the Six Nations reserves, Liberal member W. Paterson claimed to "know more of this subject than most of the members" and said he spoke from the perspective "of the more advanced tribes." The minor amendments Macdonald proposed in 1880 to then existing native legislation were "only in the direction of more firmly fastening the shackles of tutelage upon them" and argued that only solution "to the Indian question" was to give them "the rights, opportunities and privileges of citizens."

> The whole Indian law discourages the assimilation of the whites and the Indians, and the solution of the Indian problem can only be found in wiping out the distinction which exists between the races, in giving the red man all the liberties and rights enjoyed by the white man, and entailing upon him all the responsibilities which attach to those rights and responsibilities... I warn the House, as I warn the hon. the First Minister, that legislation in the direction proposed, old-time legislation, simply means that it will entail upon

the people, year after year, and for all time to come, the voting annually of hundreds of thousands of dollars to keep the Indians in the low, degraded state in which they are at present... What I advocate is this: That we should have an Indian policy, which will not only tend to relieve us from those heavy [fiscal] burdens, but will give to the Indians more rights than they now possess, and wipe out the race distinctions that now exist.[24]

At least one Conservative member, J. White, appreciated Paterson's approach arguing that "we should no longer treat the Indians as children" and if that some educated natives held the "responsibilities of members of this House, [they] could fill positions here with credit to themselves and the country."[25] G.E. Casey asked the House if the ultimate goal of native policy should not be to integrate natives into the community rather than leaving them "separate" and "in a worse condition than the negro."

> The question for us to consider is, whether it is advisable to keep the Indian tribes together, and separate from the rest of the community. That was necessary, no doubt, when the Indians were the helpless wards of the Crown, but I should be very much surprised if the country at large would think it advisable, in the case of Indians who have settled down, that they should continue in that state of tutelage for ever... I think Indians, who are equal to whites in intelligence, who are superior to many whites in wealth, and who are full grown citizens of the Dominion, should not be placed in a worse condition than the negro.[26]

As noted above in our discussion of Fisher, the Liberals fiercely opposed Macdonald's 1885 proposal to give the right to vote in federal elections to natives who could meet the financial property requirements.[27] This was consistent with their view that natives were not free under the present Act, were wards of the state, and would cast their vote under the instruction of government agents. Paterson argued that granting propertied natives the franchise

> is not intended to elevate or uplift the condition of the Indian in the social scale... If his desire is to benefit the Indians, let him give

greater facilities for them to attain the full status of their rights and liberties, to emancipate them from the guardianship of the Government of the day, to make them free agents, with the right to manage their own affairs. It gives the Indian the right to vote, but the Indian and his vote are virtually controlled by the Government of the day, and will be used by the Government as a means of retaining themselves in power.[28]

But S.J. Dawson was disappointed in Paterson's stance, particularly because he saw him as an ally in support of native rights: "I have had the greatest respect and the highest esteem for him, just on account of the fact that every Session he has stood up for the rights of the Indians, who have but few to take their part in this House..." For his part, Dawson told the Commons that natives were "naturally intelligent" and that many were "far advanced in civilisation" and "as able to exercise the franchise as white men."

In the district I represent there are many Indians who have property, and pay their taxes, who are educated, and who have been elected as members of the municipal councils. One was the reeve of a municipality, and many of them are well off... The Act now before us is intended to apply only to Indians who have left their wild life and acquired property sufficient to keep them and their families comfortable, and these men are as able to exercise the franchise as white men, for the Indian is naturally intelligent, and when he gives up his wandering habits makes a very good member of the community... The hon. gentleman has held forth the idea that the franchise is to be given to Indians who are hardly removed from the condition of savagery; but let me tell him that there are Indians throughout this Dominion who are far advanced in civilisation. There are Indians who have been in France, in England, and in other countries in Europe, for their education. I believe that the Premier of Manitoba will come under the designation of an Indian... It is a mistake to suppose that these Indians are without the affections common to other men; they are not the barbarians which many people imagine... I know of another case of an Indian in Algoma who sends his children to Paris to be educated, who has white people in his employ as servants...[29]

Not only did Dawson advocate votes for natives who met the

property qualifications for voters, he also argued that as British subjects they deserved their own representatives in Parliament.[30] It was not enough for them to rely on the "few" who spoke on their behalf in the Commons.

> I express the opinion now, as I have expressed it before, that it is contrary to the spirit of our institutions, contrary to the system existing throughout this wide Dominion, that there should be such a large number of people as the Indians without representation in this Parliament... There are several hon. members of this House who deserve great credit for the interest they have taken in these poor people; but I think the Indians will never be properly taken care of until they have, in some shape or other, parliamentary representation, like other classes of Her Majesty's subjects.[31]

Dawson's assertion that natives could count on only "few to take their part" in Commons debates was true. Many members thought like J. Charlton who judged that "we have in this Dominion 131,000 Indians, nine-tenths of whom are barbarians, and two-thirds of whom are pagans... They are grovelling barbarians, sunk in the depths of ignorance, and depravity and vice..." Charlton sarcastically inquired "...if it is reasonable or proper to give the franchise to a wild Indian of the plains, who is now flourishing the scalping knife and the tomahawk, and ravaging our settlements in the North-West. Has he the love of country and the pride in British institutions which would qualify him to exercise the franchise?" Americans had "broken down all the barriers" and given the vote "to the colored race" but had the good sense to withhold it from natives living on reserves.

> It is proposed to enfranchise Indians who are still maintaining tribal relations. But you cannot assimilate these Indians with the body politic, or make them homogeneous with our population; they are alien and foreign to us, and have no element, characteristic or qualification that will fit them to exercise the sacred right of the suffrage, which is the privilege and right of a free man... Although the United States Government have dealt generously with the Indians, although their policy has been a liberal and humane one, yet the people of the Union, who have broken down all the barriers sur-

rounding the suffrage and have given votes to the colored race, have found it inexpedient to enfranchise the Indians, except on condition that they abandon their tribal relations and become citizens. Under no conceivable circumstances are we warranted in going beyond this policy that has prevailed in the United States. It will be an act of more than folly, it will be an act fraught with dangerous consequences to the people... it is derogatory to the dignity of the people and an insult to the free white people of the country to place them on a level with pagan and barbarian Indians.[32]

A biologically determinist argument was employed by P.B. Casgrain to oppose votes for natives. They were simply "not capable of being civilized" and, anyway, were dying out because "the Indian, by his very nature is unfit to live in [the] confinement" imposed by modern society and so was "gradually disappearing from the country."

> ...if we examine the position of the Indian race in Canada, and even in the whole of British North America, it is easy to see that it is not a race which is capable of being civilised... in spite of all that has been done by the missionaries to evangelise them, it is a remarkable fact that throughout the whole of North America it has always been impossible to bring them to that state of civilisation which exists among the nations of Europe... Is he susceptible to being brought to a more advanced stage of civilisation than that in which he lives today? I do not believe it.

Even though natives would remain forever uncivilized, it was nonetheless conceivable that they might be able to determine the outcome in elections: "...if universal suffrage was to be adopted, as it is the tendency of the age, the individual vote of each of these Indians would form a casting vote and might change... the verdict of the white population." Casgrain concluded by declaring that "everybody would prefer the vote of one white man to the votes of five Indians."[33] M.C. Cameron mocked the idea of native representation in Parliament: "If we give Indians the right to vote, we cannot refuse them the right to send their own representatives to this House; and should the Government decide to give representation to the Territories, how would the hon. Minister of Public Works, for instance, like to have seated among his colleagues or near him Pi-a-pot, or Big Bear, or Strike-him-on-the-back, or any of the other Indian chiefs, about whom we hear so much these days?"[34]

LOSING THE FRANCHISE

Criticisms like these influenced Macdonald to back away from granting the franchise to property-qualified natives in the North-West and, after he left office, natives in the eastern provinces had their vote taken away as well. The Laurier Liberals came to government in 1896 pledged to abandon the federal electoral list in favour of using provincial lists in federal elections.[35] Since natives were not included in any provincial list, they would lose their federal vote.[36] Adolphe Caron objected to this "retrograde step" since it was "almost an unheard of thing for the franchise, once conceded, to be taken away from the people who have enjoyed it."[37] Laurier argued that since the existing federal legislation governing native voting was already regionally specific, he was not bringing any new principle to bear letting the provinces decide "whether or not Indians should be admitted to vote." In the 1885 debates, he said, it had been pointed out to Macdonald

> ...that, according to the Bill, as introduced, Poundmaker, who was at that time engaged in rebellion, and Big Bear, would be invested with the franchise. The Bill was modified subsequently, and Indians were granted the franchise only in the older provinces and the Indians of the North-west Territories were restrained. This shows that even according to the Act some discretion is to be exercised in this matter. Who is to exercise it? We think it should be left to the provincial legislatures. Accordingly, after this Bill becomes law... it would be for the legislatures of the different provinces to determine whether or not Indians should be admitted to vote. This is the policy of the Government on the subject.[38]

Two Liberals representing native voters enfranchised in 1885 spoke against their party's policy. C.B. Heyd told the House that while Six Nations traditionalists from his constituency generally opposed the franchise, viewing themselves as allies of Great Britain rather than as British subjects, most natives appreciated the "opportunity of getting rid of their superfluous steam at election time, and have learned to be most inveterate politicians. They take the Conservative or Liberal side in the most ardent manner, and take a most lively interest in politics, and are just as well qualified to exercise the franchise as are the whites." In the three federal elections that had been held under the 1885 Act, Heyd presented figures that showed that about 60% of eligible native votes were cast in his riding, splitting almost evenly between Liberals and Conservatives. J.F. Lister averred that it was his experience "that the Indians upon the reservation in my county have exercised that right [franchise] as wisely, as prudently and as intelligently as any other class of people in the county of Lambton." A majority of native voters had supported him in preference to the Government candidate proving "that the influence which it was supposed the Government would have had on the Indians has not in fact existed, but that the Indians, notwithstanding they are wards of the Government, have been sufficiently independent to vote as they thought proper." Lister warned that taking away the vote would be remembered as an injustice: "…once having given the franchise to a portion of the people, who have proved themselves able to exercise it intelligently, the Government should not now take away from those people that which free men all consider a boon, and do an act which the Indians will remember as one of the greatest injustices ever perpetrated upon them by any legislature in this country."[39]

As Opposition Leader, Sir Charles Tupper also supported keeping the franchise for natives and took a run at Laurier's credibility as an advocate of liberal values. Perhaps "you might find some fossilized Tory who would go back on Liberal principles," he taunted, but Laurier's

> first important act [as Prime Minister] is to take away the franchise from a large body of British subjects in this Dominion who at the

present time enjoy it. That is not a position upon which the right hon. gentleman will plume himself as leader of the Liberal Administration. One of the great principles of the Liberal party throughout the world has been to broaden and extend the franchise to all persons who could properly enjoy it... Long ago the question was decided as to whether the Indians should be enfranchised or not, and year after year they have proved that they possessed all the qualifications necessary to exercise the franchise in a wise, independent, and judicious manner in the interests of the country. For the leader of the Government to deprive them of that franchise, without being able to advance a reason for his action, is a thing for which you will search in vain for a parallel all the world over.[40]

But there is little in the record of the Debates to suggest that Laurier saw natives as one of his "races of equal rank" that should be guaranteed "equal rights and equal justice" in Canada. He, for example, observed of the Métis that they "were sprung from European hunters and the Indians, and their character partook of the character of both nations; but in point of education and experience, though vastly inferior to the whites in point of intelligence and adaptability to civilisation, they were far superior to the Indians." And so, the "rule universally applied to the Indians has been to put them upon reserves, and there to protect them and defend them against white encroachments, and to assist them by money and otherwise during their advancement from savage to civilised life."[41]

INFANTILIZED OBJECTS OF BUREAUCRATIC ADMINISTRATION

Losing the electoral franchise was an important turning point for Canadian natives because it closed a tangible path to developing greater political legitimacy and effectiveness as full British subjects. Instead, they were locked into a political world which more than ever perceived them as infantilized objects of bureaucratic administration. Robert Forke explained to the House that his heart had "bled... many a time" for the "child-like" Indians.

I have lived for a great many years in very close proximity to a

> band of Indians and I appreciate their child-like qualities... I cannot but think, Mr. Chairman, that the Indian question is one of the tragedies of our modern civilization, or perhaps it would be better to say of the progress of development in a new country, and I would like to impress upon the minister at this particular time the desirability of a most careful examination into all the conditions on our Indian reserves. I know individually the Indians in my locality, I am thoroughly familiar with their circumstances, and my heart has bled for them many a time. We sometimes blame the Indian for the condition in which he finds himself. We say that he is not as persistent as he might be, and that he does not adapt himself to our modern way of living; but where in all history, have you ever found it possible for a people who have been living in a state of semi-barbarism to adapt themselves to civilization and all its methods of living in just one generation. We must treat these people with sympathy and consideration and give them all the support and help that we possibly can. Unfortunately it is but too true that white people, to a very large extent, are blameable for a great many of the vices to which the Indians are addicted at the present time.[42]

Largely gone were the root and branch critiques of the early 1880s that sought to loosen rapidly the "shackles of tutelage" by developing new strategies to wipe out "race distinctions" and give natives "the rights, opportunities and privileges of citizens." Natives were now typically pigeonholed as "wards" of the state with uncertain prospects of ever being able to achieve 'adulthood' since supervision would be required "generation after generation." MP's would no longer have to compete for their favour as potential electors, although they might from time to time help the natives of their ridings by acting as their ombudsman with Indian Affairs officials. By 1920, any memory that natives had ever enjoyed the federal franchise seemed to have vanished from the Commons. In commenting on an overhaul of the Elections Act, then Solicitor General H. Guthrie observed that "...where a man is in the position of being a ward of the Government and is receiving public aid, I do not think he is entitled to the franchise. We have recognized that principle in our legislation in other respects, that being the way we have treated our Indian wards; they have not a vote yet and they do not get it under this Bill."[43]

The Indian Act provided the legal authority structuring the 'wardship' relationship between federal bureaucrats and native peoples. Almost nothing escaped the regulatory control of Ottawa and the local Indian agents in their pursuit of improving the "moral character" of their charges. Consider, for example, the 1914 comments of a then former Minister of the Interior, Frank Oliver, concerning two minor amendments to the Act. One amendment forbade natives to perform ceremonial dances for public entertainment. This met with Oliver's approval because while the "white man" could safely "join in a public show for money," if natives did so they would become less "amenable to reason and argument and good influence."

> The merit of the Indian is in the maintenance of his dignity, and when the Indian consents to join in a public show for money he degrades and demoralizes himself to an extent that would not be present in the case of a white man doing a similar thing. The Indian is either a gentleman or very much the reverse. As long as his dignity is maintained he is a gentleman and he is amenable to reason and argument and good influence, but when he loses his self-respect, and he certainly does lose his self-respect when he makes himself a public show, then he gets to a point where neither the Government nor anybody else can do very much with him or for him.

But the other amendment, prohibiting natives in the western provinces from marketing their livestock, he thought went too far. Indians required the civilizing influence of developing a "sense of ownership" and "selfishness."

> My objection to it would be that it establishes too great a condition of paternalism. It does not give scope to the Indian to grow in his sense of proprietorship, of personal ownership, which is really essential to his progress and civilization. The sense of ownership, after all, is the very foundation of civilization. Ownership, selfishness, which is foreign to the mind of the Indian in his normal condition, is really the foundation of civilization.[44]

Far more significant to natives were the provisions of the Indian Act that made it impossible to change the boundaries of their reserves without their consent. But the pressure from non-natives on reserve land was growing. Representing the Medicine Hat constituency, C.A. Magrath explained that settlers "were starving for land" while natives were "dying off."

> I do not believe in taking advantage of the Indian, and I do not believe anybody in Canada wishes to do so. But there is the settler starving for land; there is the Indian without the means of occupying more than probably one-third of his land; he is dying off, and as time goes on, unless we can get the Indian to sell some of his land, he will disappear without having received any benefit from his property and it will revert to the government.

Oliver, then Minister, responded sympathetically to Magrath's appeal. Although some Indians, he observed, are "indisposed to sell at any price" it is "the policy of the department as at present administered to secure the surrender of Indian lands when these lands are of no present value to the Indians and when they would be of present value in adding to the productive wealth of the country."[45] The idea was to "change the condition of that land from lying dormant and useless under the ownership of the Indians, to that of productive and tax-paying land under the ownership of white people who are willing to pay a fair market price for it."[46]

Pursuit of this policy brought with it the St. Peter's Reserve scandal. In 1907, the Peguis Nation lost 35,000 acres of first class farming land 25 miles from Winnipeg, to "a few of [the Government's] political friends for less than one-third of its actual value," according to local MP G.H. Bradbury.[47] And then there was the case of the Songhees Nation whose reserve contained valuable ocean front land within the city of Victoria. Laurier told the Commons that he "need not say… that the Indians, with their habits, did not at all improve the tract of land that was in their possession. As this land bordered the ocean it was essential to the development of the city, but the Indians would not surrender their rights and for years it was a constant battle between the Indians and white men of Victoria." Laurier determined that in future such cases needed to be "settled under general principles." This meant legislation to allow Indian Affairs to bypass the land surrender protections built into the Indian Act through direct application to the Court of the Exchequer to determine "whether or not it would be in the interests of all concerned, the Indians' interest first of all, and the interests of the communities in these growing cities, that the Indians should be dispossessed, upon fair compensation of course, and given another reserve..."[48]

Alarmed native leaders petitioned parliament to drop this bill and sympathetic members read their letters into Hansard. Two Six Nations chiefs argued that "should this Bill apply to the Six Nations it would be trampling upon our conceded rights from the British Crown... As the city of Brantford is within ten miles of this reserve we are of the opinion that an aim is being made by some unscrupulous persons to legislate us out of our reserve, by virtue, of this enactment, in a similar manner as was done on the St. Peters reserve."[49] Mohawk Chief F. McD. Jacobs wrote that his people had presented a petition to the Minister with "nearly four hundred names" asking that his reserve be excluded from the provisions to seize land. The bill, he said, showed "how utterly the natural rights of man are disregarded in special Indian legislation at the prompting of our official guardian." And then Chief Jacobs got to the heart of the matter. Not only did the Indian Act interfere with natives "natural and inherent rights" but because they were "not recognized as citizens" natives had been denied access to their own political representatives to oppose such unjust legislation.

> ...we are Indians in name only; we are self-supporting, industrious, etc. Our people of Caughnawaga are well known practically in every part of the civilized world, and still we are not recognized as citizens. The basis and scope of our Indian Act is wrong, and injurious to us, because it interferes with our enjoyments of natural and inherent rights. We have no voice whatever in legislation. We are often opposed to it and suffer from its effect... Justice is intended

> to provide for every man in this country whether his skin be white, red or any other colour.[50]

Native representations did not sway either the Laurier or the successor Borden government on this issue. Indeed, Oliver rationalized that Ottawa was protecting natives "actual rights" and from doing an "ultimate injury" to themselves "by standing on [their] treaty rights."

> ...this Bill is necessary for the mutual protection of the actual rights of the Indians and the well-being of the white people. For while we believe that the Indian, having a certain treaty right, is entitled ordinarily to stand upon that right and get the benefit of it, yet we believe also that there are certain circumstances and conditions in which the Indian by standing on his treaty rights does himself an ultimate injury as well as does an injury to the white people... The government believe that when such cases occur in the future, as they certainly will occur, it would be very much better that there should be a statutory provision having the sanction of parliament, that would adequately protect the material interests of the Indians, and at the same time would protect the interests and the welfare of the white community residing adjacent to the Indian reserve.[51]

Oliver was especially frosty to the proposal of Bradbury that native communities be allowed to choose their own lawyer to defend their desire to retain their reserve lands before the Court of the Exchequer. If natives could be trusted to protect their own interests, he posited, "then there would be no necessity for the Indian Act."

> ...I think that is a very dangerous proposal, and not in the interests of the Indians themselves. If the sound judgment of the Indians could be depended upon to be exercised in the protection of their own interests, then there would be no necessity for the Indian Act or for the supervision that parliament has placed over them. It is because it is recognized that they cannot be trusted to protect their own interests that this supervision is exercised... under those circumstances to leave the question of the choice of a counsel in the hands of the judge of the Exchequer Court, is giving them better protection than to leave the matter at their own choice.[52]

Representing Nipissing, G. Gordon echoed Oliver's line. Natives were "simply children" who "were not able to look after themselves" and it "would be a very material help to the Indians" if they could be moved from their reserve even over their objections.

> There is an Indian reserve of something over 100 square miles situated between North Bay and Sturgeon Falls. The Indians on that reserve would not be benefited if they were represented on a board to take care of their own interests. They are simply children, children of the forest, and I believe they would be protected just as well under the provisions of this Bill as they could be in any other way. I desire to see the interests of the Indians protected in every way, protected just as well as those of the white men, and even better, because they require more protection from the fact that they are not able to look after themselves. Take the case of this reserve between Sturgeon Falls and North Bay. It would help the Indians, it would help the country, and it would help the surrounding towns to have a road built through that reserve, but the Indians will not agree to it. It would be a very material help to the Indians if they were moved into some other place away from the white people, and I think the Indians are of the same opinion.[53]

Not everyone in the Commons quietly went along with allowing Indian Affairs a workaround to the reserve lands protections in the Indian Act. For example, E.A. Lancaster reminded members that even if this legislation would prove "popular from the white man's standpoint... we should remember that these Indians are in our power, and we should try to defend those who have no other defenders." The legislation would "practically set aside" native treaty rights and so was unBritish.

> They have treaties which it is suggested by this legislation we should practically set aside. It seems to me the first question involved is not the question of whether it will be better for the white men living in neighbourhood of the red man's land, but the question of breaking a pact made with the ancestors of these Indians. It will not do the country any good to start in that line. If this country has a standing in the world today, it is because it is supposed to keep its pacts; it is a child of the British nation which always keeps

its pacts. I do not want any new or twentieth century ideas in that regard; the idea which for hundreds of years have been the strength and honour of the British nation are the ideas that I would prefer to see maintained.

But there was more. The underlying issue, he held, was that Ottawa was seeking to force natives to surrender their interest in land that had appreciated in value over time and accept in compensation land that was marginal. The "white man" would never be put in a similarly unjust situation.

> The Indians have located upon certain pieces of land, and they are entitled to the luck – if you like to call it that – and the benefits derived from the fact that their land turns out to be in a progressive part of the country. If land taken up by our ancestors turned out to be valuable, we should not expect that fact to be made a reason why we should hand those lands over to somebody else. And we must give the red man the same quality of justice that we would give to the white man similarly situated.[54]

Bradbury also objected that the legislation was unBritish and suggested that while French Canadians had the political means to protect themselves from an assault on their rights, natives did not.

> ...the powers asked for in this Bill are altogether too arbitrary. They would violate treaties made with the Indians by the Crown of Great Britain. We have always boasted of the manner in which we have treated the Indians in this Dominion, contrasted with the treatment they have received in other parts of this continent; but if we enact this measure, we shall be taking power to violate every treaty that we have made with the Indians in British North America without consulting them. We shall be giving the Superintendent General powers that I do not think any Superintendent General or the Department of Indian Affairs ought to have. I think it would be just as reasonable for the minister to propose a Bill to do away with the dual language in Canada as one to deprive the Indians of their treaty rights, and if any man brought before this House a Bill for any such purpose, it would raise a howl in the country that would open the eyes of the government.[55]

Parliamentary discussions around native education provide another good illustration of how policy options were constrained by the 'wardship' consensus coming out of the Macdonald era. Clifford Sifton, responsible for Indian Affairs as Minister of the Interior, explained to the Commons that education was the portal required for a native to improve from a "savage" to a "civilized" person although "perhaps not of a high type."

> Our position with reference to the Indians is this: We have them with us, and we have to deal with them as wards of the country. There is no question that the method we have adopted of spending money to educate them is the best possible method of bringing these people to an improved state... generally speaking there is a vast difference between the Indians who have passed through the day school and are now adults or becoming adults, and the Indians who have not had that advantage. There is a difference between the savage and a person who has become civilized, though perhaps not of a high type... You cannot press the Indian children as you can the children of white people, you cannot require so much from them.[56]

In the system of native "boarding schools," Sifton said, "what we desire to do is not give a highly specialized education to half a dozen out of a large band of Indians, but if possible to distribute over the whole band a moderate amount of education and intelligence, so that the general status of the band would be raised." Opposition MP's generally supported Sifton's position on the advantages of off-reserve residential education. For example, A.A.C. LaRivière responded directly to Sifton in the House by maintaining that

> ...the education of the Indians does not merely consist in teaching them to read and write, but that in addition they have to be civilized. In that case if you keep the Indians within their reserve I am afraid the civilization of the Indians will not be attained. I believe that the best way to civilize them is to remove them from their reserves and get them to lead a civilized life at least for a certain length of time.[57]

When he was Minister of the Interior, F. Oliver emphasized the importance of delivering native education through the religious institutions that ran the residential schools as moral instruction was more necessary to their becoming 'civilized' than were the three Rs.

> ...what the Indian needs is not a knowledge of geometry, or algebra, or astronomy or of the different branches of higher education. It is not even the reading and writing and arithmetic he needs. Even a white man may live and live well and never know how to write his name or to read a book. But what the Indian does need is to have moral character instilled into his mind and heart. That, the government does not pretend to do. It looks to the churches to do that, and it is with that end in view the government has sought the co-operation of the churches in imparting education to the Indians... if we are to have an improvement in the condition of the Indians, that improvement must start in the mind, in the heart, in the soul. I do not think that even this government can satisfactorily undertake that work."[58]

Arthur Meighen, who was responsible for Indian Affairs between 1917 and 1920, agreed with his predecessors that denominational boarding schools were the answer because reserve life was "wholly alien to the purposes of education."

> The Indian, to be educated, must be in an environment that permits of education. You cannot get it on the Indian reserve; you cannot get it around his parent's home. There the Indian is under the influence of his parent; the parent is not very anxious that the child attend school, and there is a constant battle between the parent and the department in an endeavour to secure the child's attendance. The reserves are wholly alien to the purposes of education. Furthermore... I do not believe you can ever educate Indian children unaccompanied by religious instruction, and you cannot have religious instruction unless you have it, for these purposes at all events, under religious denominations.[59]

Meighen was responding here to a member who was pressing for the re-opening of the Stoney Nation Alberta reserve school that had been closed for three years awaiting construction of a residential school over 200 miles away in Edmonton. Transferring students to Edmonton, J.T. Shaw told the Commons, "will not meet with the approval of the Indians at this centre. They have a large number of children there. They want to accommodate them, and not only that, but they want the school to serve as a community centre, not only to benefit the children both intellectually and physically, but also because it is an advantage to the Indians themselves and a place, round which their community activities might centre."[60] It was rare that members questioned the assumptions behind residential schooling but Shaw threw his support behind the Stoney parents: "I am frank to say, Mr. Chairman, that I have not very much sympathy with that method of [residential school] education..."[61] Meighen, however, disclosed that when he was Minister he had developed a policy of shutting down all day schools on the reserves. "I remember very well coming to the conclusion that the day school as a means of educating young children had failed," he explained. "As to the soundness of that conclusion I had no doubt at all; and in pursuance of it, day schools one by one were closed and resorted in toto to the policy... of educating through institutional schools – large boarding schools under religious supervision. When this [Stoney] school was closed it doubtless was in pursuance of that policy..."[62]

Beyond improving the 'moral character' of natives and bringing them to 'civilization,' downloading the financial costs of providing for Ottawa's 'wards' to religious and other private organizations was another powerful influence governing the administration of native affairs. An excellent illustration of how this was understood in practice can be found in a 1922 exchange in the Commons between Charles Stewart, then minister responsible for Indian Affairs, Meighen, the former minister, and A.W. Neill, a British Columbia member. The exchange began when Meighen questioned Stewart's announcement that there would be an increase in the daily fee allowance for natives at a hospital from $1 to $1.25. As the cost of living was then in decline,

Meighen complained that his former government was being cast by the new Liberal administration as 'penurious.'

> Mr. Stewart: ...I understand that there has been a persistent request from those hospitals for increased grants for medical attention while Indians are inmates of the hospitals.
> Mr. Meighen... the minister is yielding to these demands and letting the cost of attendance to the hospitals go up. We have always allowed so much a day, why should this time be seized to increase that allowance.
> Mr. Stewart: ...I think $1 per day would not pay full compensation for attendance upon an individual in a hospital, as I think my right hon. Friend will agree. I understand that this hospital is maintained by private individuals. Perhaps I should not make the assertion, but I think that we have been trying to get off rather cheaply with the Indians who are wards of the Government. On a very superficial examination, I think that we have been delegating the care of the Indians very largely to private individuals and church organizations, when it seems to me that the responsibility is on the Canadian people...
> Mr. Meighen: Certainly we employ and co-operate with church organizations and charitable institutions, and the Indians will never be properly taken care of without that co-operation. Those are the organizations that can do the work best, as time has proved and as history has shown...
> Mr. Neill: I can heartily endorse the attitude taken by the minister in regard to increasing the grants to Indians. The question is not one of economy, it is one of justice. These local hospitals have been grossly underpaid for a number of years. I have in mind a hospital in my district, a hospital kept up partially by government grants, but largely by personal subscriptions and money contributed by means of dances or other entertainments. Every year, however, that hospital goes behind between $2,000 and $3,000. When we came to analyse the situation at a recent annual meeting, we found we were doing the Indian work at about half the cost. The question was raised – why should the white people put their hands into their pockets as a matter of charity in order to maintain the wards of the Indian Department?[63]

The estimates for Indian Affairs were closely examined on a yearly basis to see where savings could be made. Macdonald had helped set the tone here. It will be recalled that Macdonald believed that in order to encourage natives to stay on reserves and to fend for themselves there it was necessary to be "rigid, even stingy, in the distribution of food." And, in response to complaints concerning the poor and inadequate quality of food rations delivered to the reserves, Macdonald responded that "the hon. gentleman says there is fraud on the Indians because the food is imperfect. It cannot be considered a fraud on the Indians, because they have no right to that food. They are simply living on the benevolence and the charity of the Canadian Parliament, and, as the old adage goes, beggars should not be choosers."[64] Shocking to some in the Commons, even in the face of the Riel Rebellion, this "rigid, even stingy" attitude provoked severe criticism. D.M. Cameron pointed to statements made by Macdonald

> in 1880 and re-affirmed in 1885 that the policy of this Administration was a policy of submission by a policy of starvation; and in the face of the report of Agent Herchmer sent to the Department that a little starvation would do the Indians good... I should like to see the experiment tried on the officials of the Government; from the commissioner down to agent Herchmer, and from agent Herchmer down to the lower officials, and a little starvation might teach them some common sense. ...Instead of dealing fairly and honestly by the Indian, as we ought to have done; instead of maintaining unbroken our treaty obligations with the Indian, we pursued, and we still pursue that mad and reckless and inhuman policy of submission by starvation.[65]

According to Indian Affairs, one in three able-bodied native men, approximately 4,000 in total, volunteered for military service during World War I.[66] The very high rate of native participation was known to the Commons. D. Sutherland observed that

> One hundred and five thousand Indians do not forget that they have sent 2,000 volunteers to the front. The most magnificent response that has been made by any race in Canada has been made by the Indians, who have not been given very generous treatment, and who have been deprived of the franchise. One would think that if there were in this country any one who had a grievance against the

Government, or against the people of another race, it would have been the Indians of Canada.⁶⁷

When the Great War was over, W.F. Cockshutt suggested that the government set aside money for native high school students noting, based on his experience in his Ontario riding, that "the Six Nation Indians are amongst the most intelligent, if not the most intelligent, on the North American continent and they are capable of a very fine education if they have the opportunity... and [with it] a large number of them would take a place among the most advanced of the white population." But J. Best, another Ontario member, baulked at Cockshutt's idea on the grounds that more needed to be done "to assist our white people" before consideration was given to spending "a lot of unnecessary money" on natives.

> I realize that many of these Indians are capable of a very high education, but in view of the conditions in which the finances of the country are today I hope the minister will not for one moment think of laying aside tens or hundreds of thousands of dollars for any such purpose. I have brought to the notice of some of the departments instances where the parents of young white men, – young men who went overseas and fought for this country – were poor and were not able to put their sons through the high school; these had to do the best they could to get through. Why then should we set aside hundreds of thousands of dollars to give higher education to young Indians when our own white people cannot put themselves through? I realize than many Indians went overseas and fought for the Empire and we ought to treat them just the same as we would any other class of people, but we are not in a financial position to do what has been suggested; and to my mind no hon. member should get up here and advocate that we pay out a lot of unnecessary money for this purpose. I believe in fair play to everyone in the Dominion, but I am also of the opinion that if we were to do more to assist our white people we would better serve the interests of our country.⁶⁸

CONTROLLING THE MESSAGE

The twentieth century had barely begun when some members

began to express skepticism about the administration of Canada's native policies. There were suggestions that the department was not effectively working towards preparing natives for meaningful employment and thereby creating the necessary conditions for natives to get out from under government supervision. Ministers, defending their Indian Affairs bureaucrats in the House, either denied the evidence of systemic policy failure or deflected the blame onto the supposed irredeemably "savage" nature of the native "race." Milloy concludes that Department files show that it was "complicit" with the churches in covering up the dismal reality of residential schooling. "Witnessing throughout this long period the persistent mistreatment of children, the Department felt most immediately not compassion for its wards but only its own vulnerability," he said. "Evidence of neglect and mistreatment had to be carefully managed, sealed in Department records."[69]

In 1909, twenty-seven year parliamentary veteran G.E. Foster underlined the very limited attention given to developing native policy by the Commons noting that "it is only once a year in parliament that we can devote half an hour to talk on the Indian question when these [Indian Affairs] estimates are being considered." Foster complained of a "condition of drift" in Indian education, no "improvement in the last ten years" and, in fact, "no good result" from native expenditures during the previous forty years. "The Indians are our wards it is said, and we should do the square thing by them," he pronounced. "But, we ought not to go on spending a lot of money, pretending to do something and really doing nothing, and coming around this table every year and nodding to each other and all acknowledge that we have failed." Foster pointed out that the residential school system was failing since "as a rule they go back to the wild state" when graduates returned to their reserves. Instead, native education should strengthen an "esprit de corps among them" and open real career opportunities.

> You cannot make a white man out of an Indian and there is no use

of our trying that. Give the Indian boy a fair education, instill something of purposes and ambition in him and offer to him some sort of useful career. They ought to make splendid fire rangers and forest rangers and scouts. Is there any inherent disability in the Indian character which makes it impossible for him to do that kind of work? Is there no kind of police duty they can do? In the United States they do utilize the Indians in various ways, they make men out of them, not white men it is true, but they instill in the Indian a good deal of nerve and verve and they are fairly successful in several spheres.

Frank Oliver, then minister responsible for natives, argued in response to Foster that if there were shortcomings they were neither in government policy nor administration but in the especially "savage" character of the native "race." Although it might appear that money was being wasted,

> We are not negligent in the matter but we have to deal with a problem which has never yet been solved. It has not been solved in the United States, it has not been solved in Canada; under no approximately parallel conditions has it been solved in any country. Even if we take the conditions in other countries where there are savage races, there is no other savage race on the same level as the North American Indian. He is in a class by himself and has a persistence of character not possessed by any other race in the world... He has an independence of character that does not allow him to submit to the same dictation, direction and conditions that other races of men will submit to...[70]

J.E. Armstrong, inspired by his knowledge of two native reserves within his own western Ontario constituency, told the House that based on his own two year study of Ottawa's native policies, he had concluded "that the manner in which the department is administered is a blot on the fair name of our Dominion." Like Foster, he unfavourably contrasted what he believed to be American successes at integrating natives into their society with a century of failure in Canada. And like Foster, he pointed the finger of blame at the department's schools and a non-native bureaucracy that spent government funding for natives in large measure on itself.

> If he [the Minister] will investigate the United States reports he will see that their Indians are making wonderful advances toward civilization, while the Indians of the Dominion of Canada are practically where they were 100 years or more ago. They are not on the whole making any great advances towards citizenship. The minister may say that it is scarcely possible to make a good citizen of the Indian, but if he will look into the manner in which Indians are treated in the United States and see what they are accomplishing towards civilizing the Indians, he will be convinced that we as a nation should be ashamed of the manner in which we are treating the Indians, and of the slow progress they are making towards good citizenship. It is all very well to bring in Doukhobors and people of that class, with less intellect than the average of our Indians, and make them citizens of Canada and give them the franchise, but it is not worth while, apparently, judging from the minister's administration of the department, to take the Indians of this Dominion and elevate them up to the standard of citizenship.

Natives should be "taken out of these denominational schools, given superior education and assisted materially towards [their] general advancement and welfare," Armstrong declared. Concerning his own constituency, "there is not a doubt in my own mind that if these men were given proper educational facilities and looked after in a proper manner they would become civilized and take up the positions that Indians are now taking in the United States. Up to 1901 there were in the United States, 16,000 Indians who had become civilized citizens of the United States and 4,000 Indians in addition who were under probation or had received their lands in such a way that in a few years they would become citizens." Armstrong accused Oliver of knowing that Canada's native policies were not working but being unwilling to look at reforms. "…he knows that the treatment these Indians are receiving, the manner in which their schools are conducted and their funds administered, have not been for the general advancement of the Indians and are not likely to bring him

[sic] to take the civilized position he has taken in the United States."[71]

But Oliver was unpersuaded and unmoved. Since native "character" lacked "the business capacity of the white man," wardship stretching "generation after generation" (in Macdonald's words) was the only realistic alternative. "Indians are Indians," after all.

> My hon. friend complained that we were spending a million and a quarter on the Indians, the greater part of which went for management and only a small part of which actually reached the Indians. Now, that is perfectly correct. That is the policy of this government and of preceding governments: it is an obligation laid upon the government by parliament. The reason is that the Indian needs protection, care and education more than he does money. It would not be sound public policy in the interest of the Indian... to take the million and a quarter of money that we spend on the Indians in one year and hand it over to them to control and expend as they pleased. If that were a sound policy then the Indians would not be Indians, in fact they would be better than a good many white men. But inasmuch as the Indians are Indians, inasmuch as they have not a knowledge of the ways of civilization, it is necessary that money should be spent upon them in education, in medical attendance, and in instruction in agriculture, as well as the general supervision and management of their affairs. It is true that for every $2 that is voted by parliament on [sic] only $1 reaches the Indian's pocket. If this is a fault, we stand convicted of having committed it. But that is done because it is the fixed policy of the government and of the parliament of this country to take care of the Indians, and always has been the fixed policy, and I believe it always will be, so long as there are Indians to take care of. As soon as an Indian arrives at a point when he is able to manage his own business, then we will no longer have an Indian question, because there is plenty of room here for Indians as well as white men. But it is because the Indian has not the business capacity of the white man that we have to manage his business for him, and that costs a great deal of money.[72]

While general complaints from members of parliament about the administration of the Indian Affairs branch were relatively politely pushed aside, when MP's pleaded specific cases on behalf of natives they typically met with evasion from ministers and sometimes even suggestions that they were being used to further the agenda of "agitators." For example, in 1922, newly elected G.G. Coote, whose riding included the Blood Nation reserve in Alberta, explained to the House that he had promised to intercede on the band's behalf with the government.

> When I was on the reserve this winter I was interviewed by about twenty Indians, who presented me with a lengthy memorandum setting forth a list of grievances which they have against the Government. In addition to those grievances, they personally stated that they had a lot of complaints against the treatment which they were receiving, and that they had nobody to speak for them; that the means of communication between them and the department at Ottawa seemed to be closed... At their request I promised to take the matter up with the Government.

Meighen, the former Conservative minister, was provoked to rise in defence of his Liberal successor Stewart and to urge "firmness" in the face of agitators. Indian Affairs, he claimed was "entitled to the co-operation" of M.P's who represented ridings with native reserves in support of "a policy of firmness."

> ...as regards the general question of complaints from reserves. As superintendent general for something over three years, I came in contact with them frequently, and I have not the least doubt that the present superintendent general will have the same experience as I did... The Indian population, perhaps more than any other body of people, are easily susceptible to imposition at the hands of the cleverer white, and nowhere do the agitator and the charlatan reap a readier harvest than among the Indian people... Now in respect to our dealings with these people, no one is more decided than I am that these dealings must be characterized by humanity, by stern fidelity to all our treaties, by justice always – as everything we do must be just – but at the same time, by firmness. The minister in the discharge of his duties will be entitled to the co-operation, in this regard, of the members who come from the districts inhabited by Indians, and I for one propose to give him support in a policy of firmness in this matter. I purpose (sic) to support him against the operations of people who want to profit by agitation and stir up unrest among the Indians, because I came out of the department

profoundly convinced that that is the attitude of mind that will be most useful, and indeed, most just on the part of my successor.[73]

After a few years leading the Department, Stewart was singing the same song about agitators who raised complaints. "We have a great deal of trouble in the administration of the Indian Act," he declared to the House. "There are agitators in every band, and there are also outside agitators who excite the Indians and give them a false conception of their rights."[74]

Even whistleblowing reports from government insiders were blown off. In 1922, Dr. P.H. Bryce, following a career of twenty-two years as Chief Medical Officer of Ontario and fifteen years as Chief Medical Officer of Immigration and Indian Affairs, released a privately-published pamphlet entitled "The story of a national crime: being an appeal for justice to the Indians of Canada" detailing the tuberculosis crisis within native communities. Bryce referred to studies which indicated an infection rate in excess of 90 per cent among native children in Alberta and Saskatchewan and pointed to an absolute decline in Canada's native population of 1,639 persons between 1904 and 1917 whereas an expected "normal increase would have added 20,000 population." Indian Affairs' "reactionary Deputy Minister" Duncan Campbell Scott who counted "upon the ignorance and indifference of the public to the fate of the Indians" was blamed by Bryce for covering up the tuberculosis plague.[75]

Bryce's pamphlet was mailed to parliamentarians and W.C. Good stated to the House that it "contains rather serious charges of maladministration in the Department of Indian Affairs with respect to medical attention to Indians... if the facts are anywhere near as they are stated, then I think the minister ought to look into the matter without delay." Stewart, as the incoming minister responsible, denied having read Bryce's report and so could not "express any opinion upon it." But his predecessor, Meighen, immediately interjected the view that the tuberculosis "plague" was largely the natives own fault because they had chosen to lead the "life of ease" provided by the department over "hard work in the open air."

> The Indian is disposed to tuberculosis. Why? Because Indian life, through the influences of civilization, has been changed. Down through the generations the Indian has led a wild life, roaming the prairies and the woods, and just in proportion as you coddle him and enable him to lead a life of ease, to that extent is he likely to drift into tuberculosis... the educational institutions do good in teaching habits of cleanliness and the prevention and spread of the plague, and so forth. But I think that most can be done by such a policy as puts the Indian on his resources and makes it his business to work in the open to gain the livelihood he must have. The worst thing you can do for him is to provide such conditions as enable him to live at ease – although, of course, that life would not satisfy white men – and without that hard work in the open air which made the ancestors of the Indians healthy and strong.[76]

But the issue did not disappear from debate so easily. Next year R.J. Manion took note of the absolute decrease in Canada's native population due to tuberculosis observing that "...perhaps we might increase our efforts to educate these people to the importance of protecting themselves, more particularly against tuberculosis. It is important that we should teach them the means to prevent this disease to as great an extent as they possibly can." In his reply, Stewart underlined that the high financial costs necessary to "wipe out" the native tuberculosis epidemic meant that the department's efforts would be limited to public health education – "In answer to my hon. friend who has spoken of the scourge of tuberculosis among the Indians, while I would not say that we are taking adequate steps to this end, because it would cost a tremendous amount of money to wipe out this plague amongst the Indian tribes, yet we are trying by propaganda and education among the Indians to make them acquainted with the best methods of combatting the disease."[77] Stewart was later to follow in Meighen's footsteps and find a way of blaming natives for the tuberculosis crisis. In reply to a member who had read to the House a heart-rending letter from a United Church administrator graphically detailing horrendous health conditions on one reserve, Stewart claimed that the problem was that Indians would not leave their reserves for tuberculosis treatment in specialized hospitals.

> To establish on each reserve a hospital for this special purpose is out of the question; it would be too expensive... Recommendations for a nursing staff was made some three years ago, and four nurses are now travelling through the provinces examining Indian children and giving such relief as they can. I am informed that this work has been very beneficial to the Indians, and good progress is being made. It would be idle to deny that there is a great deal of tuberculosis among the Indians, not only in the western provinces but throughout Canada. It is a very serious problem for the department. That, I think, is all that I can say in reply to my hon. friend.[78]

CONCLUSION

Chapter 4 has focused on race-thinking as it related to Canada's native people. Sir John A. Macdonald's key role in framing for future generations the federal government's native policies is underlined as are the arguments of his opponents who predicted that these policies were bound to fail as they were not predicated on "giving the red man all the liberties and rights enjoyed by the white man." Losing the voting franchise in the late 1890s, it is suggested, moved natives from being legitimate subjects of politics and political contestation[79] under the British notion of *jus soli* to objects of bureaucratic administration.[80] When this happened, debate ceased about their democratic rights and became instead focused on the terms of their wardship. The underlying assumption of wardship was that of inferiority: it was said by one minister that the government was constrained to manage native affairs for them because, unlike "white men," "Indians are Indians" and therefore by definition lacked "knowledge of the ways of civilization." Within the wardship frame, the responsible bureaucrats proved adept at turning aside suggestions in the House that government needed an exit strategy to make natives less dependent and/or evidence of Indian Affairs' calamitous mismanagement of native education and health services. Not everyone was convinced, however; a few members stubbornly rejected the "savage race" excuses of department ministers and instead insisted that natives were highly intelligent and given meaningful opportunities could contribute positively to Canadian society. In our next chapter, we will turn to an account of the Commons debates concerning all other Canadians of non-European origin during our period of study.

Notes

1. Canada, House of Commons, *Debates*, April 3, 1914, pp. 2394-2395.
2. Daniel Gorman, *Imperial citizenship: Empire and the question of belonging.* Manchester: Manchester University Press, 2006. p. 20.
3. See Kenneth M. Narvey, "The Royal Proclamation of 7 October 1763. The Common Law, and Native Rights to Land within the Territory Granted to the Hudson's Bay Company," *Saskatchewan Law Review*, 1974, pp. 123-233.
4. Commons, *Debates*, May 4, 1885, p. 1582.
5. Gorman, *Imperial citizenship*, p. 20.
6. Commons, *Debates*, May 1, 1885, pp. 1504-1505.
7. Ibid., April 30, 1885, p. 1487.
8. Ibid., June 10, 1885, p. 2423.
9. Ibid., July 6, 1885, p. 3119.
10. Ibid., April 27, 1882, p. 1186.
11. Ibid., June 17, 1887, p. 1094.
12. Ibid., May 5, 1880, p. 1991.
13. Ibid., April 7, 1884, p. 1403.
14. Ibid., May 9, 1883, p. 1101.
15. Ibid., May 3, 1880, p. 1946.

16. Ibid., May 9, 1883, pp. 1107-1108. For an overview of "the founding vision" of the residential school system in Canada, see John S. Milloy, *A National Crime: The Canadian Government and the Residential School System, 1879 to 1986*. Winnipeg: University of Manitoba Press, 1999, Chapter 3.
17. Ibid., June 17, 1887, p. 1095.
18. Ibid., April 1, 1885, p. 868.
19. Ibid., June 10, 1885, p. 2422.
20. Ibid., May 3, 1880, pp. 1941-1942.
21. Ibid., May 9, 1883, p. 1107.
22. Ibid., June 10, 1885, pp. 2426-2427.
23. Ibid., May 5, 1880, pp. 1993-1994.
24. Ibid., p. 1990.
25. Ibid., p. 1990-1991.
26. Ibid., p. 1996.
27. Macdonald's Franchise Act was debated in the Commons with the 1885 Riel Rebellion as backdrop. For many weeks the Liberals held up passage of the legislation accompanied by the disruptive sounds of kazoos, cat screeches, and desk scraping "punctuated now and then with telegrams from the Northwest that Caron or Macdonald would read to the House." Peter B. Waite, *Canada 1874-1896*. Toronto: McClelland and Stewart, 1971. pp. 140-142.
28. Commons, *Debates*, April 30, 1885, p. 1489.
29. Ibid., pp. 1486-1487, 1491.
30. It is conceivable that Dawson had been inspired by knowledge of precedent elsewhere in the Empire where the New Zealand Parliament had set aside four seats for aboriginals under the Maori Representation Act of 1867. See, "The Origins of the Māori Seats," New Zealand, New Zealand Parliament, Parliamentary Library Research Paper, November 2003 (Updated May 2009). Accessed December 12, 2012.http://www.parliament.nz/en-NZ/ParlSupport/ResearchPapers/5/b/e/00PLLawRP03141-Origins-of-the-M-ori-seats.htm

31. Commons, *Debates*, April 7, 1884, p. 1403.
32. Ibid., May 1, 1885, pp. 1504, 1524.
33. Ibid., p. 1516.
34. Ibid., p. 1503.
35. A resolution supporting a return to the provincial lists had been passed unanimously by the first Liberal Party national convention in 1893 following a rousing speech by Toronto lawyer N.W. Rowell against the federal Franchise Act which he denounced as "a fraud" and a tyrannical abuse of power by the Conservatives: "The Old Flag has been dragged down from the proud place it occupied in the heart of every Briton, dragged down to wrap around the corruption and dishonesty of a corrupt and dishonest administration, dragged into the mire of fierce political conflict; it has been prostituted to base and dishonorable party purposes by those who profess to be its especial guardians. And it is left to the Liberal party, which has always been loyal to what is true and best in the British system of government, to raise that flag out of the mire and unfurl it to the world as a symbol of their belief in the principles which that flag represents — freedom of trade, justice to all classes with privileges to none, an honest, economical and truly representative government, a government of the people, by the people and for the people." *Official Report of the Liberal Convention*, June 20th and June 21st, 1893. Toronto: Budget Printing and Publishing, 1893 pp. 127-128.
36. Montgomery has argued that the 1898 Liberal withdrawal of the native right vote in federal elections was motivated in some degree by partisan vindictiveness resulting from their loss of the 1896 federal election in the South Brant riding. South Brant included the Grand River Reserve of the Six Nations and since 1872 had been in the hands of William Paterson and the Liberal Party. Montgomery observed that "while Paterson and the Liberal party had firmly opposed the extension of the franchise to the Indians, the Six Nations did not seem to put much weight upon this fact until the election of 1896." But in that election, Conservative candidate Robert Henry "waged a vigourous campaign in an attempt to woo the Six Nations voters in South Brant." Conservative

campaign literature prominently featured many "bigoted statements allegedly by Grits" in the 1885 House of Commons debate that had enfranchised property-qualified natives. Paterson's subsequent electoral loss to his Tory challenger was blamed, at least in part, on native voters by numerous Liberal party notables. Montgomery concluded that Liberal Party political payback was swift. "The Indians had committed the crime of not voting the right way. By doing so, they no doubt hastened the revocation of their franchise... the result in South Brant called for immediate action. The punishment the Indians received was that of being deprived of the right to vote for sixty-two years." Malcolm Montgomery, "The Six Nations Indians and the Macdonald Franchise," *Ontario History*, Volume LVII, No. 1, March 1965. pp. 16-17, 25. On Paterson's loss, Weaver recorded that "in the election of 1896, the last before the withdrawal of the Indian franchise, the high turnout of Six Nations voters was credited with swinging the [South Brant] riding to Robert Henry, a Conservative candidate, although the Liberals won power in Ottawa." Sally M. Weaver, "The Iroquois: The Grand River Reserve in the Late Nineteenth and Early Twentieth Centuries, 1875-1945," in *Aboriginal Ontario: Historical Perspectives on the First Nations*, Rogers, E.S. and Smith, D.B. (eds.) Toronto: Dundurn Press, 1994. p. 238. Henry's victory in South Brant was overturned in 1896 and he lost the ensuing by-election to the Liberal candidate, C.B. Heyd. Heyd, unlike Paterson, supported the federal vote for his Six Nations constituents speaking against his party's policy in the 1898 Debates.

37. Commons, *Debates*, April 21, 1898, p. 3947
38. Ibid., p. 3967.
39. Ibid., pp. 3946-3948, 3953.
40. Ibid., pp. 3968-3970.
41. Ibid., April 20, 1886, p. 810. Macdonald expressed a similar view of how race constructed the character of the Métis – "Well, the Metis are, as you know, half Indian; they have many of the characteristics of the Indians, especially the Metis of the plain... [who] are just as wild in their habits, as irregular in their conduct, and as impulsive in their actions as their full blooded red brethren." (March 26, 1885, p. 762.) And, earlier

in this Chapter, we saw Macdonald assert that "half-breeds, enticed by white men," had "their savage instinct... awakened" in the pursuit of "warlike glory" during the Riel Rebellion. (July 6, 1885, p. 3119.) But Laurier's mapping here of a path allowing for the future "advancement" of native "character" from "savage to civilized life" reflected a developmentalist, ladder of civilization ethnocentrism, in contrast to Macdonald's more deterministic focus on the weight of "blood" and "instinct" in fixing wild and impulsive "habits."

42. Ibid., April 27, 1922, pp. 1223-1224.
43. Ibid., April 29, 1920, p. 1815.
44. Ibid., May 8, 1914, pp. 3483-3484.
45. Ibid., February 12, 1909, pp. 1007-1009.
46. Ibid., April 14, 1910, p. 7073.
47. Ibid., April 13, 1910, pp. 7009-7011. In 2010 the Government of Canada signed a 6 million dollar financial settlement with the Peguis First Nation in compensation for the surrender of St. Peter's Reserve. Canada, Aboriginal Affairs and Northern Development Canada, "Fact Sheet – Peguis First Nation 1907 Surrender Specific Claim." Accessed February 27, 2013. http://www.aadnc-aandc.gc.ca/eng/1306511636962/1306511731501
48. Commons, *Debates*, April 26, 1911, pp. 7830-7831.
49. Ibid., p. 7834.
50. Ibid., April 3, 1914, pp. 2394-2395.
51. Ibid., April 26, 1911, p. 7827.
52. Ibid., May 4, 1911, p. 8407.
53. Ibid., April 26, 1911, pp. 7841-7842.
54. Ibid., p. 7840.
55. Ibid., pp. 7835-7836.
56. Ibid., April 18, 1902. pp. 3045-3046.
57. Ibid., July 18, 1904, pp. 6946-6947.
58. Ibid., June 22, 1908, p. 11056.

59. Ibid., April 27, 1922, pp. 1229-1230. Statistics do not support Meighen's claim that residential schools were effective educators. As late as 1930, "three quarters of Amerindian pupils across Canada were in grades one to three. Only three in 100 went past grade six." Olive Patricia Dickason (adapted by Moira Jean Calder), *A Concise History of Canada's First Nations*. Toronto: Oxford University Press, 2006. p. 227.
60. Commons, *Debates*, June 24, 1922, p. 3536.
61. Ibid., April 27, 1922, p. 1227.
62. Ibid., p. 1229.
63. Ibid., pp. 1218-1219.
64. Ibid., July 11, 1885, p. 3319.
65. Ibid., April 15, 1886, pp. 725, 729.
66. Janice Summerby, "Native Soldiers – Foreign Battlefields," Canada, Veterans Affairs Canada, 2005. p. 5. (See footnote 7 for the original source for the number 4,000)
67. Commons, *Debates*, June 26, 1917, p. 2686.
68. Ibid., June 8, 1920, p. 3280.
69. Milloy, *A National Crime*. p. 149.
70. Commons, *Debates*, February 12, 1909. pp. 980-982. Two years later Foster's opinion of native administration had not improved. "I have not as much confidence in the Superintendent General of Indian Affairs as I had when I was much younger. I used to think that he was a sort of God in equity, whose whole object was to conserve the rights of the Indians first and entirely. I have now modified my opinion, and look upon that official now as the paid officer of a party government, and certain things which have occurred within the experience of men who have been in public life the last 25 years would, I think, bear out that conclusion." April 26, 1911, p. 7838.
71. Ibid., June 22, 1908, pp. 11026, 11037-11038, 11044.
72. Ibid., pp. 11052-11053.
73. Ibid., April 27, 1922. pp. 1219, 1223. Meighen here was reading from much the same script as that employed four decades earlier by Sir John

A. Macdonald, who it will be recalled, had claimed that "coaxing and firmness at the same time" were required to "manage" natives. May 9, 1883, p. 1107.

74. Ibid., February 15, 1927, p. 317.
75. Dr. P.H. Bryce, ""The story of a national crime: being an appeal for justice to the Indians of Canada; the wards of the nation, our allies in the Revolutionary War, our brothers-in-arms in the Great War," Ottawa: James Hope & Sons, 1922. Accessed January 14, 2013. http://archive.org/stream/storyofnationalc00brycuoft/storyofnationalc00brycuoft_djvu.txt
76. Commons, *Debates*, April 27, 1922, pp. 1220 1224-1225, 1230.
77. Ibid., April 24, 1923, pp. 2152-2153.
78. Ibid., June 4, 1926, p. 4032.
79. To illustrate, consider the account given of the 1896 federal election campaign in South Brant by Montgomery in "Six Nations Indians and the Macdonald Franchise."
80. Some parallel might be discovered in the movement of the contentious politics of Canadian tariff policy during this era "from the arena of explosive partisan politics into the routine operation of a state bureaucracy." See Keiko Sueuchi, "Tariff out of Politics: Political Economy of Tariff Policy in Canada, 1875-1935," Ph.D. dissertation, Carleton University, 1992. p. 410.

CHAPTER 5.

DOMINION ANGLO-SAXONISM AND CANADIANS OF NON-EUROPEAN ORIGIN: ASIANS, SOUTH ASIANS, AND AFRICANS

I cannot reconcile it to my views to vote in favor of the exclusion of any condition, class or race from the rights of citizenship... If a Chinaman becomes a British subject it is not right that a brand should be placed on his forehead, so that other men may avoid him. As a member of this House, and as a Radical, I enter my protest against this reactionary proposal... This is a new country; we should invite all classes of settlers to it, and make them feel, when they come here and make it their home, that they stand on the same footing as the people born here. The old exclusive idea has vanished. I enter my protest against this amendment. I am in favor of any one who has become a British subject and has the necessary qualifications having the right to exercise the franchise....[1]
–L.H. DAVIES, 1885.

As noted in Chapter 4, Canadians of African, Asian, and South Asian descent shared a claim on the "equal rights and equal justice" that in rhetorical principle attended British subjecthood within the Empire. Lacking the group claim of natives to the protection of *jus soli* British subject rights, non-whites were vulnerable to being portrayed in Commons debates as either backward and uncivilized or biologically inferior and antagonistic. In either case, they were often judged to be difficult or impossible to "assimilate" or Canadianize to British standards. Therefore, as D. Mills put it when speaking of "Asiatics," many argued that the most that need be offered them in the way of individual rights was a protective status for their "life and property."

> Their standard of civil morality, their views of government and of society, are all wholly different from ours; their training is different, and I think if we give them security for life and property for the short time they remain here – and very few become British subjects or acquire property in the country – we do all that is done for them in the country of their birth... We are seeking to promote immigration from Europe and not from Asia, and it seems to me that we are perfectly justified in extending the elective franchise... to every person who comes from Europe to this country and is naturalised, and withholding it from a class of people that we may be disposed to tolerate, to give security to when they come here, but that we do not regard as desirable citizens to have among us.[2]

Still, non-white subjects of the Empire could point to the 1857 Queen's Proclamation declaring that her subjects in India should "all alike enjoy the equal and impartial protection of the Law" and that "Our Subjects, of whatever Race or Creed; be freely and impartially admitted to Offices in Our Service, the Duties of which they may be qualified, by their education, ability, and integrity, duly to observe." Banerjee observes that this Proclamation "became the rallying point for British Indians during the latter decades of the nineteenth century, being hailed – be it in London, Natal, or Calcutta – as the Magna Carta for Indians."[3]

With three-quarters of the British Empire's total population in 1913[4], the equality rights of Indian subjects were a very sensitive topic especially given the rising tide of race-thinking in the self-governing white settler colonies. According to Huttenback, attempts by the Dominions to restrict the entry of Indians risked "affronting a British government charged with the guardianship of the imperial philosophy of equality." The answer was found in the Natal Act of 1897 where an administrative barrier was employed – in this case literacy in a European language – rather than exclusionary legislation directed explicitly towards immigrants from the Indian subcontinent. Through this bureaucratic device, according to the Colonial Office in London, Natal was able to conform with the British Secretary of State's "opinion that it was desirable that a law should be passed in that colony in a form which was not open to objection that it persecuted persons of a particular colour."[5]

BRITISH COLUMBIAN EPICENTRE

British Columbia was the epicentre of anti-Asian agitation in Canada's House of Commons during the period of our study. Scarcely a year passed in which not one, but several, B.C. members did not rise to complain bitterly about the Asians in their midst.[6] As early as 1880, setting out arguments that were to be frequently repeated during the next half century, Vancouver's A. Bunster asked for legislation forbidding the Canadian Pacific Railway from employing Chinese workers. Inexpensive Chinese labour would, he claimed, squeeze out white labour and "swarm the country." Further, the Chinese did not contribute to building societal institutions in British Columbia, repatriated all their earnings rather than recycling them within the provincial economy, and were, in addition to all else, morally corrupt.

> I hold in my hand resolutions from the Workmen's Association [of B.C.], praying the Government for the insertion of a clause in the Railway contract prohibiting the employment of Chinese labour in the construction of the Canadian Pacific Railway. This exclusion is desirable for various reasons. The Chinese, as a rule, hoard their money and send it to China; hence its scarcity to some extent in the Pacific Province and Canada generally. We have no idea of the magnitude of the evil befalling and certain to befall us in consequence of the importation of these people. They will swarm the whole country along the line of the road as contractors will employ the cheapest labour. White labourers, English, Irish and Scotch would settle along the road and add to the revenue and prosperity of the country. Chinese would contribute nothing, except rice were taxed more heavily... we will have to struggle before very long to protect our own race against four hundred and eighty millions of Chinamen

who can send fifty millions to swarm us out, an operation already commencing, perhaps. Are we to protect a race that has no respect for our laws, religion or institutions, and does not contribute to our revenue, but robs us in various ways, while guilty of practices not to be described? I hope the Government will, before we meet again, watching over the interests of the Dominion, pass orders preventing the immigration of the Chinese. In California they nearly had a civil war on their account.[7]

Representing Victoria, E.C. Baker sensationalized for his fellow parliamentarians the supposed moral degeneracy of the Chinese. "Whenever a Chinaman or a gang of Chinamen are suspected of a theft or murder, or any other atrocious crime," he claimed, "there is always a difficulty in getting sufficient evidence among them to convict the offender, or even to discover who the principal culprit is." Drug use and drug trafficking were also said to be endemic: "...there exists among the Chinamen the excessive use of opium, which is being disseminated to a great extent among the juniors of the white population. I think these facts speak for themselves, and show that it is highly desirable that a class whose habits are such as described here should, if possible, be prohibited from coming into a civilized country at all." Chinese sexual licentiousness was also professed to be so scandalous as to be "almost beyond description."

> ...Chinese women are not, like Cesar's (sic) wife above suspicion, and that there exists among the Chinese, both male and female, a very low scale of morality... I know, from living in a part of the world where they are to be found in great numbers, that their morals are almost beyond description. In fact, to thoroughly describe their state of immorality I should have to use language that would entitle me to be called to order; and I shall therefore not attempt it, but leave hon. gentlemen to draw their own conclusions.[8]

In 1882, Amor de Cosmos, a former Premier of British Columbia, warned the Commons that because of tougher new U.S. restrictions on Asian immigrants, Chinese labourers would flood the province so as to "outnumber the entire white population."[9]

Following an existing model of prohibitive Australian immigration legislation, another B.C. member, N. Shakespeare, subsequently proposed a motion to exclude Chinese migrants from Canada. This was perceived by some to be a radical measure and created a stir within the House. As Joseph-Adolphe Chapleau, who had served previously as Premier of Quebec, later remembered, he "...was rather struck with a feeling of surprise, which I am sure has been shared by many hon. Members of this House, that a demand was made for legislation to provide that one of the first principles which have always guided the English people in the enactment of their laws and regulations for the maintenance of the peace and prosperity of the country, should be violated in excluding from the shores of this great country, which is a part of the British Empire, members of the human family."[10]

Two New Brunswick members condemned Shakespeare's motion to bar Chinese from Canada. A.H. Gillmor offered several lines of opposition. Excluding the Chinese, he said, was an attack on liberal principles of free trade.

> ...being in favor of Protection and, being in favor of the proverb that 'Canada should be for the Canadians.' I think the hon. gentleman is quite consistent. Besides, he is not in favor of free goods. Being neither in favor of free goods nor of free labor, he is, I say, consistent in seeking to shut out the Chinese. I think the real reason why they do not want the Chinese in British Columbia is because they interfere with the labor market and afford cheap labor... In China, there are... five hundred millions of the human race, who are crowded together, and are starving for want of food. It does not cost our Minister of Agriculture millions of dollars to bring them into Canada. They come at their own expense, they work at cheap rates, and they can live for twenty-five cents a day, while it will cost the white man a dollar. What wrong is done by these men eating rice and sleeping on boards? What crime is there in wearing cheap clothing? There is nothing wrong in these things.

It was unchristian.

> The Chinese are disciples of Confucius, but they are not destitute of ability and of inventive power. The Chinese, long before the Euro-

peans, invented the mariners' compass, the art of printing, gunpowder, and the manufacture of the finest silk and porcelain. They are not destitute of ability, but they are capable of improvement. Our institutions are based on Christian principles... and the institutions which are founded under him [Christ] are bound to triumph, and Chinamen will become Christians rather than the Christians will become Chinese... If the Chinese are educated and given a good example by white men, paid for their labor, and taught morality and religion, they will become good subjects.

It was an expression of regional prejudice that ran counter to the national interest, Gillmor observed: "the hon. mover of the resolution has stated that no candidate need present himself in a constituency in British Columbia who was not opposed to the free importation of Chinese. But I think there are other parts of this Dominion that are interested in this matter as well as British Columbia..." He noted that Canada was spending 100 million dollars in building a transcontinental railway to fulfil its Confederation obligations to B.C. "and in order to get the road built we have been under the necessity of importing Chinese to do the work; and, notwithstanding all the boasted superiority of Canadians and British Columbians, if there are any dangerous place in the canons [sic] of the Fraser, or any mud-holes, you will find the Chinese in those dangerous and uncomfortable positions..." Finally, Gillmor argued, excluding the Chinese was short-sighted because in time they would become good British subjects.

> ...really, I think we have listened long enough to this sort of thing from British Columbia. The more that come in the better, and we want them to come and stay; we will give them something to do. Let some of them come here. We want them in this country, we are expending millions to bring immigrants here. I do not know what sort of citizens these people from China make; but I think, judging from their past history, if they come here and become acclimatised and accustomed to our society, they will fall into our ways. They are an ingenious and imitative people, and I do not think that they will do us any harm.[11]

Summarizing an 1876 joint U.S. Senate/House of Representatives report that had examined Chinese immigration in San Francisco, G.E. Foster explained to the Commons that the Chinese were found to be industrious taking on work unwanted by 'white people,' that they were honest in business, that they lived in crowded but clean conditions, and that they had an "infinitely" lower crime rate than whites. "I draw the conclusion," he declared, "that as the Chinese as a whole cannot be shown to be idle and ignorant, but that as a large proportion are shown to be good and law-abiding citizens, it is not proper for us to raise this Chinese wall of exclusion..." Since Canada needed "a class of immigrants" that are "not only industrious, intelligent and strong, but... good, honest and true," then excluding the Chinese was nothing more than a reflection of old-fashioned prejudice.

> That is where I would draw the line... not a line of race, creed or color... I think that is a better line to draw than to say that after these centuries of progress and refinement, during which the tendency has always been to break down the Chinese walls of exclusion and weld divided humanity into one common whole, we should go back to abandoned prejudices and raise again barriers of color, race and creed. If there are intelligent, moral and industrious Chinamen, why in the name of goodness should a wall be raised to exclude them from this country?[12]

Sir John A. Macdonald acknowledged that there were two sides to this debate about Chinese immigration to Canada through asking the Commons "who will decide, when doctors disagree?" He claimed that his government would take the "middle path" allowing for some immigration for the time being because Chinese labour was temporarily required to compensate for the lack of "white labor" in building the railway. But, putting on his 'race scientist' hat, Macdonald judged that since the Mongolian and Arian races "cannot combine," "no permanent immigration" could be allowed.

> I am one of those who have a great sympathy with the cry both of California and Australia, against the permanent introduction or

entry into a country of a foreign race. I am sufficient of a physiologist to believe that the two races cannot combine, and that no great middle race can arise from the mixture of the Mongolian and the Asian. [sic] I believe it would be a great mistake, and would tend to the degradation of the people of the Pacific; and that no permanent immigration of the Chinese people into Canada is to be encouraged as a body of settlers...[13]

ROYAL COMMISSION OF 1885

Macdonald's government did act with some speed to accommodate British Columbian opinion, appointing a two person Royal Commission in 1884 on Chinese immigration and introducing legislation in 1885 to impose both a head tax on immigrants from China and to deny those of Chinese origins the federal vote. Joseph-Adolphe Chapleau was at the same time a co-Chair of the Royal Commission and the cabinet minister responsible for introducing the head tax in parliament. Considering the evidence and testimony, Chapleau dismissed most of the favourite arguments employed by the B.C. critics of Chinese immigrants: he concluded that they were not spreading disease; that they lived abstemiously and morally without noticeably high crime rates; that they were extremely hard working and made possible economic development through doing work that white workers refused; and that they spent most of their earned money in B.C. rather than returning it to China.

Unlike Macdonald, Chapleau was no biological determinist, but he nonetheless came to similar policy conclusions concerning the Chinese. Both in his presentation of the head tax legislation to parliament and in his signed analysis in the Royal Commission Report, Chapleau characterized race as a socially constructed phenomenon rather than a biological fact. In reference to the Chinese, he told the Commons, "some people say they are a degraded race; they are a mischievous race; they are an uncivilized race; they are barbarians of some kind; and the advanced civilization developed under British institutions, cannot suffer such an element on British territory." But race was a product of politics, he countered, and often found expression in "very idle and senseless" "prejudices" based in "physical peculiarities." Political opportunists then worked to stoke these prejudices into "race enmities."

> Physical peculiarities tend to make other and less important divergencies conspicuous, and in this and in other ways are constantly operating to isolate the race possessing them from other races. I am inclined to think that physical peculiarities which now pass unnoticed might, if a prejudice were aroused against them, ultimately result in the separation and isolation of new races and septs now unknown. Upon the whole, I doubt if there is any obstacle in the way of the fraternisation of races so difficult to overcome as this one of physical peculiarities, and the prejudices, sometimes very idle and senseless, which are begotten of them... We are prone to generalise the fault of the individual culprit and attach its stigma to the whole nation to which it belongs. A Chinese servant runs off with my spoons; I hasten to vociferate that all Chinamen will steal. An Indian horse-trader tells me a falsehood I feel safe to say that no Indian ever told the truth. Worse than this, the sin committed against me is taken up by my race as a sin committed against our whole family, and individual crimes are thus catalogued into national grievances. This sort of race hostility is materially strengthened by a large class of men who find their principal scope feeling and fostering race enmities.[14]

Rather than biological, then, above all else the barriers separating Chinese and English Canadians were social and cultural.

> ...if Chinamen dispensed with those conditions of Asiatic civilization which they have hitherto insisted on taking with them everywhere; if their children were found more often than at present dressed in western garb and their books under their arm going to an English school, hostility to them would gradually disappear. In fact, a few bright Chinese school boys would do more for assimilation than all the measures of statesmen. There is little difference in appearance between a Chinaman who wears western clothes and makes a western toilet and the Portuguese or the Italian, who would be welcomed on whatever shores immigration was needed.[15]

But the key, Chapleau argued, was that the "prejudices" that separated the two "races" in Canada were politically active in the real world and therefore presented a long-term danger to the country's peace and stability. Politics is about choice and many choices in politics reflect "prejudice" of one kind or another.

> I am satisfied that my statement will not be contradicted when I say that prejudice and [labour] rivalry are the main sources of opposition to their presence amongst us. But are we for that reason not to take into consideration the social and moral condition of the country where they are living? Are we to ignore feelings and antipathies? Is it not necessary for a Government dealing with questions on its responsibilities, to respect even prejudices? Are we not obliged very often to respect prejudices? Do we not respect them very often in our legislation? I think that this would alone constitute a sufficient reason for any legislation the Government may choose to enact in respect to the Chinese. ...it is a natural and well-founded desire of British subjects, of the white population of this Dominion, who came from either Britain or the other European States and settle in this country, that their country should be spoken of abroad as being inhabited by a vigorous, energetic, white race of people; I say that it would be much more pleasant to have this said of the Province of British Columbia than to have that Province even if it grew richer than it is, with two-thirds of its population composed of a race which is not similar to ours, and which cannot assimilate with ours.[16]

And, Chapleau concluded, what in the end justified legislative restrictions on Chinese immigration was that the prejudice was mutual and between two "races" each convinced of their superiority over the other. "They do not want to assimilate with us, and we do not want to assimilate with them," he explained. "As a piece of wood in the tissues of the human body, unless it is removed, must cause disease in the places around it, and ultimately to the whole body, so the civilisation of Chinese, introduced into Christian civilization, must disappear, or it will be a cause of danger to the community." No "fusion" of Asians and Europeans was possible because of the legacy of group inequality and oppression along with social barriers against intermarriage.

These groups stand apart. No such fusion can take place between them as takes place between the Irish, German, French, etc. The yellow and white or the black and white will not mix, and the antagonism of race is always intensified if one of two peoples has oppressed the other, or regarded it with social scorn. On the hypothesis of a permanent settlement of Chinese they would soon resent being deprived of the right to vote and as they became stronger in numbers and wealth, would treasure up the memory of past contempt. In the case of the Chinese the feeling would, perhaps, be stronger than in any other instance known to history. For the contrast between the whites and the Chinese is not as their enemies fondly and foolishly say, the contrast between the civilized and the barbarian, but between two kinds of civilization, the one modern and of the West the other ancient and of the East. It is not merely that the Chinaman comes as a competitor in the labor market, or that he is of another race, differentiated by physical, intellectual, moral and religious characteristics, the whole stamped and sealed by color. He comes a highly civilized man, proud of those things which distinguish him as one of the sons of Han full of contempt for the "barbarians" amongst whom he means for a time at least to cast his lot, and ready to despise their institutions... Regard race antagonism how you will; treat it as a natural instinct or as an unreasonable prejudice; there it is and will not down; and if nothing happened more than outbreaks of violence amongst the whites, a case would be made out for considering the expediency of regulating this immigration.[17]

LOSING THE VOTE

A key ingredient in Chapleau's prescription to avoid the unpleasant political consequences of "race antagonism" was keeping the vote out of the hands of Chinese Canadians. He assured the Commons that if this was done there would be "no danger... to our politics."[18] And so, the franchise was taken away from naturalized Chinese Canadians in the same 1885 legislation in which the Macdonald government gave the vote to property qualified natives (see Chapter 4). Where Chapleau explained "race antagonism" as largely socially constructed, Macdonald, the "physiologist," set out the lessons of pseudo-scientific biological determinism. He warned parliament that if the Chinese "...came in great numbers and settled on the Pacific coast they might control the vote of that whole Province, and they would send Chinese representatives to sit here, who would represent Chinese eccentricities, Chinese immorality, Asiatic principles altogether opposite to our wishes; and, in the even balance of parties, they might enforce those Asiatic principles, those immoralities... which are abhorrent to the Aryan race and Aryan principles, upon this House."

> ...all natural history, all ethnology, shows that while the crosses of the Aryan races are successful – while a mixture of all those races which are known or believed to spring from a common origin is more or less successful – they will amalgamate. If you look around the world you will see that the Aryan races will not wholesomely amalgamate with the Africans or the Asiatics. It is not desired that they should come; that we should have a mongrel race; that the Aryan character of the future of British America should be destroyed by a cross or crosses of that kind... Let us encourage all the races which are cognate races, which cross and amalgamate naturally, and we shall see that such an amalgamation will produce, as the result, a race, equal, if not superior, to the two races which mingle. But the cross of [Aryan and non-Aryan] races, like the cross of the dog and the fox, is not successful; it cannot be, and never will be... We are in the course of progress; this country is going on and developing, and we will have plenty of labor of our own kindred races, without introducing this element of a mongrel race to disturb the labor market, and certainly we ought not to allow them to share the Government of the country.[19]

While native peoples were British subjects by birth under the doctrine of *jus soli*, Macdonald told the Commons, Chinese Canadians were "foreigners" and lacked "British instincts" and "British feelings." The parliamentary exchange where Macdonald introduced the motion to deny the franchise to naturalized Chinese illustrates a regional divide between B.C. members like J.A.R. Homer who feared the Chinese vote would upset the political balance in his province and eastern and central Canadians like M.H. Gault and Peter Mitchell who supported in principle equality rights for all British subjects. Mitchell, a father of Confederation and former premier of New Brunswick, went so far as to call out B.C. members for their "prejudiced" attitudes.

> Sir John A. Macdonald: The Chinese are not like the Indians, sons of the soil. They come from a foreign country... they are, besides, natives of a country where representative institutions are unknown, and I think we cannot safely give them the franchise... a Chinaman gives us his labor and gets his money, but that money does not fructify in Canada; he does not invest it here, but takes it with him and returns to China; and if he cannot, his executors or his friends send his body back to the flowery land. But he has no British instincts or British feelings or aspirations, and therefore ought not to have a vote.
> Mr. Mitchell: The idea I have is that every person who comes and lives in the country, even if he is a foreigner – a Chinaman if you like, the most disliked class of foreigners – if he comes to make Canada his home, we ought to make Canada free enough to include even the Chinaman... I can see no reason why we should exclude the Chinamen. Of course, I know there are gentlemen who are prejudiced against the Chinamen.
> Mr. Shakespeare: No.
> Mr. Mitchell: Yes, there are hon. gentlemen here who are prejudiced against the Chinamen; there is a strong feeling on the Pacific coast against them... we have a number of them in the city of Montreal, and they are spoken of as a respectable body of men – good, peace-loving citizens. True they are economical, and some of them are penurious; but what they do with their money after they earn it is not our business. If we can make Canada sufficiently attractive to them, I am not sure that they will go back to China; and we should make our laws comprehensive enough to include all classes of foreigners. So long as they comply with the naturalization laws, they can become British subjects, and I would give them a vote.
> Mr. Casey: I would ask the hon. gentleman what is the technical meaning of the word Chinaman. As I understand, there is nothing to prevent a Chinaman being a British subject; would he be called a Chinaman? Of course, while he is an alien he cannot vote, whether he is excluded expressly by this Act or not. But the case many arise when a Chinaman becomes naturalised. Would a naturalised Chinaman be a Chinaman, in the meaning of this clause, or would he be a Canadian or a British subject? I should think he ceased to be a Chinaman when he became a British subject.
> Sir John A. Macdonald: If I thought so, I would alter the words. I

> used the word Chinaman to designate a race. However, I am obliged to the hon. gentleman for the suggestion, and I shall word it – "Excluding a person of Mongolian or Chinese race."
>
> Mr. Gault: There are a number of Chinamen in Montreal who are industrious people. I believe they voted at the last election, and I think they should not be deprived of their votes.
>
> Mr. Homer: In British Columbia there are 30,000 whites and upwards of 15,000 Chinese, who are controlled by some half dozen or ten of their principals. Those principals could be induced, probably, by some political aspiration, to convert some 4,000 or 5,000 of those Chinese into British subjects. If allowed to vote, the entire control of the Province will be in the hands of the Chinese...[20]

Louis Henry Davies, later to become Chief Justice of the Supreme Court, told the Commons that he could not "vote in favor of the exclusion of any condition, class or race from the rights of citizenship... If a Chinaman becomes a British subject it is not right that a brand should be placed on his forehead, so that other men may avoid him." Davies complained that the "prejudices" of B.C. "whites" were being allowed to override the established principle of equal rights for all British subjects in Canada.

> It is not right or fair that a broad question of principle should be decided by the passion or prejudice of those who come from one section of the Dominion alone. I have every regard and respect for the 10,000 or 15,000 whites who live in British Columbia, but decline to admit that their prejudices... dictate to the whole Dominion a principle which in itself is vicious, which I am sorry to see incorporated in our law, namely, the exclusion of any one race or color from participating in the political franchises and privileges of the people of this Dominion. My contention is, that a Chinaman who has become a British subject by naturalisation, who resides in the country and has acquired the necessary qualification, has as good a right to be allowed to vote as any other British subject of foreign extraction.[21]

Another member from the Maritimes, P-A Landry, also saw the franchise question as a regional issue. Even though he was in general agreement with Davies concerning the principle of equal rights for all British subjects, he was prepared to defer to B.C. opinion on this question.

> ...theoretically it would be more in keeping with my own views that a Chinaman should have a vote, if he can place himself on the same footing as a white man. I do not hesitate to say that that is my view in regard to a Chinaman or any other man, I do not care of what country or nationality. I am not, however, willing to carry that feeling to the extent of going against hon. gentlemen who know the condition of their Province better than I do... if I give a vote on this subject it is in deference to the people of British Columbia...[22]

Perhaps stung by the accusations of "prejudice" against his party, D.B. Woodworth contemptuously mocked those who defended equal citizenship rights for Chinese Canadians. The government initiative to strip Chinese Canadians of the vote at this point was a pre-emptive strike against any future debate initiated by sentimental members featuring

> ...stacks of books brought in here upon the Chinese pigtail; we would have had copious tears from the hon. gentleman from Queen's P.E.I. (Mr. Davies), and other members, over the injustice of the Chinese being denied the right to vote; and they would have argued in favor of giving votes to a dirty, greasy man, a man with a long pigtail hanging down his back, unfit for human society, with a forbidding countenance, with a flat head, with pinched toes. We would have been told – that not only did they not send their money that they earn across the water, that they lived not on a penny a day, that they sent not their bones away to China, that they would even be buried in the soil of Canada – that they were British subjects.[23]

A.H. Gillmor rebuked Woodward for his "tirade against the Chinese. I believe they have just as good a right to wear a pig tail as my hon. friend has to wear a bald head... If it is no disqualification for citizenship for a man to have a bald head, I do not see why it should be a disqualification for a man to wear a pig tail." The 1885 Royal Commission report had dispelled many of the untrue negative stereotypes about Chinese Canadians, Gillmor claimed, and it demonstrated that "since they have been in

British Columbia they have been more moral and industrious than the white population..." But British Columbians had denied them both the chance to assimilate and to enjoy political representation. "If the Chinese had had votes we would not have hear the members from British Columbia railing about them during twelve years," he observed. "Is it fair to treat these people as you propose?," he continued, "for my part, I believe in a unity of the human race; I believe that of one blood God made all nations of the earth, and I should be sorry to see any man, of whatever race, receiving anything but fair play in a British colony."[24]

In the previous Chapter, it was suggested that when native peoples lost the electoral franchise in 1898 it blocked a significant path leading towards their full equality as British subjects and increasingly confined them to a role as infantilized objects of bureaucratic administration. For Chinese and other Asian Canadians, being denied the franchise in 1885 was significant in the same fashion because it disconnected them from the electoral market place where they could have rewarded or punished candidates or parties seeking their votes. It also left Asian Canadians exposed without their own local B.C. defenders to counter the racist attacks of a unified and increasingly belligerent provincial parliamentary caucus. This caucus employed every opportunity to lobby against Asian Canadians in Ottawa and claimed for itself the legitimacy of representing the totality of B.C. public opinion.

EXCLUSION AND WHITE CANADA

Imposing a $50 head tax in 1885 to deter Chinese immigration did little to assuage the B.C. anti-Asian caucus. They wanted legislated exclusion but they were not going to get it. Both Conservative and Liberal governments recognized that exclusion would have significant foreign policy implications. Macdonald told the Commons that

> we are just finishing the Pacific Railway, and one of the objects of that enterprise is to enable Canada to compete with the United States for the Chinese and Japanese trade... it might seriously

impede the success of that line if we legislated in a manner to offend the Chinese government. The Chinese government is well informed on everything that goes on in the outer world... Now, it might greatly impede the initiation of any trade between Canada and China if the Chinese Government found that when we approached them to make commercial arrangements we had shut down the gate and said: 'We want to trade with you, but we won't allow any of you to come to us.'[25]

In a similar fashion, Laurier argued that the success of Canadian trade to Asia would be threatened by any "hostile legislation" to exclude Japanese. Instead, "negotiation and diplomatic action" should be employed to get the Japanese government to voluntarily restrict emigration of its citizens to Canada.[26] As well, after the Anglo-Japanese Alliance of 1902 directed towards containing Russian ambitions in Asia, Canadian governments wished to take care to avoid offending a British ally.[27]

There was also the fact that the most intense lobbying for Asian exclusion was confined to the parliamentary representatives of one province, British Columbia. For some outspoken members from other provinces, the B.C. campaign against Asian Canadians was anti-liberal, anti-Christian, and, anti-British since it undermined the imperial vision of a universally inclusive British citizenship. In 1892, for example, T. Christie opined, in reference to the head tax, that he held

> no sympathy with any legislation which discriminates against any class, creed or nationality, and I hold that all classes and all nationalities should be placed on the same basis... If the Chinese government should retaliate... and if the same treatment should be extended to white men going to China, a storm of indignation would arise at their barbarous action... If we were to treat these people kindly, if we were to throw open our schools and allow their children to be educated, they would become just as good citizens as people of other nationalities... Personally, I am an out-and-out free trader, and I am in favour of free trade in labour as well as in anything else.[28]

In 1900, W.C. Edwards invoked free trade, Christian charity, the rights of British subjects, and Empire foreign policy in a spirited attack on the "retrograde and inhuman legislation" of the Chinese head tax. Recognizing that his was a minority position in both parties, Edwards remarked that

> When any attack is made on the principle of free trade, on the principle of freedom... I am bound to speak. Why, Sir, if Chinamen were made by another Creator than the one who made us, then this principle is right; but if they are the offspring of the same Creator, then the underlying principle of this legislation is entirely wrong; it is barbarism and nothing else... I offer my sincere protest against this kind of legislation, and if I were able to muster up members enough to vote it down I would certainly do so, because I consider it abhorrent to the principles of free trade and to the commonest rights of all men who occupy this earth... Especially is that true in a new country like Canada, with such boundless and unlimited resources that are waiting to be developed. If we had a hundred million more labourers to develop Canada, so much the better for Canada... Let labour come in from all parts of the world, and the only effect will be that our commerce will be enlarged... But beside altogether from an economic point of view, just think of Canada, the right arm of an empire who proclaims freedom the world over, who is trying to maintain everywhere an open door, introducing legislation of this kind.[29]

In the same debate, T. Christie revisited his 1892 assault on the head tax.

> We should let these poor oppressed and persecuted Chinamen come in free, we should treat them like men, and make Canada a free country... I hold that this measure is not in accordance with our free, liberal institutions in Canada. It is not at all in accord with the principles of free trade; nay more, it is not in harmony with our Christian civilization, with the fatherhood of God, the brotherhood of man and the golden rule. It is both unjust and un-British, and, therefore, cannot fail to be detrimental and injurious to the best interests of Canada and be a reproach to the good name of our country.[30]

While these arguments did not carry the day, they nevertheless could encourage a certain element of defensiveness in the positions of their opponents. For example, J. Charlton conceded that Christie's anti-head tax oration had reflected

> credit to his heart and aspirations in favour of humanity and his love for freedom; and speaking in the abstract, his arguments may perhaps be considered unanswerable. It was long ago declared by a very high authority, that God made of one blood, all nations of men, to dwell upon the face of the earth, and I suppose that warrants us in the belief that there should be such a thing as the brotherhood of man... Abstractly... the government are wrong, perhaps in placing restrictions upon the immigration to this country. But while a thing may be right or wrong in the abstract, it may be exactly the reverse in the concrete... We have that same sentiment in eastern Canada, which we find exhibited in the eastern parts of the United States – a sentiment in favour of the equality of man, of his right to better his condition, the right of a down-trodden people to come to a free country... But against that we have the sentiment of the people who have been brought into contact with this Mongolian immigration, who know its character, and who for some reason, sufficient or insufficient, are bitterly opposed to permitting these Mongolians entering [sic] the country.[31]

Even Sir John A. Macdonald was prepared to acknowledge that the Chinese head tax was a concession to racial prejudice which "may be right, or it may be wrong."

> ...it is not considered advantageous to the country that the Chinese should come and settle in Canada, producing a mongrel race, and interfering very much with white labor in Canada. That may be right, or it may be wrong; it may be a prejudice or otherwise; but the prejudice is universal. Whether it be in the United States, in Australia, or in Canada, white labor and Chinese labor will never work harmoniously together, and we shall have the same scenes in Canada, if that immigration is permitted, that we have seen so lamentably exhibited in the United States.[32]

And so, when Laurier introduced legislation in 1900 increasing the head tax from $50 to $100, he took care to distance himself from it through shifting responsibility to B.C. public opinion calling it a "legitimate concession to the aspirations of the people of British Columbia, who, upon this question, entertain views peculiarly their own, views which are not shared by the people of the east, who are represented by a majority in this House, and who are not prepared to go as far as the people of British Columbia would go in this matter." Laurier further rationalized that the head tax was meant to apply to a specific Chinese class rather than the Chinese as a "race."

> The Bill is not intended to apply to men of science. It is intended to apply to labourers who come into competition with our own workmen... There are Chinamen who are very able men in their own way. If possibly Confucius were to come here and settle in Canada there would be no objection to his doing so.[33]

Increasing the head tax was not enough for some members. A.M. Morrison, who represented New Westminster and later served as Chief Justice of the British Columbia Supreme Court between 1929 and 1942, unsuccessfully attempted to piggy-back the terms of the Natal Act as an amendment to Laurier's bill. "...If we had legislation on the lines of the Natal Act – we should not have today such a question as the Chinese question; we should not have had a yellow blot on the map of Canada, as we have today," he explained to the Commons, because "the main point of the Natal Act is that it provides an educational test for immigrants going into that country, and it would not be a bad thing if Canada should have a test of the same kind... I do not think that it can be seriously objected that by introducing legislation on the lines of the Natal Act we are violating any treaty obligation." In Morrison's opinion, the Chinese were "virtually slaves" in an economic sense and not "rational beings." They stubbornly resisted conversion to Christianity and were filthy plague-bearers, he claimed.

> These people come in, they are virtually slaves, they are entirely and humbly submissive, they do not live like rational beings. That is incontrovertible and nobody will deny it. For a great number of years they have been in the province of British Columbia, mingling with the people of that province, have the advantage... of receiving instruction from the missionaries and yet, can anybody in this assemblage... point out the beneficial results of the sojourn of these

people in British Columbia? By saying that there is no evidence of improvement in these people... it is an evidence that these people consider themselves, as they are the older civilization, and the stronger characters. They ignore the people of this country, and... they will never be converted in the sense which we are attempting to convert them. If they pretend to be christianized they are not sincere, and that is evidenced by people who have lived amongst them as missionaries... To give an idea of the manner in which these people live in British Columbia... to show their inherent nature, which certainly is most objectionable, and un-British, I will read a short extract from a sanitary report of the health inspector of the city of Vancouver... Attention was directed to the existence of these Chinese and Japanese who, it was said, were living in a very unsanitary way, by the report of bubonic plague across the border in some of the American towns and by the report that the disease had been brought to the continent of America by immigrants from China and Japan.[34]

As the twentieth century began to unfold, the incessant anti-Asian lobbying of both Liberal and Conservative B.C. parliamentarians began to turn away somewhat from sociologically-oriented themes such as wage competition, morality, religion, and hygiene towards biologically-oriented themes like race competition and miscegenation. For example, Comox member W. Sloan warned that the rise of Japan to the status of a world power meant that as a future "mistress of the Pacific and with rapidly increasing colonies on our western shores," it had become a serious threat to British and Canadian security. In the context of the rivalry between the races based in "their undying ambitions," it was "unnatural" to think that Japanese Canadians in British Columbia could "assimilate" with loyal British whites.

> The All Red Line from which we expect so much is a bond drawing together the outposts of the British dominions. It narrows to a slender thread in the defiles of the Rockies. Guard well then the west; fill it with people who will be loyal to our ideals of national life. Guard well the strategic position which is not only of dominion but of empire... England has made an alliance with this new world power [Japan], but this alliance and all other treaties or compacts of an Eurasian complexion can never endure. They can at best possess

only the elements of expediency. They can never possess the elements of permanence or stability. It is impossible, it is impractical, it is unnatural. As individuals the races do not and never will assimilate. As nations their ultimate individual destiny, their world-wide interests, their undying ambitions centre in channels as opposite as the poles.[35]

Vancouver member R.G. Macpherson warned the Commons of "the yellow peril" and explained the strategic threat to the Empire if Asian immigration was to his province was not quickly halted

> we will soon find a greater number of orientals in British Columbia than white people. I maintain that in a very short time, we would lose a very important part of Canada if any trouble should ever arise between the orient and Great Britain. The Japanese, Chinese, and Hindus would have a surplus of population as compared with the white people in our province, and they would have no difficulty in taking possession of the Pacific coast. It is my opinion that the yellow peril is much closer than the people of this country have any appreciation of.

Race mixing was akin to mixing "oil and water," he opined.

> You cannot build up a great country by mixing the occident and the orient together. It is impossible to bring about cohesion between races which are so directly opposite in views as the oriental and the Caucasian. It is just as impossible to do this as to mix oil and water. Perhaps in two hundred, three hundred or four hundred years, some amalgamation may take place, but in that time your history will be written in bloodshed, and we cannot afford to allow any considerable number of people who come to our shores out of whom we cannot make good Canadian subjects. That may seem to some members of this House to be exceedingly strong language, but I am convinced that if we are to have a great nation in Canada, if we are to have such a country as we would wish to leave to our children and our children's children, it must be a country developed by the white races of our land; it never can be done by letting down the bars to the free and easy access of the hundreds and thousands and millions of orientals who are ready to come to our shores.[36]

Representing his Victoria constituents, G.H. Barnard denied that B.C. members were "local or provincial" in their views but were, he claimed, instead expressing the Canadian national interest through being

> imperialists in the truest significance... speaking to men in the old land and following the more recent articles in the leading papers and reviews of Great Britain, the thoughtful opinions of the mother country have become fundamentally changed on the question of the influx of the Oriental race. The day is coming, even if it has not come already, when... it is recognized more and more every day to be the duty of the home government and the imperial authorities, no matter what conditions they have to face in other parts of the world, to stand by even the most distant and smallest portions of the British empire to build up a nation that should be Anglo-Saxon in race and tradition.[37]

In a similar fashion, Kootenay member W.A. Galliher told the House that B.C. should be "preserved essentially as a white man's country... a country wherein not only those who are employers and can live without doing actual manual labour are white, but a country where the white man who has to earn his livelihood by the sweat of his brow may call his home." Two classes of immigrants were desirable: those who were "British born and have a love of British institutions inbred in them" or "assimilable" Europeans like the "Germans or the French, or other nations of that character." On the other hand, Galliher averred, the Japanese people possessed an "unassimilable nature."

> We all know that the Jap is an excessively patriotic man; we know that the love for the Mikado and that obedience to his will exists in the Jap from the cradle to the grave. And we know that no matter what country he may emigrate to, his emigration is not looked upon even by himself as a permanent departure from Nippon or as a permanent residence in the land he goes to. He comes there for a time. He may take the oath of allegiance of that country, but that oath... is not as binding upon him as the traditions which have been instilled into his mind from his early infancy... instead of looking forward to his children and his children's children inhabiting it as subjects of his rulers, the Jap is always looking forward to the day when he can

return to the land of the Rising Sun and end his life under the rule of his beloved Mikado. I say that citizens of that character, no matter how estimable they may be in other respects, are not the material with which we can preserve the Pacific province for a white race that will be true and loyal to the British flag.[38]

B.C.'s anti-Asian lobby was given a significant boost by Vancouver's anti-Asian riots of 1907.[39] In its wake, both national political parties curried favour with intolerant voters in the province. On the eve of the 1908 federal election, Borden sent a telegram to the *Victoria Colonist* newspaper stating that "the Conservative party stands for a white Canada and the absolute protection of white labour."[40] Pushed by electoral realities and by his own B.C. caucus,[41] Laurier climbed down from his earlier-expressed opinion that British Columbians entertained anti-Asian "views peculiarly their own" and at variance with those of eastern Canadians. Instead, he now found "no fault with the view maintained in British Columbia that that province should be maintained as a country for the white race." Indeed, the call for a "white man's country," Laurier continued, was not an expression of racial prejudice but was merely a natural and understandable reaction against "an economic disturbance" that had resulted from "many generations" of Asian "despotism."

> I have no hesitation in saying also that I do not attribute the attitude of British Columbia in its passionate desire for a white man's country to anything like prejudice – prejudice of colour or anything else. No; I recognize that the origin and cause for the feeling which prevails and predominates in British Columbia is to be found in economic laws which would produce the same result in any other place in which the conditions were similar to those of British Columbia. The races of Asia, whether they be Japanese or Chinese, East Indian, have been for many generations… subjected to despotism which has reduced them to a condition of penury. In their lodgings, in their food, in their garments, they are content with the most simple necessaries of life which can be supplied with only a fraction of the wages necessary to maintain a workingman in respectability in this country. So, when these races come to this country in such large

numbers as to compete with white labour, they accept wages so low that they create at once an economic disturbance.[42]

Even while the "white Canada" tide was rising, some members continued to speak out against it. For example, S.A. Fisher, Laurier's Minister of Agriculture from 1896 to 1911, told the Commons that after having studied and visited Japan, there was "nobody in Canada who has a higher opinion of the Japanese people than I have." He observed that when Japan first opened itself to the west, the Japanese were seen as "barbarians" and "held to little account." But there was great irony to be found, Fisher pointed out, in the fact that after having studied and adapted western methods of warfare, and defeating the Russian Empire, they were admired by the western nations.

> Then, for the first time, the Christian world began to admire the Japanese because they know how to fight, not because they had excelled in art, not because they had a literature of a thousand years, not because when our forefathers were barbarians their forefathers were highly civilized, not because they had a history, traditions and inspirations of patriotism that western nations cannot emulate and cannot equal, but when they were able to show in the barbarism of war they were equal and superior to the western nations the western nations bowed down and worshipped them. It is a commentary on western civilization and on Christianity but it is the truth.

Even if "hundreds of thousands" of Japanese immigrants were to enter Canada, he suggested, all of the alarmist talk about a yellow peril would turn out to be as wrong as the stereotypes of Japanese as barbarians. British ideas of political liberty and democratic representative institutions would prove powerful enough to prevail in the end. Confronting Japan through enacting exclusionary legislation against Japanese immigrants "would bring about a condition of affairs which would be disastrous to Canada, disastrous to the entente cordiale between the motherland and Japan and also of that cohesion in the British empire, which we on this side of the House, desire so much to uphold."

I still have confidence that whether it be on the Pacific coast, whether it be on the continent of America, whether it be on the broad Pacific or whether it be on the Asiatic continent itself, the Anglo-Saxon will come out on top and will be able to hold his own against Chinese, Japanese or anybody else. It may be at times we will falter, that we will be behind, but I have no doubt that as has often been said of the Briton he will blunder through and we will come out the victors in the end. I am not afraid on this continent of America of the inroads of these people or that hundreds and thousands of Japanese may come to Canada and rule this continent – not a bit of it. Many of them may come in. I am not so much afraid as some people that many of them will come in... I do not know that it would hurt, and I have confidence that if a few thousands, or I do not hesitate to say, if a few hundreds of thousands of Japanese came into Canada the present Canadian people will still rule this land and our ideas of constitutional and representative government will be maintained and the Japanese will have to come to our ideas and our views if they are going to become citizens of Canada and we not to theirs. For these reasons I am not so very much afraid of Japanese immigration as some people are...[43]

R. Lemieux, another prominent Liberal who held numerous cabinet posts under Laurier, explained that he was "always surprised to hear fair-minded people speak of the Japanese as an inferior race" when they are "a rising race, a rising people, indeed the greatest race today in far Asia. Sir, the Japanese are not an inferior race." Japan, he reminded members, began its "march towards nationhood with the Dominion of Canada" in 1867 and was now "the ally par excellence of Great Britain in the far east." Accordingly, it served imperial interests for Canada to maintain good relations with Japan.

The Canadian government, he seemed to say, had been caught in the middle between B.C. racism and its threat to public order on the one side and diplomatic and commercial interests on the other. And so, Lemieux cautioned against extremes when dealing with Japanese immigration. "I am against any large influx of Japanese into British Columbia" as it would disturb the labour market, he said, "but I am also against that other extreme of total exclusion, of a foreign race indeed but belonging to a friendly power." It was embarrassing, he pointed out, that while Canadian and American missionaries

> are leaving every year to preach the Gospel of Christ to the pagan races of Japan. They preach a religion of toleration; they preach principles of liberty and principles of charity, and the first thing the Japanese hear on the other side is that those who send missionaries to Japan – missionaries well received, well treated, and highly respected – are demanding their expulsion from the ports of Canada.[44]

In urging moderation, Lemieux nonetheless conceded that "the problem of Asiatic immigration" was a disruptive political issue "not only in Canada but in the British Empire of which Canada is a component part."

> In Australia and New Zealand the Asiatic races are considered as the most imminent peril, and it is admitted that the action taken by Australia and New Zealand in matters of naval defence, namely in the establishment of local navies in those commonwealths, was due to the apprehension that some day those dominions might be invaded by the Asiatic races. As regards South Africa, it was only a few weeks ago that we were the witnesses – distant if you will – of a struggle between the Hindu residents and the Government of the Union. We know that as a result of the drastic legislation passed by the Union Government passive resistance was offered by the Hindu subjects of South Africa, and the troops had to be called so as to maintain peace and order in the veldt. This question of Asiatic immigration is therefore causing grave concern in the dominions and in the mother country, and Canada is also highly interested in the settlement, one way or another, of that problem.[45]

PREJUDICE AND BIGOTRY

For their part, B.C. members regularly complained that their attacks against Asian Canadians were misunderstood in central and eastern Canada. W.G. McQuarrie, for example, told the House that he wished he could put the shoe on the other foot by having "the Chinese... come down here [Ontario] in large numbers... I know how you fell about it here in Ontario. You have no sympathy with us, when we speak against Oriental immigration." Asians who were British subjects were Canadians "only in name" who used their "naturalized" status to take unfair advantage of "the white man."

> We call these men foreigners, but as a matter of fact they are not foreigners. According to the law, they are naturalized British subjects. Now you know what that means; anybody in British Columbia knows what that means. These men are citizens of this country only in name and only for the particular purpose of securing a fishing license. They take the oath of allegiance to His Majesty the King, but remain loyal subjects of their own emperor.[46]

Similarly, T.G. McBride complained about "people down here who do not know" that Asian Canadian children were sitting alongside and talking to "our white boys and girls" in B.C. schools.

> Why should we in British Columbia be compelled by this government to allow those people to come to this country, and have them sit in the same schools with our white boys and girls... But I do say that this government should stop, and stop once and for all, those people coming in and placing themselves alongside our children in the schools, where our children will have a chance to talk with them. It is all very good for people down here who do not know, but it is a serious question out in British Columbia...[47]

Sensitive to the more liberal opinion of other provinces, B.C. members frequently began their anti-Asian tirades by gainsaying that they were expressing racial prejudice. In 1922, Vancouver member H.H. Stevens explained to the Commons that "this is not... a racial question; I desire to lay that down at the very outset of my remarks. In approaching the question, I treat it, as I think all do who understand it thoroughly, as a sociological, an ethical and essentially an economic problem."[48] He had made nearly the same statement the year before when he assured other members that "whatever I say regarding the Chinese or Japanese is not with any racial prejudice; my remarks are based upon exceedingly sound economic grounds and reasons." But then Stevens had gone on to denounce miscegenation as producing "a lower and inferior type."

> Generations of experience on the Pacific coast, as well as the experience of innumerable other countries, shows beyond all peradventure that the Orientals, and the Chinese in particular, cannot be assimilated. They are not assimilating, and they do not assimilate. I have but to refer hon. Members who have visited the Pacific coast to San Francisco, where there are Chinese of the second and third generations, some of them intermarried with whites, and their national traits and characteristics are still there distinct and clear. Indeed I will say this, and I say it advisedly; if anything, the offspring of an intermarriage between an Oriental and a white invariably results in a lower and inferior type than either of the parent races. I have had some considerable experience in watching this in other countries, as well as in Canada and the United States, and that is invariably the case.[49]

Miscegenation figured prominently in the debate around a 1922 motion supported by all the B.C. members asking the Mackenzie King government to "secure the exclusion" of "oriental aliens." C.H. Dickie declared that he believed "that an immigration policy can be enacted that will keep from obtaining a foothold in our country people with whose descendants cannot intermarry. We cannot conceive of a commingling of the blood of our Canadians with that of the Ethiopians; we cannot conceive of a commingling of our blood with that of Asiatics." Striking a similar note, McQuarrie opined that Asians

> cannot be assimilated. They will always exist as a foreign element in our midst. The real test of assimilation is intermarriage. The divergence of characteristics of the two races is so marked that intermarriage does not tend to perpetuate the good qualities of either race. The races are fundamentally different. Their morals are different, and language, heredity, religion and ideals will militate against and prevent even sociological assimilation of orientals… So far as I am aware, intermarriage between the white and the oriental has always produced unsatisfactory results.

G. Black challenged the "sentimentalist" with a "practical" question.

> Canada wants settlers; but she wants only settlers who will adopt Canadian and British ideals, people who will become Canadians. We want only races which will intermingle and which can intermarry with our people and become not only with us, but of us... Some sentimentalist has referred to these people as our 'little brown brothers'... But it has been said, with a great deal more practical force – 'what about these people for brothers-in-law?' It is all very well to refer to them as brothers; but would any hon. Gentleman of this House consider an alliance between a sister or daughter of his and a Chinaman or a Japanese? [50]

As Opposition Leader, Meighen threw his weight behind the bipartisan B.C. caucus' demand for "exclusion." Meighen asserted this was "not out of any disrespect" but it was in the interest of preserving Canada's "racial purity" since "the two races will not assimilate."

> ...we ask for the exclusion, not out of any disrespect for the Japanese empire or the Chinese empire. We ask for it because it is for the permanent interest of the people of both those countries, that we maintain here our racial purity, just as they have considered it in their permanent interest to maintain their racial purity. It is not that we consider them and inferior race. Who can consider the Japanese people an inferior race? They have different standards of living from ours, standards of living that we describe as lower; but the Japanese nation in the last thirty years has, perhaps, made the greatest progress of any people of the world. It has made great progress in the advancement, not only of their military standards, but of their science, in the development of their arts and literature. In all that goes to make the highest type of a civilized nation the Japanese have gone ahead in the last thirty years faster than has any other great nation in the world. It is simply because they as a people so differ from us that the two races will not assimilate.[51]

For his part, King did not object so much to the objective of "exclusion" as to the word itself. Going back to the 1890s and the Natal Act, it had been established British diplomatic practice to avoid directly confronting South Asians or Asians, especially their Japanese allies, with hot-button legislative language considered insulting like "exclusion." King in pre-debate negotiations with the thirteen member B.C. caucus insisted that "exclusion" be dropped in favour of a euphemistic phrase like "bringing to an end further such immigration for residence purposes." This exchange in the Commons illuminates the way in which the outcome of this 'non-partisan' issue was mediated not only by race-thinking and the sway of a united provincial caucus but also by international politics.

> Mr. Mackenzie King: Are we in this Parliament going to create an international problem not only affecting the British Empire but other countries, simply that hon. Gentlemen opposite may be able to point to the word 'exclusion' when they go before their constituents in the province of British Columbia. Let us be honest...
>
> Mr. Stevens: ...I took the initiative in bringing the British Columbia members together, and we have presented this resolution without the slightest tinge of partisanship.
>
> Mr. Mackenzie King: ...A few days ago I spoke to the mover of this resolution (Mr. McQuarrie) about the serious international consequences involved in the use of the word 'exclusion,' and I told him we would gladly accept his resolution if he used language acceptable to the different countries comprising the British Empire. He came to me a day or two ago and told me he regretted that step could not be taken because the British Columbia members attached so much importance to the word 'exclusion.'
>
> Mr. Stevens: Our action was non-political; the supporters of my hon. Friend and the supporters of the hon. Leader of the Progressive party (Mr. Crerar) were included in a joint meeting – the whole of the members from British Columbia, of whom we here number seven and the others six.
>
> Mr. Mackenzie King: Then I accept my hon. Friend's interpretation that it was non-political; I will appeal to him now on the ground of national interest as against sectional interest.[52]

Employing language similar to that used in 1909 by Laurier in accepting the legitimacy of B.C. demands for a "white man's country," King characterized this issue as "fundamentally an economic problem" in the sense that "it is a great economic law that the lower [standard of living] civilization will, if permitted to compete with the higher, tend to drive the higher out of existence, or drag it down to a lower level..." However, King went beyond Laurier's economism by lending comfort to the biologically-based argument of racial purity being made by B.C. members.

> There is another important national aspect that claims our attention – the desirability of a country having a homogenous people. It must be admitted that every country should have the right to control the composition of its own population. That is a fundamental right which I think we are in duty bound to assert. As has been said over and over again in this debate, it is impossible ever to hope to assimilate a white population with the Orient; the two will not assimilate. We wisely recognize that, we realize that if the question of oriental immigration ever became one of any considerable magnitude, we would be face to face at once with the loss of that homogeneity which ought to characterize the people of this country if we are to be a great nation.[53]

But there was third factor in King's considerations here; "the obligation" to preserve civil peace from "the danger" of any repetition of the Anti-Asian riots of 1907. As noted in Chapter 1, this factor was a likely catalyst in his government's decision to intern Japanese Canadians in 1942.

> we cannot consider too seriously... the obligation that exists at all times to avoid as far as possible the danger of social and industrial unrest, to say nothing of the vaster possibility of international strife. It is futile to contend that the danger is not pregnant where the oriental races are brought into competition to any great extent with the white races. Some fourteen or fifteen years ago I had the privilege of investigating the causes of Asiatic riots on our Pacific coast, and in the light of what I learned at that time, it would be impossible for me to do other than assert that danger is existent whenever these two competing industrial standards make their effect felt the one upon the other.[54]

In the year following the 1922 "exclusion" motion, King quietened the protests of B.C. members through sponsoring legislation effectively preventing the immigration of Chinese other than students and merchants while at the same time abolishing the Chinese head tax. Seemingly without irony, King presented this as a progressive social measure in keeping with Christian values as it was designed to remove the "indignity" of discrimination against the Chinese.

> ...it was objectionable that a country calling itself a Christian nation, should attempt in such a manner to deal with a problem which immediately affects oriental civilization. I could never see how Canada, from any self respecting point of view, could impose a poll tax on working people coming from another country, and at the same time have its population subscribe to funds for missionary purposes to teach the heathen the most elementary principles of Christianity. The government has shared that view, and has felt that any indignity of the character of the imposition of a poll tax upon a people in any other part of the world was something to which we, as a Christian community, should not lend our approval. So we have decided to abolish the head tax for that reason if for no other.

King stressed to the Commons that the language of his bill imposed restriction and not exclusion. In this way, he claimed, the dignity of the Chinese government had been respected and it had accordingly declared it was prepared to accept a Canadian ban on Chinese labour. Again, King tried to lay claim to a higher moral ground suggesting that the new law would be in harmony both with Empire foreign policy goals and "the conception of British freedom as I understand it."

> I do not think it is possible to talk of excluding the peoples of any country, of excluding all of the people – regardless altogether of what their standing or standards may be – and not offend the entire nation concerned; I do not think it is in the interest of Canada, or of any part of the British Empire, that any Dominion of the Empire should knowingly pass an act, which is certain to be regarded as an act of offence to an entire nation... I am speaking of the conception of British freedom as I understand it: I have never known a time when the British flag has stood for inflicting anything in the nature of an indignity upon the people of any country in the world.[55]

The combative anti-Asian Canadian character of these debates generated criticism from J.S. Woodsworth who had recently been elected as the Independent Labour Party member representing the Winnipeg North constituency. "A good deal has been said that showed racial prejudice and an appeal made to racial bigotry," he judged.[56] In this exchange, Woodsworth underlined the grim reality that this "racial bigotry" targeted Canadians rather than foreigners.

> Mr. Woodsworth: …any one who has listened dispassionately to the discussions on the floor of this House from time to time will recognize that there is an immense amount of prejudice towards the orientals. For example, not only on the floor of the House but in the West we have complaints about the low sanitary standards of the Chinese, and yet a year or two ago the oriental nurses or girls who wished to train as nurses were excluded from the Vancouver general hospital.
> An hon. Member: Hear, hear.
> Mr. Woodsworth: An hon. Member says 'hear, hear'. It may be well from one standpoint, that the white nurses shall not be contaminated by the presence of yellow nurses – Chinese or Japanese – but I submit, since we have large numbers of orientals already in the country, that in some way or another we ought to permit them to live up to our standards. We fail to do so with danger to ourselves and to our civilization.[57]

Rather than grounding his critique solely in Christian principles or liberal values, Woodsworth referenced contemporary anthropological studies asserting that the differences between "the different races" had been exaggerated.

> It seems to me that we must very definitely and consciously attempt to overcome the prejudices which we have against men of other races and other colours than our own. All students of ethnology will recognize that after all there are a great many more things in common between the different races than things which separate us, and the apparent divergences are not so great as sometimes we imagine. The stranger has always been regarded as more or less of an enemy, and we are naturally content to look down upon those who are not of our own kind.

Woodsworth further undercut social Darwinist pseudo-science by substituting a realist account of the dominance of "the west" over "the Orient" for one based in biological racial superiority. Early access to scientific advances and the industrial revolution had given "the west" a temporary military advantage over the "the coloured and darker people of the world," he observed.

> We in the west have been superior very largely because of the industrial revolution with all that it has brought to us in the advancement of science, and in the possibility of large-scale production, and may I add also in the possibility of our securing arms which from the military standpoint have made us dominant throughout the world. But now, as thoughtful students have observed, we are losing that advantage which we have had for the last hundred years or more, and the Orient is beginning to open its doors to western science, to western civilization, to western industry, and to western militarism. When the hundreds of millions of people across the ocean have gained possession of the tools of production and destruction, we have no advantage, or comparatively little advantage over them. There is not much wonder that some writers are afraid of this 'rising tide of colour'. It is a real danger; yet there are other ways of meeting it than by attempting to turn back the rising tide. It is a dangerous proceeding for a comparatively small portion of the human race to attempt by physical force to beat back the great masses of the coloured and darker people of the world.[58]

Woodsworth also asked members to consider the implications of globalized markets for those who imagined Canada as "a white man's country." B.C. workers were already competing with cheaper Asian labour because of expanding international trade and simply halting Chinese or Japanese immigration would not change this new reality.

> We are trading in all parts of the world; goods from the Orient as well as from other parts of the world are coming into Canada; and if we maintain our trading and financial interests with other parts of the world, I cannot see how we are to adopt a rigid policy of exclusion of the people who are coming here. Some people say that this ought to be a white man's country. What about South Africa or India today? We claim the right to go in and dominate India, and

yet at the very same time refuse to let the races of India come into Canada in any numbers at all. I am not pleading for permission for them to enter this country, but we must have regard to the larger international issues.

In the end, while Woodsworth deplored the language of "racial prejudice" in the House, he blamed "large corporations and financial organizations" for importing Asian labour into Canada and supported Asian immigration restrictions as "very essential."[59]

> While I am not opposed to a certain measure of precaution in this direction, feeling as I do that we have a right to protect the standards of this young country, at the same time I cannot let this opportunity pass without pleading with the government and the House that they treat this question in a broad way. Do not let our prejudice blind us to the greatness of the question or to the possibilities that are open to us, as a people, of making our contribution to the solution of the great world problems which are pressing upon us in these days as never before.[60]

SOUTH ASIANS AS BRITISH SUBJECTS

Hostility towards South Asians found voice in Ottawa coincident with the first major wave of "Hindu" immigrants[61] to land in British Columbia. As Ward notes, when these migrants from India began to arrive in noticeable numbers during 1906 and 1907, they "entered a community of heightened racial awareness, enduring racial cleavage, and recurring racial tension [where] white perceptions of East Indians were framed by the community's fixed assumptions about previous Asian immigrants."[62] In other words, they fell into a well already poisoned by three decades of hatred directed towards Chinese and Japanese Canadians.

H.H. Stevens warned the House that South Asians were a threat to public health as "the bulk of the Hindus" lived in "absolutely disgraceful" conditions. In support of this opinion, he read into Hansard "an extract from the report of the medical health officer for Vancouver" stating that "from a sanitary point of view, I consider the Hindu worse than the lowest class of Chinese. It is impossible to conceive a more filthy condition than the manner in which these men live." Consequently, Stevens argued, serious infections like hookworms were being introduced from India that would "devitalize our population." South Asians were also a threat to public morals as they practiced polygamy and married child-brides. Some British Columbia "Hindus" were a security threat to the Empire, he charged, because they had formed "a society which was organized in Canada for the purpose of participating in the mutiny in India." Overall, he averred, South Asians could not be 'assimilated' into Canadian life – socially, politically or biologically.

> Physically, mentally, morally, socially, and in domestic matters, they are entirely distinct from us. They may have their own civilization, about which I have nothing to say at the moment, but I hold that it is distinct from that civilization which we hold dear. They have no conception of our ideals or of democracy; they are totally unfit to exercise the rights and privileges of citizenship as we understand it; and on that score they should not be admitted. Lastly, we cannot hope to preserve out national type if we allow Asiatics to enter Canada in any large number, and it is the sacred duty of the Government and of the people of Canada to preserve that type so far as we are able.[63]

Awkwardly and inconveniently, however, South Asians were British subjects who claimed equality rights within the Empire in accordance with the 1857 Queen's Proclamation. Several other MP's joined Stevens in disputing the idea that Indian migrants deserved special consideration because they were fellow British subjects. The fact that some of these British subjects had previously served as British soldiers also failed to sway. Kootenay member W.A. Galliher, declaring that his province should be "preserved essentially as a white man's country," professed that he did

> not care if the Hindu is a British subject. He may be a British subject, and have fought the battles of Great Britain on many occasions. He

is a soldier and a good soldier, I admit all that; and I have as much respect for a British subject as any other man in this House, and I think I am as good a British subject, too. But... I say in all fairness, without wishing to reflect upon the Hindus, that they are not suitable citizens for British Columbia or for any other part of Canada; they are not suited to the climate or to the work they are called upon to perform.[64]

Vancouver member R.G. Macpherson, lobbying "to keep Canada a white country," observed that

Because a man has been a soldier it is no reason why we should admit him. There is no difficulty in getting a man to be a soldier in India because a Hindu would rather swell around in brass buttons than work. He does not like to work. Even if you are a British subject many times over and wear stripes and be a soldier that does not fit you to become a Canadian citizen of a type such as that to which we believe Canadian citizens should conform. I think we can never expect to maintain a high standard of nationality unless we keep the strain white.[65]

W.E. Knowles reasoned that

even though these people are British subjects, that does not settle the matter. There is many a British subject taken out and hanged until he is dead; many a British subject gets the lash for villainous conduct of which he has been proven guilty. For my part, I think that, British subjects though they may be, the less of the Hindus we have in Canada the better. And... [the Liberal party] record justifies me in saying that every man on this side believes as I do, that the less of the Hindus we have the better.[66]

H.H. Stevens argued that while these were British *subjects* and entitled to the protection of the British Crown, they were not really British *citizens* because they did not enjoy the vote in their own country. "I hold that before the Hindu has the right to come to Canada or any part of the empire and claim the privileges of citizenship," Stevens suggested, "he should at least attain that right in his own country." Moreover, if

these men are serious in their desire to pioneer on behalf of the empire, there is a vast hinterland in India, very sparsely settled; they can go into Thibet, Egypt, or northern Africa, where climatic, social and labour conditions and economic and industrial conditions are peculiarly suited to their race. They can go into these countries and pioneer and build up the British Empire. But they do not do that, and never have exhibited any tendency along that line; they simply wish to enter those countries where they can pluck the plums of civilization with the greatest ease.

The bottom line, Stevens concluded, was racial. South Asian British subjects did not share the higher civilization of white Europeans and, so, were incapable of making an effective contribution to the march of progress in the Empire.

> I speak strongly on this question, but it is not because of any feeling against them individually or as a people; it is because I hold that civilization finds its best exemplification in the civilization which we see in the British Empire and the other countries of northern Europe. I hold that it is the sacred trust of the Anglo-Saxon and kindred peoples to hold that civilization and to cherish it. I ask you or any other intelligent member what would be the effect in the British Empire, what would be the effect in the Dominion of Canada, if we gave unreservedly to 340,000,000 Asiatics the same rights in the empire as we enjoy ourselves. You know that 340,000,000 of these people against the 60,000,000 Anglo-Saxon of the British Empire would undoubtedly mean that within the space of a generation our most cherished traditions and customs and doctrines would be set aside.[67]

CONTINUOUS PASSAGE

As the entry of South Asians had been coincident with the Vancouver anti-Asian riots of 1907, the Laurier government was determined to shut it down quickly. Laurier cabinet minister Rodolphe Lemieux dispatched Mackenzie King to London charged with working out a formula to prevent South Asian immigrants from landing in British Columbia while at the same time saving face for the Empire. Some years later, Lemieux explained to the Commons how the diplomatic niceties had been managed without resorting to exclusionary legislation that would explicitly name British subjects of Indian origin. Immigrants to Canada were now required to sail non-stop from their country of origin and since there was no direct passenger service from India to Canada then there could consequently be no further South Asian immigration to British Columbia. Lemieux noted that the British subject status of South Asians had made

> the problem still more complex. Some years ago when the Hindus began to come into British Columbia, I, as Minister of Labour, dispatched to England the then deputy minister (Mr. Mackenzie King), and a very satisfactory arrangement was made with the British authorities. This arrangement was followed by Orders in Council which were incorporated later on in the Immigration Act. No Hindus were admitted unless they had come to Canada by a continuous passage and unless they were in possession of a sum of $200.[68]

Laurier also portrayed this policy as a concession to political expediency "in accordance with the wish of the people of British Columbia." "If these Hindus are allowed to come into British Columbia," he clarified, "there may be riots on the streets of Vancouver and Victoria; that has happened, and it may happen again." As we previously witnessed, Laurier preferred to see this as an economic clash rather than a racial one.

> We find that there is a condition in which one class of British subjects want to gain entrance into the country and other class of British subjects do not want to let them in. The people of Canada want to have a white country, and certain of our fellow subjects who are not of the white race want to come into Canada and be admitted to all the rights of Canadian citizenship. They say: We are British subjects, as you are; we were born under the British flag; some of us have worn British uniforms; some of us have fought under the British flag; you should open your gates to us as you would if we were of the white race. There are other British subjects who say: we will not have them. What is the cause of this? The question is not altogether a racial one: the basis of the objection is not wholly antipathy to the yellow races. When members of the Asiatic races go to South Africa, to the Straits Settlements, to British Columbia, to California, to Australia, or anywhere, the moment they come into

contact with white labour and white workingmen, there is conflict. The reason is altogether an economic one.

The other side of this, of course, was preserving as far as possible the unity of the Empire. Towards this end, diplomacy and administrative exclusion was far preferable to explicit legislative exclusion. If South Asians were barred by a specific law

> they will go back to India with bitterness in their hearts, and the unity of the empire must suffer. These men have been taught by a certain school of politics that they are the equal of British subjects; unfortunately, they are brought face to face with the hard facts only when it is too late. In my humble judgment, while the Government will do well to keep them out, the best method is to resort, not to law, but, if possible, to diplomacy. Let arrangements be made with the Government of India whereby they will do as the Japanese government have done: try to keep their own people at home. They may say: The white people come to our country; why should not the people of our country go to yours? That is logical, but, unfortunately, this is a matter in which such logic will not count...[69]

A non-confrontational approach similarly recommended itself to the Conservative government when they were forced to take up the issue of South Asian immigration in 1914. J. Roche, Minister of the Interior, counselled against "any undue harshness or severity" in dealing with the "Hindus."

> I quite agree with my hon. friend that our Immigration Act should be enforced; we desire to see that it is enforced without any undue harshness or severity. It must be recognized that those people being British subjects have, perhaps, more claim upon us than the average person coming from an alien country. We do not desire to do anything that will be unduly harsh, or that will grate upon their feelings, but at the same time we are taking steps under the provisions of the Immigration Act for self-protection; we are carrying out our own immigration laws to protect our own people.[70]

In saying this, Roche was echoing Lemieux who admitted that Canada was being "rather harsh" in barring fellow British subjects, some of whom were former British soldiers.

it is rather harsh to debar them and keep them out of the country when we know they are British subjects as we are British subjects. When I was coming back from Japan a few years ago, there were Hindus on board the steamer and very many of them were wearing the King's uniform; mostly all of them are British soldiers. This feature of the case makes the problem still more complex.[71]

The hypocrisy inherent in this "harsh" approach was challenged by A. Haggart on the grounds that Canada's parliament lacked authority to take away "the rights" or "the privileges" of British subjects "to land in this country" except in certain exceptional circumstances.

> I may be wrong in my law but... this parliament cannot deprive a British subject of his allegiance or of his right to land in this country except for certain causes... that is he must not be diseased, idiotic or subject to lunacy. Nor must he be a criminal. Nor must he be an indigent person... It is proposed that the Hindus shall be excluded, not because they are Hindus; their crime consists in not coming direct from Hindustan, but in landing in a British colony [Hong Kong] on the way. I may have old-fashioned ideas as to the power of this country to deprive a British subject of his allegiance or of his rights as a British subject. I do not think that this parliament can do either... I may be wrong in my law. But suppose we had the power that is claimed, is it judicious or right for us to legislate against British subjects in any other part of the empire? Is it in the interest of this country or of the empire as a whole? While it is right that we should protect ourselves against immigration that is detrimental to the interests of the country, when a man is a good subject of the empire in one part of it, he has the right to all the privileges as a subject of the empire on landing in this country.[72]

Laurier politely turned aside Haggart's spirited intervention suggesting that "on reflection the hon. gentleman... will agree with me that he has carried a principle which is very good in itself a little too far..." The continuous passage rule, he rationalized, merely provided Canada with necessary "protection" against those classes of British subjects who Haggart had admitted could be excluded – "paupers, criminals, and those physically tainted or mentally unsound." The power to exclude would be "nugatory" unless such an individual could be returned "to the place from which he came" and this was impossible to do where indirect passage had been booked.[73] Indeed, Laurier went to some lengths to explain to the Commons that the continuous passage rule was universal applying to immigrants from "Asia, or Europe or anywhere else" and was not meant to single out "Hindus."

> ...the Minister of the Interior, in order to have the machinery under his hand to send back to the country of origin any man who did not come up to our regulations physically, mentally or otherwise, passed a regulation whereby no one would be admitted unless he came on a through ticket from the country of his origin. This applies to Hindus, to British subjects and to foreigners of all nationalities. A Hindu, for instance, coming from Hong Kong could not be sent back to Hong Kong if he was physically or mentally unfit... because the authorities at Hong Kong would not receive him there... therefore these regulations were adopted in order to have absolute control of the steamship companies bring immigrants to Canada so that we could compel them to take them back to the country of origin. The Hindus are in that condition, they are not in any different condition from anyone else. The regulations applying to them apply to all other immigrants from whatever country they may come in Asia, or Europe or anywhere else.[74]

B.C. members like Galliher acknowledged that the continuous passage requirement would be effective in getting around the British subject status of "Hindu" immigrants.

> I know of no other way by which we can keep out these undesirable Orientals, and I have thought the matter over a good deal, unless you are going to discriminate against one or more nations. But if you put a provision of this kind in the law, all nations are then treated alike; and all we ask of any nation whether they be British subjects, or Frenchmen, or Germans, or any one else, is that they come direct from their own country to Canada.[75]

At the same time, however, Frank Oliver, the Minister responsible for immigration, was able to insist that the requirement was *not* specifically designed to bar South Asians and that "it applies to all people."[76] This raised a problem. Would Europeans who travelled to Canada through third countries be prevented from entering Canada? The following exchange is highly instructive as it clearly indicates that it was anticipated that Canadian immigration officers would administer the supposedly racially neutral regulations in a racially selective manner.

> Mr. Sproule: Within the last couple of weeks a German went on board a vessel at New Zealand and went to Vancouver; but he was not allowed to land because he did not come from the country of his origin. There was no contention that he was not a good citizen; but he was excluded, and was forced to go to the United States...
> Mr. Oliver: ...Cases of hardship have arisen under the application of the regulation, because our officers have not thoroughly understood how we desired to apply it...
> Mr. Macpherson: I think the object of the amendment brought in by the minister is quite plain.
> Mr. Hughes: To exclude Hindus, that is all.
> Mr. Macpherson: Yes, to exclude Hindus and all kinds of Asiatics, and all kinds of undesirable people.
> Mr. Sproule: Will it not exclude desirable classes as well?
> Mr. Macpherson: Possibly if we gain in one respect we may suffer in another. In the case the hon. gentleman speaks of, I fancy the good sense of the immigration officer would allow the German to come in.
> Mr. Fowler: That is giving a good deal of latitude to the immigration officer.
> Mr. Macpherson. If I or my hon. friend were an immigration officer, we would use the good sense the Lord has given us...[77]

SELF-GOVERNMENT AND EMPIRE CITIZENSHIP

Several years later, Oliver claimed that the real issue involved in controlling South Asian immigration was self-government for the Dominion. "Under the plea of being fellow-citizens of the empire," the whole issue was being pushed along by an "organized movement" of "highly intelligent and wealthy men" who were seeking to dictate Canada's immigration policy under the cover of "the principle of world-wide empire." "To say that we in Canada shall not be able to say who shall join us in the work of building up the country, that we must accept the dictation of other people as to who shall join in that work," he explained to the Commons, "places us in the position, not of a self-governing state in a free empire, but... a subordinate dependency not in control of its own affairs." Accordingly, Canada was simply exercising its "imperial responsibility" in determining not to admit South Asians. Canadians were not thereby declaring any "individual or national superiority... over any other nation, country or race."

> We are in occupation of the country; we are in control of its affairs, and there is nothing that is of such intimate, immediate and ultimate, future concern as the character of the population that goes to make up the country. The country is the people; the people are the country, and it is the first duty of the country, as it is the first duty of the Government, to take such measures as may be right and expedient to prevent, if prevention is necessary, the occupation of this country by population that shall hamper and deter in any material degree the development of those ideals of civilization which we believe ourselves to be here for the purpose of working out to their highest degree.[78]

Taking a similar tack on Canadian autonomy within the British Empire, Lemieux used the incident to mock the hypocrisy of the "jingos" and the "ultra-jingo-movement" in advocating an imperial federation under a central parliament.

> We know the difficulties of British Columbia, but it all goes to emphasise the fact that there is a wide margin between jingoistic theories and Canadian conditions... The advocates of imperial federation say that the time is ripe for a central parliament for the empire... Yet, Sir, speaking as a Canadian who thinks that it is quite easy to expound theories but very hard to apply them to conditions, I say that this same gentlemen who parades his imperialism, who claims to be a better Britisher than his opponents, is the one who bangs, bars and bolts the gate of Canada against his fellow subjects, the Hindus. Sir, there are people who believe in imperialism, but in sane imperialism; and the sane imperialists, in my judgment, are those who stand at all times for the autonomy of the dominions and not those who preach centralization and one parliament for the empire, and yet who, at the first opportunity, if it suits their politi-

cal purposes, are ready to fling their so-called imperialist principles to the winds.[79]

The issue of South Asian immigration re-emerged in Commons debate during World War I. India had massively backed the Imperial war effort, fielding over one million troops fighting in Europe – almost as many as from the four "white Dominions" put together.[80] India's remarkable war contribution was recognized in part through a resolution of the 1917 Imperial War Conference in London recommending "reciprocity of treatment between India and the Dominions" on immigration policy. In his study of this issue, E.T. Yarwood concluded that the Indian government had found it "increasingly necessary to refute the impression" that the "low status" accorded to Indians "as emigrants to and citizens of the empire" was a "consequence of India's subjection to an alien ruler."[81] Prime Minister Borden returned to the Canadian Commons from London declaring his moral support for its resolution on immigration policy.

> Its basis is the idea that the self-respect of India shall be maintained... India has been splendidly loyal in this war and has contributed of her manhood and of her treasure for the purpose of enabling us to win it. We must take that all into account. Her civilization is different from ours; it is more ancient, in some respects it may be said to be on a higher plane... There is more of idealism in their civilization; more perhaps of materialism in ours. I am not disposed to discuss the question as to whether one of the other civilization is superior; but I do say that the Indian civilization is entitled to our respect, and that we must do our part in making the inhabitants of that great dependency of the Empire feel that they are not treated with contumely or injustice by the people of any of the Dominions.

For his part, Laurier, as Leader of the Opposition, endorsed the idea of "overcoming" the "difficulties" standing in the way of giving "the subjects of India fair and proper treatment when they ask for it."

> ...it is one of the most important subjects that we have to deal with

in order to maintain the unity of the British Empire. If representatives of the people of India shall attend future Imperial Conferences, we must be prepared to give the subjects of India fair and proper treatment when they ask for it. This is a very serious subject. And I do not see how it can be successfully dealt with unless a very wise and prudent course is adopted. At the bottom of it there is an economic condition which we must not lose sight of. What is the reason why Asiatic and Hindu labourers, our fellow-subjects, have not been admitted into some parts of the British Empire? ...The reason is that they were accustomed to such a low wage and they could live so cheaply that they could compete with white labour on conditions which no white man could accept. We should not close our eyes to this situation. I approve of the idea that we should endeavour to overcome these difficulties...[82]

The idea that the Canada's doors were about to be opened to South Asian immigrants as a result of the Imperial War Conference resolution put a chill down the spine of the former Laurier minister, Frank Oliver. He, remember, had a decade earlier put the continuous passage restriction in place. Reprising his argument for Dominion self-government in regards to immigration policy, he strongly objected to "our hands" being "tied by Imperial authority." What was at stake for Oliver was nothing less than maintaining the British Empire "finally and completely as a white man's empire."

> The question of Oriental immigration has been serious in Canada in years past, and if the Prime Minister truly expressed the attitude of this new cabinet of the Empire towards the subject of Hindu immigration into Canada, I would say that our position will be very much more dangerous in the future than it has been in the past... Our purpose in this country is to establish firmly, to build up and improve our civilization according to our best ideals, and we can only do that by retaining the control and direction of affairs in our own country so that we may direct them in the interests of upbuilding of that civilization. If, in dealing with those older civilizations [China, Japan, and India] which come amongst us, our hands are tied by Imperial authority, then we are handicapped in the purpose we had in view in establishing ourselves in this country. We claim that this Empire of ours is the most perfect fruit of the civi-

lization of which we are a part. Our claim is that it stands today at the head of a white civilization. It can only retain that position by being maintained by a white civilization, and that white civilization must be maintained in the self-governing dominions of the Empire, or this Empire cannot be maintained finally and completely as a white man's empire... India is fighting for her liberty, to do what she pleases within her own area. Canada is fighting for the same purpose. The fact that we are fighting to protect our rights and interests in our own country gives us no right or authority to dictate to the peoples in some other part of the Empire what they shall do in their own county and under their own conditions. So we say, however well the soldiers of India may fight, however much India may do in the cause of the Empire, we still have the same right to protect ourselves and our own country, to protect the civilization our fathers established here...

Oliver need not have been overly concerned. In the reply to his speech by Robert Rogers, Borden's Minister of Public Works, it was made clear that the Imperial War Conference resolution on immigration reciprocity had made a symbolic, rather than substantive, commitment. Irrespective of its wording, the resolution would change nothing on the ground in Canada and this had been made clear on the spot to the representatives of the Indian government. "Let me assure my hon. Friend that no rights have been given away, that there has been no thought of any rights as likely to be given away," Rogers said. "We did discuss with the Indian representatives the question of immigration, and we distinctly and clearly informed them that it would be impossible to hold out any hope of any particular change in respect to immigration to the province of British Columbia."[83]

Behind the scenes, Borden had informally told the British that in return for a prohibition on future South Asian immigration Canada would agree that "Indians already settled should be accepted as a permanent part of the population and placed on exactly the same footing as whites" including the right to vote. However, Borden did not fulfil this commitment "largely because of [his] insecure parliamentary support."[84] With an eye to his party's fortunes in British Columba, his successor, Mackenzie

King, also proved unwilling to force the issue on the province. As he explained to the Commons, a policy that would create "unrest" in British Columbia over votes for South Asian British subjects could not serve the interests of the British Empire.

> ...if the members from the province of British Columbia regardless of political party were to be favourable to having the franchise granted to the Indians in British Columbia, the rest of parliament would fall cordially into harmony with their view, that on the other hand if there was no agreement among the members of the province of British Columbia on this question, if it were clear to the members of this House that so far as British Columbia was concerned instead of being in favour of granting the franchise they were all pretty much the other way, it was hardly probable that the members of parliament generally would seek to impose any view upon them which would be contrary to their wishes. In other words, that it was very doubtful how any situation of unrest in one part of the British Empire could be improved by creating a new condition of unrest in another part.[85]

King was very well aware, of course, that the British Columbia members would never agree to give the vote to South Asian Canadians. Although he was not endorsing their view, he was certainly prepared to bend to it. Comox-Alberni member A.W. Neill argued that giving South Asians the vote would upend the politics of the province as the "Hindus" would demand political representation and could hold members electorally accountable if they failed to provide it.

> Now, he says that there are only twelve hundred of these people that would be affected. We will say that there are five thousand; according to my hon. Friend's argument we would grant them the franchise and that would be the end of it. Well, that would not be the end of it. Five thousand voters in British Columbia would have a very powerful influence on the electorate and on the result of the election. They would be skilfully handled: they would vote in a mass and for one object, and the result would be to swing perhaps two or three seats. What would that object be? Would it be the advancement of Canada as a whole or of British Columbia as a province,

or would it be to secure some advantage for that colony of Hindus? Would it not be for the latter?

Worse, for Neill, was his acknowledgement of the fact that if South Asians were enfranchised, then Japanese and Chinese Canadians – British subjects too – could no longer "logically and with any sense of decency" be denied the vote. British Columbia's decades-long political monopoly held by "white Canada" advocates would be in this way surrendered.

> another point is this: If you grant this privilege to the Hindus, can you deny it to others under similar conditions? The hon. Member says there is a difference between these people; that the Hindus are British-born subjects and that differentiates them from Orientals such as Japanese and Chinese. But Japanese and Chinese are born in British Columbia, which is far more than the Hindu is. He too is a British subject, I admit; but when the oriental is born in British Columbia of naturalized parents how can we logically and with any sense of decency withhold the vote from him when he attains the age of twenty-one when we have given it to the Hindu, a worse fitted man, a man untrained, unaccustomed to our language? If we grant it to the Hindu how can we deny it to the oriental born in British Columbia who speaks the same tongue as we do? It follows as the night the day that if we grant it to Hindus we must grant it to the other orientals.[86]

J.S. Woodsworth took Neill, along with another B.C. member, to task for the "narrow bigotry" of their remarks and asked "why not" respect the "fundamental rights of citizenship" of South Asian and Asian Canadians.

> I cannot but deprecate the attitude taken by the hon. Member for Comox-Alberni (Mr. Neill) with regard to the orientals. He has tried to disparage almost every other nationality but our own, the Chinese, the Japanese and the Greeks and the Jews. No, I think it was the hon. Member for Cariboo (Mr. McBride) who enumerated these particular groups. I cannot see that we are going to get very far by a narrow bigotry of that kind. The member for Comox-Alberni, in referring to the fact that the orientals have no vote, said he was afraid that if the Indians should be given a vote it would result in a vote being given to other orientals. I should like to ask why not?

> I admit that I do not believe in admitting large numbers of these people at the present time because we are not in a fit position to take care of them. I do not believe that we can have intermingling of these races under present conditions but it is one thing to say to the orientals 'it is not well for you to come in at the present time' and it is quite another thing after we have allowed them to come in and they are citizens with us, rate-payers with us and all the rest of it, to deny them the fundamental rights of citizenship.[87]

S.W. Jacobs forcefully argued the position that the views of British Columbia were outside the mainstream of Canadian public opinion and that they should not be allowed to dictate national policy on the voting rights of South Asian "British subjects domiciled in Canada."

> No matter what the views of the people of any particular province on a matter of this kind, I submit they ought to give way to the generally accepted views of the people of the Dominion of Canada as a whole and to the views of the Empire of which we are always proud to say that we form an integral part. The question of the Hindu franchise is of great interest to this country. There is no reason in the wide world... why British subjects domiciled in Canada should be deprived of the franchise. They are British-born. Their skins may be a little duskier than ours, but they belong to the Aryan race, and in all respects they are quite as capable of using the franchise as any person who resides in this country. .. there is a vast difference between the Chinese and the Japanese and the Hindu. The first difference is that these latter people are British subjects and are part of the British Empire.

The idea that South Asian Canadians would use their vote to "work some injury to the white people" of British Columbia was nothing more than racial prejudice and Neill had proved himself to be "one of the most prejudiced members in this House."

> Mr. Jacobs: ...As I say, these people [Indians] are there now. They are tax-payers. There is nothing against their receiving a franchise except the fear on the part of the people of British Columbia that when they do receive this franchise... they might work some injury to the white people of that province. I trust this parliament will rise above these narrow considerations which have been mentioned by

> the member for Comox-Alberni and do its duty. I think it will be generally admitted that my hon. Friend (Mr. Neill) is perhaps not the best person to speak on this matter without prejudice. He is one of the most prejudiced members in this House –
> Some hon. Members: Order.
> Mr. Jacobs: – from British Columbia on the question –
> Some hon. Members: Order.
> Mr. Jacobs: – of orientals. He positively glories in it. He says: 'I am against orientals in every form; I am against their immigration, I am against their franchise.' He has constituted himself the authority in matters of this kind; I think he would look upon it as a piece of flattery if I were to tell him publically as I do now, that in the matter of oriental immigration and oriental franchise there is no more prejudiced person in the House than he is.

Jacobs' speech was interrupted several times but he was unbowed. At one point, he was challenged by the Cariboo member T.G. McBride who tried to personalize the issue and make it about miscegenation.

> Mr. McBride: If my hon. friend had a daughter would he want her to live and associate with the Hindu?
> Mr. Jabobs: I would say this: I have three daughters, and I would rather see them associate with respectable Hindus than with some white men I know. But that is not the question which comes up here tonight. It is not a question of the association of white men with the duskier races or anything of that kind. The question –
> Mr. McBride: That is exactly what it is, Mr. Chairman. It is forcing these coloured races in among white people, and making the people of British Columbia associate with them.[88]

AFRICAN CANADIANS AS "SONS OF CANADA"

Compared to Asian Canadians, there is little to be found in the Commons debates about Canadians of African origins. Unlike native peoples they were not special subjects of federal legislation. And, unlike Europe, Asia, and South Asia there was no continuing immigration pressure from Africa that would have engaged debates over a politics of federal regulation. African Canadians first came to the British North American provinces in the seventeenth and eighteenth centuries as slaves and as Loyalist settlers. However intensely they suffered from economic and social discrimination, and were the victims of racialist provincial legislation (such as segregated schools in Ontario and Nova Scotia), generally African Canadians formally enjoyed legal and political citizenship rights as British subjects.[89] Indeed, the formal equality enjoyed by Canada's Blacks as British subjects was an important and historically recurring marker for many Canadians of the moral superiority of their political system in comparison to that of the republic to their south.[90] Nevertheless, many Canadians also became nervous on those occasions when it appeared that large numbers of African Americans might cross the border and settle amongst them. R.W. Winks has noted that "prejudice rose as the numbers of Negroes rose."[91]

And so it was that 1910 reports that U.S. Blacks were seeking free land in the Canadian west was soon followed by news that their entry was being restricted by the federal government. A.H. Clarke, representing the southern Ontario riding of South Essex with its sizeable community of African Canadians "who are honest, law-abiding, good citizens" rose in the Commons to express concern that Black settlers were being turned back at the border.

> Coloured people in my experience have been amongst the most loyal citizens of this country. They have been true to the British flag and I think they are worthy to be reckoned amongst the people of Canada. Surely, the large areas of Canada are sufficient to entitle us to take in this class of people who have not the privileges of other classes. It has always been the boast of British institutions that unfortunate men will find a haven within our borders. Representing a large number of the coloured people, I certainly protest against any rule which would exclude them on account of their colour...[92]

Others, while they also defended of the rights of African Canadians as British subjects, and, by implication, our moral superiority to the Americans in the area of race relations, were far less welcoming to these immigrants. George Foster claimed he

> would be very sorry indeed to see any colour line drawn in the

> Dominion of Canada. We have quite a large negro population in Canada... most of whom are descendants of those who came in the old days, when slavery flourished in the United States. We gave them a hearty welcome and a hospitable one... they have enjoyed all the rights and privileges of free men here. We are glad that they are doing so.

Still, Foster raised the spectre of a mass influx of "tens of millions" of American Blacks "the result of which we have not the least idea at present."[93] Others were more direct in calling for exclusion. W. Thoburn warned of

> negro immigration from the southern states into our Canadian Northwest. We find by the newspaper reports that these people are coming over into Canada by the hundreds; later on they will come by the thousands, and so long as we give them free homesteads in the Canadian Northwest they will come by the tens of thousands... Would it not be preferable to preserve for the sons of Canada the lands they propose to give to niggers?[94]

While the Asian and South Asian communities in Canada had been denied the voting franchise and therefore lacked both the leverage and legitimacy to call upon their MP's to protect their dignity, African Canadians did not suffer under any such liability. When in 1885 Sir John A. Macdonald delivered a pseudo-scientific racial outburst where he proclaimed that "crosses" between the Aryan, African and "Asiatic" races, "like the cross of the dog and the fox," would never be successful, he was immediately challenged to explain if this meant he planned to remove the franchise from African Canadians in the same fashion as he was proposing to do with Chinese Canadians. D. Mills observed that Macdonald had introduced to Commons debate the lessons of polygenetic race thinking on

> ...the very large and complicated question of miscegenation. The hon. gentleman has given us a lecture upon the subject. He tells us what races may properly mingle and what races may not. The hon. gentleman has expressed views that are not exactly in accord with the views of Prichard and Latham, though they may be in accord

> with the views of Morton, Gliddon and Agassiz... The hon. gentleman says that the African race never can mingle with the Caucasian or Aryan race.
>   Sir John A. Macdonald: I did not say that; I know they do mingle.
>   Mr. Mills: He said, not successfully. He has deprecated such miscegenation. He says their immigration into the country is to be discouraged, and, if I were to follow the hon. gentleman's argument to its logical conclusion, we must infer that it is his intention to disfranchise the colored men of this country as well as the Chinese.
>   Sir John A. Macdonald: No.[95]

A significant number of MP's acknowledged African Canadians as "sons of Canada" and would, from time to time, lobby openly on behalf of what they perceived as their interests. In 1906, for example, the right of African Canadians to civil service jobs in Ottawa had been advanced by H.S. Clements who proudly claimed a large number of his constituents as Black.

> We are proud of the coloured people in that section of the country. They are intelligent, respectable and thoroughly good Canadian citizens. We have... coloured men who are practising at the bar, men who hold first-class certificates and men who occupy honoured positions in the medical professions... If we are true Canadians I think we should see to it that all classes of people are represented in the public service of this country. In the various departments of this government there are positions in which these people could be employed with most beneficial results to the public service... I would ask in their behalf that this government might take into consideration that large and intelligent section of people, who, I am sure will prove themselves to be worthy of any confidence reposed in them... I feel it my duty as a representative of that section of the people to advocate their interests here and I trust these people will be represented as well as other nationalities in this Dominion.

Representing the Ontario Essex South constituency of historic African Canadian settlement, A.H. Clarke added his voice to Clements' appeal noting that "the coloured people"

> have had a harder struggle than the white man in this country. They have obstacles to overcome which the white man has not. They have prejudices against them. They have not had the facilities for educa-

tion which the white man has... My hon. friend is quite right in saying that the coloured race in Canada ought to be recognized by the government and given their fair share of the public positions which are open to the people of this country. [96]

In the same vein, J.W. Daniel (representing the "coloured constituents" of his St. John constituency) along with J.D. Reid questioned the cases of two African Canadians who had shone in federal civil service exams only to be later assigned work that was inferior to their qualifications. Despite making a direct appeal to Prime Minister Laurier to "not allow that kind of thing to spread throughout the departments," their questions were shrugged off in the Commons by the government.[97]

And, likewise, during World War I, W. Pugsley, Daniel's successor in the St. John constituency, raised the possibility of a "colour line" in military recruitment which had informally prevented the enlistment of twenty of his constituents. Sam Hughes, Minister of Militia and Defence, denied that this was the case. "From the city of St. John a large number of coloured men have enlisted in the various regiments raised in that vicinity," he said. "There is scarcely a regiment in the Dominion, or at the front, but has coloured men in the ranks, and they are splendid soldiers; very excellent soldiers indeed."[98]

It was this liberal tradition, recognizing African Canadians as a legitimate part of the Canadian community with a valid claim to the rights of British subjects, which inspired E.M. Macdonald's rejection of Thoburn's call in the Commons to keep "niggers" out of the country.

> Of course, if a man be undesirable within the meaning of the [Immigration] statute, he should be excluded, whether he is coloured or white; but I trust that my hon. friends opposite do not propose to exclude a man simply because of his colour, whether from the United States of any other part of the world... does my hon. friend pretend that we should exclude a man simply because he is coloured, regardless whether he be an undesirable or not in other respects.[99]

R.L. Borden, then Leader of the Opposition, pleaded that the feelings of African Canadians be spared in this matter and that there be no explicit colour barriers to the entry of Black immigrants.

> It would be very unfortunate if any impression got abroad that any person, coming as an immigrant, was to be excluded simply because of his colour. There are a great many people of that race in different parts of Canada. They are good, honest, law abiding citizens and a credit to the communities in which they live. Some of their settlements have existed in this country for 150 years and others – I am speaking more particularly of my own province of Nova Scotia – for about 100 years. There are many communities of these excellent citizens in Nova Scotia, and it would be most unfortunate if the impression got abroad that these regulations were to be construed so as to exclude any immigrant by reason of his colour.[100]

A.B. McCoig, a government backbencher whose Kent West constituents included "a good many coloured farmers who are amongst the most industrious and successful citizens in the Dominion," claimed that he had received written assurances from the Minister that

> so long as these coloured people were entitled to enter under the law, they would be admitted as freely as any other people who came to our country. I am glad to know that the government has taken that stand, because I would regret deeply if this government of which I am so proud and which I am so glad to support should in any way discriminate against coloured people, especially when we have amongst us men of that race who are doing their share to build up this Dominion.[101]

And so, these calls to avoid offering insult to African Canadians appear to have played a significant role in dampening within the state the effect of the widespread western agitation for formal measures to exclude U.S. blacks.[102] African Americans were indeed denied entry to Canada, but not by special legislation: an Order-in-Council prohibiting "any immigrant belonging to the Negro race, which race is deemed unsuitable to the climate and requirements of Canada" was actually prepared during 1911 but was never proclaimed.[103] As it was with South Asians, but for different reasons in this case, the state's preferred solution was to aver formally race neutral legal instruments while encouraging racially selective administrative determination of the entry regulations.[104] F. Oliver, the Minister, declared that Canadian immigration law operated "without any distinction of race, colour, or previous condition of servitude." He also "absolutely and entirely" denied that there was any policy to bar Blacks[105] and declared that special legislation would be necessary to accomplish that purpose.

> When these people came to Canada they get the same rights as anybody else. Any person coming from another country into Canada and having the necessary qualifications is entitled to a homestead, and negroes get free homesteads the same as any other people. So far they have been treated exactly the same as other people have been, both in their admission to the country and in regard to taking up land in the country. They will have to be continued in that treatment until parliament authorizes some other action on the part of the government.

In practically the same breath, however, Oliver referred vaguely to "the distinction between legislation and administration."[106]

> there are many cases where the admission or exclusion of an immigrant depends on a strict or lax interpretation of the law, so that if the immigrant is of what we would call the desirable class then they are administered laxly, and if he is of the presumably less desirable class then they are administered more restrictedly. Beyond that there are no instructions to the immigration officers, but they are expected to act according to the instructions they have.[107]

The research of H. Troper has shown that an "informal exclusionary programme adopted by the Minister of the Interior and his Immigration Branch" was put into effect against potential African American immigrants to Canada during this period. As Troper concludes, this episode was to have continuing significance as it "forced the Immigration Branch to adapt administration of existing legislation to meet ends not perceived by those who had enacted that legislation."[108]

CONCLUSION

Chapter 5 has focused on race-thinking as it related to Canadians of Asian, South Asian and African origins. British Columbia is identified as the Canadian epicentre of anti-Asian race-thinking and 'white Canada' agitation. Throughout the entire period covered in our study, it can be seen that the racist political ideas of B.C. members were challenged by members from other Canadian regions who articulated ideas based on principles of Christian or liberal equality. Although they protested that one province should not be able to dictate Dominion policy in regards to "Orientals," it is nonetheless apparent that over time the B.C. members enjoyed a growing influence in determining immigration policy and excluding Asians from the voting franchise. By 1908, the leadership of both the Conservatives and Liberals were declaring their party's support for a "White Canada" policy, at least at the rhetorical level. As the twentieth century unfolded, there was evidence in the Commons debates of increasing use of social Darwinist pseudo-science in the form of dire warnings against miscegenation. This supposed authority of this 'science' did not deter parliamentary opponents of discriminatory policies as they continued to argue forcefully against "prejudice" and for liberal equality principles. In our next and final chapter, our discussion will look back over the four previous chapters and argue that the late nineteenth and early twentieth century Canadian race-thinking represented in parliamentary debate cannot be confined within watertight European, Native, and non-European categories but must instead be understood as whole taking place within and between these 'racial' categories.

Notes

1. Canada, House of Commons, *Debates*, May 4, 1885, p. 1583. Davies was a former Premier of Prince Edward Island and went on to serve as a Justice of the Supreme Court of Canada between 1901 and 1918 and Chief Justice between 1918 and 1924.
2. Ibid., May 4, 1885, p. 1583.
3. Sukanya Banerjee, *Becoming Imperial Citizens: Indians in the Late-Victorian Empire*. Durham, N.C.: Duke University Press, 2010. p. 22.
4. Angus Madison, *The World Economy: A Millennial Perspective*. Paris: OECD Development Centre, 2001. p. 97.
5. R.A. Huttenback, "The British Empire as a 'White Man's Country' – Racial Attitudes and Immigration Legislation in the Colonies of White Settlement," *Journal of British Studies*, November 1973, pp. 110-111. See also Jeremy Martens, "A transnational history of immigration restriction: Natal and New South Wales, 1896-97," *The Journal of Imperial and Commonwealth History*, September 2006, pp. 332-333.
6. Patricia Roy, *A White Man's Province: British Columbia Politicians and Chinese and Japanese Immigrants, 1858-1914*. Vancouver: UBC Press, 1989 has provided a wonderfully rich account of the province's political culture during the later nineteenth century. Anti-Asian sentiment, she concluded, was first and foremost an expression of economic and cultural insecurity rather than biological racism. "To argue ...that nineteenth-century British Columbians 'shared the firm conviction that intellectually, socially and culturally, the Chinese were their inferiors' is to oversimplify. Whites wanted to belong to a superior race; they doubted their ability to compete with the Chinese, who were 'too smart for us.' Not only might China's 'immense population' easily 'swamp us,' but, if unchecked, the Chinese could absorb 'every industry and trade in the province . . . and those who are now the masters will become the servants,' Roy wrote. Further, "...race, that is, in its narrow sense of skin colour and other visible physical characteristics, though present, had never been the sole source of their antipathy to Asians, and few would

have ever argued that Asian peoples were innately inferior...British Columbians had been inspired by fears that the presence of Asian sojourners would inhibit the development of a stable and prosperous province, that the low wages and inferior working conditions Asians seemed willing to accept would drive down standards of living; that Asians might take over particular industries; that weak white people, particularly the young, could be corrupted by Asian vices; and, above all, that through their potentially overwhelming numbers, Asian immigrants might turn British Columbia into a settlement where Asian rather than western standards prevailed. The campaign for a 'white man's province,' though blatantly racist in appearance, was, in fact, a catch phrase that covered a wide variety of concerns and transcended particular economic interests." pp. 57-58, 286.

7. Commons, *Debates*, February 15, 1880, p. 28.
8. Ibid., July 2, 1885, p. 3016.
9. Ibid., May 12, 1882, p. 1477.
10. Ibid., July 2, 1885, p. 3003.
11. Ibid., March 29, 1883, pp. 326-328.
12. Ibid., pp. 329-330.
13. Ibid., April 30, 1883, p. 905.
14. Ibid., July 2, 1885, pp. 3006-3007.
15. Canada, Royal Commission on Chinese Immigration, Honourable Commissioner Chapleau's Report Respecting Chinese Immigration in British Columbia, Ottawa, February 21, 1885, p. ciii.
16. Commons, *Debates*, July 2, 1885, pp. 3009-3010.
17. Royal Commission on Chinese Immigration, Honourable Commissioner Chapleau's Report, p. xcix.
18. Commons, *Debates*, July 2, 1885, p. 3010.
19. Ibid., May 4, 1885, pp. 1588-1589.
20. Ibid., p. 1582. Gault was a financier and founder of Sun Life Financial.
21. Ibid., p. 1583.

22. Ibid., p. 1584.
23. Ibid.
24. Ibid., pp. 1585-1586
25. Ibid., April 2, 1884, p. 1287.
26. Ibid., January 22, 1909, p. 35.
27. Christina L. Davis, "Linkage Diplomacy: Economic and Security Bargaining in the Anglo-Japanese Alliance, 1902–23," *International Security*, Vol. 33, No. 3 (Winter 2008/09).
28. Commons, *Debates*, July 5, 1892, pp. 4637-4638.
29. Ibid., June 25, 1900, pp. 8166-8167.
30. Ibid., pp. 8190-8191.
31. Ibid., pp. 8191-8192.
32. Ibid., May 31, 1887, p.642.
33. Ibid., June 25, 1900, pp. 8163, 8185-8186.
34. Ibid., pp. 8101, 8165-8166, 8198-8199.
35. Ibid., December 16, 1907, p. 729.
36. Ibid., pp. 722, 726.
37. Ibid., January 22, 1909. pp. 75-76.
38. Ibid., January 28, 1908, pp. 2045-2046.
39. For a discussion of the riots see P. Ward, *White Canada Forever*, Third Edition, Chapter 4.
40. Commons, *Debates*, January 22, 1909, p. 46
41. Ward, *White Canada Forever*, Third Edition, p. 75. In his statement to the Commons, Laurier gave every appearance of the Liberals having been backed into a political corner by B.C. voters on this question: "…in British Columbia, the problem of Asiatic immigration is the one question that interests all sections of public opinion; and all classes of the people in British Columbia, to whatever party they may belong, unite in the opinion which is expressed in the words now current in the politics of the province, 'A white British Columbia; a white Canada,' meaning that British Columbia should be preserved as a home of the

white race. To this opinion, to this fact, we on this side of the House have no opposition to offer, and to it we take no exception whatever." Commons, *Debates*, January 22, 1909, p. 35. Both the political calculation and the lack of enthusiasm ("no opposition to offer") shine through here. Nevertheless, it should be remembered that the unity in B.C. public opinion that Laurier describes here and that had led both parties to climb on the 'white Canada' bandwagon, was constructed politically upon the condition of Asian Canadians being denied the franchise.

42. Commons, *Debates*, January 22, 1909, pp. 35-36. But Laurier continued to understand these questions from a developmental perspective rather than through the prism of biological or racial determinism. To illustrate, this is how he explained to the Commons Japan's then current position within the international system. Japan, he said, "has suddenly become one of the world's greatest powers. Sir, everybody will concede that no event during the last fifty years of the history of the human race has been more remarkable than the sudden revolution which has changed the institutions of Japan… Japan has adopted our system of education, our methods of trade and industry, and in the art and science of war, both on land and sea, she has shown herself the peer of the most famous nations of the present day." January 28, 1908 p. 2092.

43. Ibid., January 28, 1908, pp. 2130-2132, 2148.

44. Ibid., January 22, 1909, p. 83-85.

45. Ibid., March 2, 1914, pp. 1225-1226.

46. Ibid., March 13, 1919, p. 427.

47. Ibid., April 2, 1925, p. 1815.

48. Ibid., May 8, 1922, p. 1548.

49. Ibid., April 26, 1921, p. 2597.

50. Ibid., May 8, 1922, pp. 1516, 1521, 1524.

51. Ibid., p. 1564.

52. Ibid., pp. 1574-1575.

53. Ibid., pp. 1555-1556.

54. Ibid., p. 1556.
55. Ibid., April 30, 1923, pp. 2312-2313.
56. Ibid., May 8, 1922, p. 1571.
57. Ibid., May 4, 1923, p. 2485.
58. Ibid., pp. 2485-2486.
59. Ibid., May 8, 1922, pp. 1571-1572.
60. Ibid., May 4, 1923, p. 2487.
61. In fact, these immigrants were overwhelmingly Sikh in religion.
62. Ward, *White Canada Forever*, Third Edition, p. 82.
63. Commons, *Debates*, March 2, 1914, pp. 1240, 1245.
64. Ibid., April 8, 1908, pp. 6441-6442.
65. Ibid., pp. 6444-6445.
66. Ibid., March 2, 1914, p. 1245.
67. Ibid., p. 1242.
68. Ibid., pp. 1227-1228.
69. Ibid., June 1, 1914, pp. 4564-4566.
70. Ibid., pp. 4563-4564.
71. Ibid., March 2, 1914, pp. 1227-1228.
72. Ibid., April 8, 1908, p. 6439.
73. Ibid., p. 6439-6440.
74. Ibid., March 24, 1908, pp. 5489-5490.
75. Ibid., April 8, 1908, p. 6442.
76. Ibid., p. 6431.
77. Ibid., pp. 6434-6435.
78. Ibid., June 1, 1914, pp. 4561-4562.
79. Ibid., March 2, 1914, pp. 1230-1231.
80. N. Ferguson, *Empire: The Rise and Demise of the British World Order*, p. 303.
81. A.T. Yarwood, "The Overseas Indians as a Problem in Indian and

Imperial Politics at the End of World War One," *The Australian Journal of Politics and History*, August 1968, p. 204.

82. Commons, *Debates*, May 18, 1917, pp. 1535, 1545-1546.
83. Ibid., May 25, 1917, pp. 1764-1765.
84. Yarwood, "The Overseas Indians as a Problem in Indian and Imperial Politics," pp. 212, 216-217.
85. Commons, *Debates*, June 29, 1923, pp. 4665-4666.
86. Ibid., p. 4646.
87. Ibid., p. 4651.
88. Ibid., pp. 4641, 4649-4650.
89. R.W. Winks, *The Blacks in Canada*. Montreal: McGill-Queen's University Press, 1971. pp. 251-252.
90. Ibid., pp. 112, 149, 262, 381.
91. Ibid., pp. 142-143. See also pp. 289, 298.
92. Commons, *Debates*, March 22, 1911, p. 5911.
93. Ibid., April 3, 1911, p. 6526.
94. Ibid., p. 6524.
95. Ibid., May 4, 1885, p. 1589.
96. Ibid., July 9, 1906, pp. 7503-05. Clements represented the nearby West Kent constituency.
97. Ibid., March 2, 1911, p. 4470; March 9, 1911, p. 4930; March 10, 1911, pp. 5038-5039.
98. Ibid., Feb 3, 1916, p. 557.
99. Ibid., April 3, 1911, p. 6527.
100. Ibid., March 23, 1911, p. 5947.
101. Ibid., p. 5944.
102. An account of this anti-Black agitation can be found in R. Bruce Shepard, "Plain Racism: The Reaction Against Oklahoma Black Immigration To the Canadian Plains," in Ormond McKague, ed. *Racism in Canada*, Saskatoon: Fifth House Publishers, 1991. p. 29.

103. H. Troper, "The Creek-Negroes of Oklahoma and Canadian Immigration, 1909-11", *Canadian Historical Review*, September 1972, p. 282. See also Troper, *Only Farmers Need Apply*, Chapter 7, "Closing the Door (The Issue of Negro Immigration)"

104. Shepard and Troper both suggest that beyond the domestic political factors outlined here, a desire to avoid diplomatic problems with the U.S. may have also played a role in deterring restrictive legislation. Shepard speculates that "Action on the problem was difficult... since the reciprocity negotiations with the United States had only recently concluded, and remarks by President Taft on the subject had fanned Canadian nationalism. A volatile subject like black immigration could easily become involved, upsetting an already precarious situation." p. 29

105. Commons, *Debates*, March 22, 1911, p. 5912

106. Ibid., April 3, 1911, pp. 6525-26.

107. Ibid., March 22, 1911, p. 5911.

108. Troper, "The Creek-Negroes of Oklahoma", pp. 283, 288; see also Shepard, "Plain Racism" for an outline of the administrative measures taken by the Immigration Branch.

CHAPTER 6.

CONCLUSION

Physical peculiarities tend to make other and less important divergencies conspicuous, and in this and in other ways are constantly operating to isolate the race possessing them from other races. I am inclined to think that physical peculiarities which now pass unnoticed might, if a prejudice were aroused against them, ultimately result in the separation and isolation of new races and septs now unknown. Upon the whole, I doubt if there is any obstacle in the way of the fraternisation of races so difficult to overcome as this one of physical peculiarities, and the prejudices, sometimes very idle and senseless, which are begotten of them... This sort of race hostility is materially strengthened by a large class of men who find their principal scope feeling and fostering race enmities.[1]
–JOSEPH-ADOLPHE CHAPLEAU, 1885

Surveying four and a half decades around the turn of the twentieth century, this book seeks to provide the reader with a wide angle photograph of the formation, representation and contestation of race-thinking in Canadian political society. Any notion that biologically determinist race-thinking was universally, or even commonly, accepted as unassailable truth in this era's political society has been shown to be mistaken. While there can be no denying that racist ideas were openly and habitually articulated by parliamentarians during this formative period in Canada's political culture, it is also true that racial determinists met with resolute opposition from defenders of the ideals of liberal and Christian equality. In fact, it was not unusual to see racist statements challenged on the spot and to hear members call each other out for being prejudiced. Political ideas of racial equality and multiculturalism were by no means newly discovered in Canada sometime after World War II. They were already there, and were well positioned to become hegemonic when ideas of biological politics became overshadowed by the totalizing Cold War conflict between communism and liberal democracy and discredited through the revulsive crimes of the Nazis.

One way to approach the task of presenting the reader with an organized overview of the material set out in the previous chapters would be to construct here a list of factors that reinforced race-thinking in this era and contrast it with a list of factors that promoted equality and undermined racial determinism. No matter how elegant the simplicity of this approach, our subject did not typically manifest itself in Commons debates as a set of neat binary opposites. Because of the many years that are surveyed, the many influences that are represented, the many parliamentarians who are canvassed, and the many issues that are discussed, debates were typically multi-sided affairs rather than a simple two-sided bout between the racial determinists on one side and the anti-racists on the other. And, underlining that there were many influences simultaneously at play here in the minds of parliamentarians, readers may have noted that members sometimes struggled to find internal consistency and clarity in their own remarks on racial issues. In keeping with the complexity of our material, then, this concluding chapter will survey our findings within four of the most significant themes that emerged within the Commons debates of this era concerning race and identity: the British Empire, Christianity and liberalism, racial pseudo-science and biological determinism, and political representation.

THE BRITISH EMPIRE

Lowry has persuasively argued that Canada was the British Empire's "prototype Dominion" pioneering both democratic self-government and a multicultural political citizenship which promised full equality for French-speaking Roman Catholics.[2] As Sir John A. Macdonald put it, "we have a constitution... under which all British subjects are in a position of absolute equality, having equal rights of every kind – of language, of religion, of property and of person. There is no paramount race in this country; we are all British subjects..." The British Empire in Canada embodied "the idea of unity in diversity and diversity towards unity" for Sir Wilfred Laurier.[3] Canada's 'racial' diversity required its political leadership to smother intercommunal conflicts through "conciliation and tolerance," contended R. Lemieux.

> Let us not forget that we live in a country composed of diverse elements, enjoying equal rights. The races which inhabit it have the same interests and are entitled to the same share of liberty, to the same right to bask in the sunshine of liberty. But if conflicts arise between them, conciliation and tolerance should be resorted to, above everything else, to dissipate prejudice, hatred and passion.[4]

If followed, Laurier judged, that it was "particularly odious that any person in this country, where there are delicate questions of race and religion, should accuse any man in public life of hatred against or insults to, the race or religion of any citizen." There could be "no worse charge... against any public man in this country... in respect of his parliamentary duties" other than personal corruption.[5]

Canada's political elites characteristically projected this understanding of their own situation onto the rest of the British Empire. Political liberty rather than race was said to be the glue holding the Empire together. R.B. Bennett claimed that "wherever the British flag has gone, wherever Englishmen have planted the outposts of Empire, there has followed order, justice, liberty, freedom, equality under the law... Whether they be Mahomedans, or Hindoos, Buddhists or Catholics, Protestants or atheists, it matters not, all have equal rights under that great flag..."[6]

Under this theory of British subjecthood, minorities in Canada possessed a strong claim to equal political rights. C. Amyot told the Commons that "diverse races" who keep their laws, language and customs could unite "to form a strong nation" under the liberty guaranteed by the British flag.

> Yes, we are able to form a strong nation with diverse races. That is true. That is the way England does with her colonies all over the world. She gives most ample liberty to the new peoples enrolled under her flag. You study the history of England, that great colonizing power, and you will find that it is not by tyranny, it is not be imposing false and bad laws, that she progresses. No. She tells the people of all her new colonies, as if they were speaking to allies: Keep your laws, your language, your customs, and be a happy people; work out your destiny with England for the honour of humanity and for the glory of the British flag.[7]

Minorities sometimes employed their political voice in the Commons to support the general principle of minority rights. Legislative attacks on "any minority" or "a class of people" were "outrageous" according to Joseph Lavergne.

> Not only as a French Canadian, not only as a Roman Catholic, but on broader grounds, as a Canadian, I shall always refuse to pass legislation which places not a Roman Catholic minority, not a French minority, but any minority, a class of people or a certain religious denomination in an unfair situation as compared with the balance of the population. It is humiliating, it is outrageous, I will never assent to that...[8]

At the end of World War I, W.D. Euler reminded fellow parliamentarians that German Canadians, like his son, had served at the front and had as good a claim to 'Canadian blood' as those of either French or English ancestry.

> Mr. Speaker, I have only contempt for the men who will deny his

father or his racial origin. I want to say that the blood that flows in my veins is exactly the same kind of blood that courses in the veins of every other hon. Member of this House. It is not English, it is not French, it is not German; it is Canadian. Now, I want to speak so plainly that there can be no misapprehension. The man who is my father came from Germany at the age of two and a half years, long before Confederation, and has lived in this country for nearly seventy-five years, and what is much more important, he is today just as good a Canadian as is his grandson, who is still carrying arms overseas.[9]

Individuals could also make a claim to political equality under the concept of British subjecthood. L.H. Davies, who later served on the Supreme Court of Canada as its Chief Justice, held that he would be "sorry to see" legislation that incorporated the "vicious" principle of excluding "any one race or color from participating in the political franchises and privileges of the people of this Dominion. My contention is, that a Chinaman who has become a British subject by naturalisation, who resides in the country and has acquired the necessary qualification, has as good a right to be allowed to vote as any other British subject of foreign extraction."[10]

But for many parliamentarians there was a catch in the fine print. Laurier, for example, maintained that a policy of "equal rights and equal justice" giving to every citizen "without any questions of birth or origin, the same rights, the same liberties, the same privileges" was reserved for "races of equal rank."[11] For Laurier, the "equal rank" races did not include the "Mongolian races which do not assimilate with us, but as to the Caucasian races and European races – not all of them, but all those who readily assimilate with us – it is our duty to open our doors to them and follow the example of the mother country in that respect."[12] Natives were also not "equal rank" races in Laurier's opinion as they came from "savage nations" who "roamed over rather than possessed" North America before the arrival of the Europeans.[13]

Macdonald stripped property-qualified Chinese Canadians of

their vote in 1885 observing that "a Chinaman... has no British instincts or British feelings or aspirations, and therefore ought not to have a vote."[14] And when South Asian British subjects tried to claim equality rights both for entry as immigrants and for voting as citizens, they were denied. Some members pointed to the realpolitik of the difference between British subjects in colonies of settlement and British subjects in colonies of military occupation. Along these lines, J.H. Burnham noted simply that "India is not part of the empire as we are... It is not necessary to go into the history of India to show that it is not on the same basis in the empire as we are."[15] W.F. Cockshutt elaborated:

> India... stands in a different relation to the empire from Canada, South Africa, New Zealand, or any of the other overseas dominions. I know my hon. friend will probably tell me that I should not allow colour or skin or class or creed or anything of that kind to enter into my imperialism. That may be very good doctrine to preach but whether it is sound in practice is another question, and whether we would be wise in endeavouring to draw a line of demarcation between the different subjects of the empire is not a question on which I am prepared to give an opinion.[16]

Other members rationalized that in the real world British subjects were sometimes denied full liberty. Even though South Asians "are British subjects, that does not settle the matter," opined W.E. Knowles. "There is many a British subject taken out and hanged until he is dead; many a British subject gets the lash for villainous conduct of which he has been proven guilty."[17]

Members often stumbled over the confusing discrepancy between the theory and real world practice of British subject equality rights for those of non-European origin in Canada. This confusion is well illustrated in the following 1917 exchange between Arthur Meighen, then Secretary of State, and W.E. Knowles, representing the Moose Jaw constituency.

> Mr. Knowles: When any man is naturalized and becomes a naturalized British subject, is he not given a pledge that 'he is, within

Canada, entitled to all political and other rights, powers and privileges to which a natural-born British subject is entitled.'

Mr. Meighen: Yes, but it adds at the same time they must assume all our obligations. Does the hon. Member say that... there cannot be a limitation of the franchise? If so, how does he justify the Government of Saskatchewan, which he supports, and which disfranchised British subjects, naturalized, coming from China?

Mr. Knowles: What has that to do with this?

Mr. Meighen: If there is a pledge, is not that pledge violated by that Act?

Mr. Knowles: Let us grant, for the sake of argument, that the legislature did very wrong.

Mr. Meighen: I have not heard the hon. Member complain of that legislature doing wrong in this matter. Why? Because he never until today interpreted naturalization in such a way.

Mr. Knowles: A pretty weak argument.

Mr. Meighen: The rights of British subjects here are rights given under the law of Canada. The law of Canada must be dictated by the needs of the hour, for the safety of Canada. Does the hon. Member say that in British Columbia there has been a breach of faith because for years past, if not since the birth of that province, they have refused the franchise to British subjects naturalized by the very same certificate, the Japanese and men of alien birth? Is it a breach of faith that those two provinces have done this for years? There is not a shadow of a breach of faith.[18]

Mindful of maintaining the power differential between colonies of British settlement and the Empire's colonies of military occupation, Vancouver member H.H. Stevens declared that granting South Asian British subjects full equality rights in Canada, rather than dealing "firmly with these people," could "stir up mutiny in India." This was because "the Hindus" would lose their respect for the "greater influence and power" of Europeans.

It has been stated here and in different places in Canada that our attitude on this Hindu question is such as to stir up this mutiny in India. I wish to affirm, and I am sure that anyone who understands the Oriental races will agree with me, that the fact that we have not dealt firmly with these people – kindly, but firmly and in a dignified manner – is doing more to stir up a mutiny in India than anything we might do in what may be called a harsh manner. The Hindus of the Pacific coast a few months ago sent a despatch to India in which they said: 'We have all along thought that these Britishers were men of greater influence and power than ourselves, but since we have come to British Columbia we find we can jostle them off the sidewalks if we wish to do so; we can ride in the street cars and sit while their women stand; we have absolutely equal privileges with them, and so on.' They submit this as an argument that the time has arrived when the Hindu should drive the British out of India... when you extend to this race the courtesies which we think should be extended to a person of our own race, they simply take advantage of such courtesies and treat them with contempt.[19]

CHRISTIANITY AND LIBERALISM

The political liberty that was said to characterize the British Empire was grounded in Christian morality and the ideology of liberalism. Insofar as both doctrines stressed the worth of the individual along with a claim to compassionate and equal treatment, they could be said to reinforce each other.[20] Indeed, some parliamentarians conflated Christian and liberal ideas in their appeals for non-discriminatory policies. For example, W.C. Edwards railed against the "retrograde and inhuman" head tax on Chinese because

> when any attack is made on the principle of free trade, on the principle of freedom... I am bound to speak. Why, Sir, if Chinamen were made by another Creator than the one who made us, then this principle is right; but if they are the offspring of the same Creator, then the underlying principle of this legislation is entirely wrong; it is barbarism and nothing else... I consider it abhorrent to the principles of free trade and to the commonest rights of all men who occupy this earth... just think of Canada, the right arm of an empire who proclaims freedom the world over, who is trying to maintain everywhere an open door, introducing legislation of this kind.[21]

But some protectionists objected that applying liberal economic theories of free trade to China lacked "common sense." J.H. Burnham argued that both Chinese persons and Chinese manufactures must be excluded from Canada in order to prevent the standard of living of "workingmen" from sinking to "the lowest levels" thereby ruining "our civilization."

> When China develops, when the men who are paid from 18 to 20 cents a day and who are capable of all sorts of skillful culture, turn their energies to producing steel and other manufactured goods, we shall be swept off the decks if we admit them into Canada... To keep out the people and yet allow their goods to come in, is simply solving half the problem. We must be prepared to maintain by judicious exclusion our own civilization as much as possible, and we must be prepared to maintain the rate of wages in this country so that the workingmen, the artisans and the labourers, may preserve that high civilization for which they are working and struggling so manfully. It is impossible to be consistent if you will not afford some protection for the rate of wages in this country and yet allow the products of cheap labour to come in, because that happens to be your idea of free trade. It is the old question all over again. It is all very well to interchange with a country like Great Britain, with a civilization like our own if not higher; but free interchange with a civilization which is lower and where the rate of wages is lower, tends to depress and ruin our civilization. It would be far better for us to put a Chinese wall around this country than to submit to such a degradation. The centre of gravity would be changed from the northern hemisphere to the oriental countries, and in 200 years, or less, we would see those countries producing a magnificent civilization while we had sunk to the lowest levels, because we had stuck to a theory which in itself has neither common sense nor consistency.[22]

Still, T. Christie protested against the head tax since it was "not in accordance with our free, liberal institutions in Canada. It is not at all in accord with the principles of free trade; nay more, it is not in harmony with our Christian civilization, with the fatherhood of God, the brotherhood of man and the golden rule. It is both unjust and un-British..."[23] In a similar fashion, A.H. Gillmor declared that he believed "in a unity of the human race; I believe that of one blood God made all nations of the earth, and I should be sorry to see any man, of whatever race, receiving anything but fair play in a British colony."[24] W.M. Ross decried the narrowness of members who criticized Eastern European immigrants and urged them to "get some expansion in their views." He was sorry, he said, "to hear intelligent men preach such doctrines." Canadians should deal with these immigrants "in a broad-minded and Christian spirit and not treat them as outcasts and publicans."[25]

But God could also be asked to play for the other team. As J. Charlton explained to the Commons, the calling of "the English race" was to be "the dominant race of the world so that the Anglo-Saxon will fulfil the destiny which God has evidently designed he shall fulfil."[26] For native Canadians, this bellicose brand of Christianity required their religious conversion as a necessary gateway to releasing them from barbarism, improving their moral character, and bringing them to civilization. Macdonald, as Prime Minister and Superintendent-General of Indian Affairs, told the Commons that the policy of all Canadian governments toward natives was to respect their rights as British subjects and to offer "as Christians" the necessary assistance over "the course of ages" to develop their level of civilization to the standard of "the general population."[27] Following a U.S. policy design in vogue during the 1880s, Macdonald began in Canada the residential schools movement that removed children from the reserves to place them in boarding institutions run by Christian denominations. "Secular education is a good thing among white men," he explained, "but among Indians the first object is to make them better men, and, if possible, good Christian men by applying proper moral restraints, and appealing to the instinct for worship which is to be found in all nations, whether civilized or uncivilized."[28] More than two decades later this view had not changed. F. Oliver when he was the Minister responsible for natives, contended that

> ...what the Indian does need is to have moral character instilled into his mind and heart. That, the government does not pretend to do. It looks to the churches to do that, and it is with that end in view the government has sought the co-operation of the churches in imparting education to the Indians... if we are to have an improvement

in the condition of the Indians, that improvement must start in the mind, in the heart, in the soul.[29]

One of the arguments employed by supporters of Asian Canadians was that "Chinamen will become Christians" thereby opening the door to their becoming "good subjects."[30] The counter-argument paraded their 'heathen' beliefs, denied that they would ever convert to Christianity, or declared that if they did convert it would be for show only. For example, T.S. Sproule suggested that although Chinese Canadians had for many years enjoyed "the advantage" of "receiving instruction from the missionaries," they would "never be converted... If they pretend to be christianized they are not sincere..."[31] According to A.W. Neill, since Japan had deliberately turned away from "the gospel message," Canada was courting divine retribution if it allowed an "influx" of heathen Japanese immigrants.

> I know it is unpopular in this day and generation, and considered old fashioned, to introduce any question of our relation to God in a matter of public or even private affairs; but perhaps we might for one minute turn aside from the pursuits of the material and ask ourselves: Do we, can we, should we, expect Providence to bless this nation in our undertakings when we deliberately open our doors to an influx of an alien, heathen population in ever-increasing numbers? ...Japan is not a nation living in ignorance or for lack of opportunity concerning the gospel message at all. Japan is heathen today by solemn and deliberate choice.[32]

Those parliamentarians who promoted Christian and liberal equality values had no qualms about characterizing their opponents as being prejudiced. And so, in the mid-1880s, the "hon. gentlemen" who supported stripping Chinese Canadians of their federal vote were judged by P. Mitchell to be "prejudiced against the Chinamen."[33] Nearly four decades later, J.S. Woodsworth complained that "a good deal" of what was said in several anti-Asian Canadian speeches in the Commons "showed racial prejudice and... racial bigotry."[34] French Canadian members like J.A.C. Ethier complained about the "racial and religious prejudices" stirred up against them "by some Ontario jingoes who, to serve their hatred for everything that is French Canadian and Catholic, do not even hesitate to endanger the fabric of Confederation and the national unity."[35] During World War I, W.G. Weichel told members that his German ancestry had left him open to "discrimination along race lines."

> I never knew what racial prejudice meant until August, 1914. From that time on, I have known what it is to have insult and ridicule and everything else that makes life unenviable heaped upon one. When I hear the hon. Gentlemen from the province of Quebec speaking about racial prejudice, I came to the conclusion that the prejudice against my race must be of a different brand from that against theirs. Discrimination along the lines of religion, of birthplace, of race, of language, is un-British and absolutely wrong. We must not forget that this is a cosmopolitan country.[36]

Speaking near the beginning of this book's period of coverage, G.E. Foster considered racial prejudice to be old-fashioned and socially unacceptable. He advised the House that it was unwise to "go back to abandoned prejudices and raise again barriers of color, race and creed" after "centuries of progress and refinement, during which the tendency has always been to... weld divided humanity into one common whole."[37] Opinions like Foster's continually wrong-footed members who advocated discriminatory policies. For example, in the midst of a long speech advocating Asian exclusion in 1907, Nanaimo member R. Smith felt constrained to excuse himself by declaring that he too "practice[d] a belief in the equality of races and men."

> ...this discussion has been associated by its opponents with race prejudice... I have been trying all my life to practice a belief in the equality of races and men, and I am not easily influenced to do anything or to say anything contrary to the principle of the equality of races. But... race prejudice is part and parcel of the inequalities existing as a consequence of the depravity of the human race, and is seen not only in the conflict of man against man but of race against race...[38]

H.H. Stevens was fond of introducing his anti-Asian and anti-miscegenation speeches with a disclaimer that his remarks should not be misunderstood as "racial prejudice." In 1921, he explained that "Whatever I say regarding the Chinese or Japanese is not with any racial prejudice; my remarks are based upon exceedingly sound economic grounds and reasons."[39] In commenting on the 1910 debate over the Naval Service Bill, Ernest Lapointe observed that "every means have been resorted to in order to discredit it; even appeals to race prejudice have been made, a tactic so odious and despicable that even those who resort to it emphatically deny that they do so."[40]

RACIAL PSEUDO-SCIENCE AND BIOLOGICAL DETERMINISM

Chapter 1 explores two branches within nineteenth century Anglo-Saxon race-thinking. One set out a 'ladder of civilization' perspective where it was held that Britain had progressed through stages to the apex of political and economic development. The possibility that even 'barbarian' or 'semi-barbarian' peoples could themselves progress to higher civilization through these same stages was not precluded. Indeed, within this branch, the expansion and dominance of the British Empire over 'lesser' peoples was justified by the idea that it was the special responsibility of the Anglo-Saxon to tutor those further down the ladder. As H.B. Ames explained to the Commons, "...we believe there are other races under the flag more backward than ours, struggling towards the light, who need this system of government, to come into the full stature of manhood as we have done."[41]

Competing with the developmental perspective was a biological determinism that divided humanity into separate racial species with heredity creating differing instinctual, intellectual, and physical endowments. Grounding itself in several pseudo-sciences, biological race-thinking first gathered significant influence in British political culture in the later decades of the nineteenth century. In spite of the fact that Darwin had ruled out that humans with different skin colors were different species or that some human groups were closer to apes than others, social Darwinists argued that the international political order corresponded to nature's model of species competition and survival of the fittest with more genetically gifted races dominating lesser races. "The avowed purpose of the Anglo-Saxon is to make the Anglo-Saxon race the greatest race on the earth," according to J. Charlton.[42] Or as Frank Oliver put it, "we claim that this Empire of ours is the most perfect fruit of the civilization of which we are a part. Our claim is that it stands today at the head of a white civilization. I can only retain that position by being maintained by a white civilization, and that white civilization must be maintained in the self-governing dominions of the Empire, or this Empire cannot be maintained finally and completely as a white man's empire..."[43]

Sir John A. Macdonald was an early exponent of biological race-thinking in Commons debates referring to himself as a "physiologist" and a "Darwinian" while claiming the authority of "all natural history, all ethnology" to bolster his arguments.[44] He portrayed different "races" as different species. Referring to native Canadians, he observed that "we have seen individuals of this race succeed, by means of education, but the exception proves the rule. The general rule is that you cannot make the Indian a white man. An Indian once said to myself: 'We are the wild animals; you cannot make an ox of the deer.'"[45] Elsewhere, he claimed that the "cross" of "the Africans or the Asiatics" with the "Aryan races" could not ever be "successful" as it was "like the cross of the dog and the fox."[46] Chinese males could safely be employed on a temporary basis to finish building the transcontinental railway but they should not be allowed to bring "women" and become "permanent settlers." Macdonald judged there was little "danger" in this arrangement of "miscegenation or a mingling of the races" although he warned that the Chinese were "an alien race in every sense, that would not and could not be expected to assimilate with our Arian population..."[47]

The idea that those of Asian origins could not be assimilated into Canadian society was repeated over and over again by their opponents. While Macdonald understood assimilation in relation to biology and miscegenation, it was more typically employed in the late nineteenth century to refer to intractable barriers of economics, culture, politics and religion. This was the way in which Joseph-Adolphe Chapleau, Macdonald's Secretary of State and Royal Commissioner reporting on Chinese immigration in 1885, understood assimilation. Race, for Chapleau, was a social and political construction rather than a biological fact. Although Chapleau dismissed most of the stereotypical complaints against Chinese Canadians as untrue and the result of "prejudice," he nevertheless agreed that assimilation was improbable due to mutual "race antagonism." Since both civilizations were convinced of their superiority over the other, "they do not want to assimilate with us, and we do not want to assimilate with them," he explained.[48] G.E. Casey likewise stressed the supposed cultural and social gap between the Chinese and "all races possessing any kind of modern civilization" to judge them unassimilable.

> We have a right, as every other people inhabiting a country have, to object to the introduction among our population of any race whom we may consider hopelessly barbarian, or not capable of assimilating with the population... The question is, what races should we exclude? I have no doubt personally, that it would be much better for this country if no Chinese ever came here. They may be a convenience as domestic servants, or as labourers in the construction of certain public works; but on the whole I consider them an element that can never be assimilated with the rest of our population. They are so totally different, not only from us, but from other civilized races – I will not say from European races only, but all races possessing any kind of modern civilization – that I do not believe they can ever become citizens of this country.[49]

While in the nineteenth century a sociological and cultural chasm was said to prevent Asians from assimilating with other Canadians, as the twentieth century progressed anti-Asian parliamentarians increasing gave their arguments about the impossibility of assimilation a biological cast. W. Sloan assured the Commons that "as individuals the races do not and never will assimilate."[50] R.G. Macpherson portrayed race-mixing as "impossible... as to mix oil and water." The "yellow peril," he warned was much closer than Canadians realized and that if Canada was to become "a great nation" it "must be a country developed by the white races of our land."[51]

On the heels of the Vancouver anti-Asian riots of 1907, the leadership of the national political parties fell progressively more in line with racial determinism. Borden endorsed the call for a "white Canada" in the election of 1908 and Laurier found "no fault" with the view that British Columbia "should be maintained as a country for the white race."[52] After World War I, the language of anti-Asian members became more explicitly biologized. W.G. McQuarrie told the Commons that "intermarriage" was the "real test of assimilation."

> The divergence of characteristics of the two races is so marked that intermarriage does not tend to perpetuate the good qualities of either race. The races are fundamentally different. Their morals are different, and language, heredity, religion and ideals will militate against and prevent even sociological assimilation of orientals... So far as I am aware, intermarriage between the white and the oriental has always produced unsatisfactory results.[53]

T.G. McBride was vexed that interracial marriage was "bringing into existence a mongrel race" and this "should not be allowed."

> And when you bring the oriental race and the white race together, what do you have? In the first case, they will not assimilate, but they are getting married, and they are bringing into existence a mongrel race that is not a credit to any country. It is certainly not a credit to Canada, and should not be allowed[54]

Even mixed-race children could be targeted. J.B.M. Baxter, for example, objected to a clause exempting the children of "Englishmen" fathers and Chinese mothers from the 1923 legislation barring most Chinese from entering Canada. His exchange with Charles Stewart, then Acting Minister of Immigration and Colonization, is instructive in the way that it illustrates how biological race-thinking could challenge established British legal norms.

> Mr. Baxter: "After all, we do not want any more Chinese here than we can help. Well, do we want half any more than we want full-blooded Chinese?
> Mr. Stewart: Is it not generally understood that nationality descends on the father's side.
> Mr. Baxter: So far as the national status is concerned it would depend on the father, yes but-
> Mr. Stewart: There are many cases where Englishmen are married to Chinese women. Their offspring would be barred if there were not such a clause in the bill.
> Mr. Baxter: If whites choose to let down the racial standard to that extent, should not they keep their progeny in the East instead of bringing them in here?[55]

Beginning in the 1890s, pseudo-scientific race-thinking was also applied to relations between Canadians of European origins with explosive results. Its assumptions directly challenged the nineteenth century view of Canada's multicultural political citizenship that promised "equal rights of every kind" for all British subjects. Also challenged was the narrative of several of the Fathers of Confederation still holding seats in Ottawa who held that the federation was a compact of provinces and several ethnic communities. On this latter point, Hector Langevin explained that "the French race went hand in hand with the English, the Scotch, the Irish, and the Germans, and the other races of this country – all went together to secure the [federal] institutions which we enjoy today."[56]

On one side, a militant Anglo-Saxonism promoted the assimilation of French Canadians in order to unify and strengthen the country. In this view, divisions between the English and French were judged to be sociological rather than biological and therefore French Canadians, although somewhat backward, were 'assimilable.' A. McNeil maintained that countries made up of a "bundle of distinct peoples" were weak but

> if our races were amalgamated, we should be stronger than we are at the present moment. We all know that our French Canadian friends have many qualities characteristic of their race, great and good qualities, which are not characteristic of the race to which we belong; and I think we may say, on the other hand, that we have good qualities characteristic of our race which are not so highly developed in theirs; and I think we may fairly conclude that if there were a blending of the races, that blending would be beneficial to both; but in any case it cannot be doubted that it would add to the solidarity of the Dominion.[57]

The fixed determination of "the Anglo-Saxon," J. Charlton declared, was that "assimilation and homogeneity shall be the characteristics of every part of the land over which he bears sway."[58]

On the other side, the Ligue nationaliste of Henri Bourassa asserted that the Confederation compact was a compact restricted to "two elements," English and French Canadians. Accordingly, Bourassa asserted that Canada was a "dual country" made up of two equal races that shared a common British genetic, cultural, and political heritage through their Norman ancestors. Immigration, as it introduced "the scum of all nations," threatened the "founders" intended balance between the "two races."

> it never was in the minds of the founders of this nation... [that] we ought to change a providential condition of our partly French and partly English country to make it a land of refuge for the scum of all nations... we should not give the better half of our continent to people who have nothing in common with us – nothing in common with us in history, nothing in common with us in blood, nothing in common with us in education or economics...[59]

Similarly, A. Lavergne wanted to source Canada's immigration only from Britain, France and Belgium and keep out "the scum of continental Europe" and "a mongrel population, a population that comes in by flocks" including "the Polish Jews, the Prussians, the Galicians and the Doukhobors."[60] On this issue, Bourassa and Lavergne made common cause with T.S. Sproule who, in addition to his parliamentary duties, served as the Orange Order's "Most Worshipful Grand Master and Sovereign of British America" between 1901 and 1911.[61] Sproule told the Commons that "people coming from England, from Ireland, Scotland, Germany or France," were welcome to come to Canada, "because we know what they are. They belong to the races to which we belong..." But "Galicians or Doukhobors or Finns or Russian Jews or Poles or Mexicans" have made Canada "the dumping ground for the refuse of every country in the world."[62] W.F. Cockshutt cut the list of desirables even further claiming that "Englishmen, Irishmen, and Scotchmen [were] the best of all settlers for Canada." "I believe that if we can get Anglo-Saxon immigrants we want no other class," he averred. "I believe it is only our failure to get these which causes us to turn our eyes to the other nations of the earth."[63]

There was strong push-back in parliament directed toward the triumphalist "anglo-saxons," the "two races" *nationalistes*, and the nativists. Laurier denounced the assimilationist ambitions of the anglo-saxonists as "vicious" and "wicked" and "a crime." "We ought to remember this – French, English, Liberals, Conservatives – that no race in this country has absolute rights, only the rights which do not invade the rights of any other race," he declared. "We ought to remember that the expression of race feelings and race sentiments should be well restrained to a point, beyond which... they might hurt the feelings and sentiments of other races."[64] Contesting Bourassa's "two races" theory of Canada, W. McIntyre reasserted the view that Confederation was meant to "bury" French-English "racial differences" and give "liberty of conscience and liberty of race" to "every nationality that should seek our shores."[65] Those who had stirred up "senseless talk about the alien and the foreigner," were decried by T.W. Scott. "It is no disgrace to be an alien and a foreigner... We had not formerly the same idea about the alien and foreigner that has grown up in recent years."[66]

The enormous stress of World War I heated Canada's simmering early twentieth century conflicts embedded in deterministic race thinking to the boil. Most serious was the dispute between English Canadians and Québécois over military recruitment. While "the call of the blood" in the defence of "liberty" explained to imperialists why many English Canadians volunteered for service, enlistment rates in Quebec were by comparison very poor. Working from history, there was nothing remarkable in this: French Quebec's self-narrative highlighted pride and satisfaction in twice defending and saving militarily the British Empire in North America from foreign invasion. But fighting Britain's wars outside North America was a political non-starter. This had been made clear most recently in the Boer War where Bourassa affirmed that "Canada is not bound and should not be called to any other military action than the defence of her territory."[67]

While the history was clear, from a social Darwinist perspective Quebec's relatively poor recruitment nonetheless proved difficult to understand. France was under attack and the French had a glorious history as a "military people." Bravery, G.E. Foster declared was "inherent in the French blood."[68] In Ontario, the Orange Order along with some newspapers had "branded... [Quebec] as a province of shrinkers, of slackers, of cowards!"[69] G. Boyer complained to the Commons that a military problem had been transformed into an issue of race. "The conscription issue has been completely set aside by some hon. Members on the other side of the House, who saw fit to base their arguments upon racial grounds. Truly, one might be led to believe that conscription is not a military question but rather a racial issue," he observed.[70] So seriously was the matter of collective cowardice taken that Laurier found it necessary to confront the question of a supposed "degeneration" of French Canadian "blood." "The fact that the men of Quebec have not enlisted in larger numbers does not mean that they have degenerated," he declared and then went on to offer a sociological explanation as an alternative. The longer a "portion of the community" had been in Canada, the less urgently they felt drawn to joining the war in Europe, he said.[71]

Blood also factored into wartime relations between the anglo-saxonists and the immigrant communities from east and central Europe. Under the Wartime Elections Act of 1917, "enemy alien" British subjects, including German Canadians and Austrian Empire Canadians like the Galicians, who had been naturalized less than fifteen years and did not a relative serving in the military, were stripped of their right to vote. Racial instinct was employed by two future Conservative Prime Ministers to explain and defend this legislation. For Arthur Meighen it was "human nature" for "blood" to determine that "the German and Austrian in Canada" were potentially disloyal. R.B. Bennett assured the Commons "that the call, the insistent call of the blood is ever upon them" and that "blood ranks first in the motives influencing the minds of men."[72] J.A. Currie demurred from this line of thinking by arguing that political socialization was a more significant determinant of human behaviour than heredity.

> Blood is certainly a powerful tie; we all admit that. But there is a tie still more powerful, and that is the tie of home; the associations connected with home are more potent than the ties of blood. When a man leaves his country to settle elsewhere, though the land of his ancestors may be dear to him, the land of his children is still dearer.[73]

POLITICAL REPRESENTATION

The parliamentary debates surrounding the political rights of British subjects, Christian and liberal values, and pseudo-scientific racial determinism all played a part in deciding who was able to vote in Canada's elections. Voting rules reflected the power of political parties, regions, and political ideas and could to no small extent fix institutionally the political fates of winners and losers. Once a community was denied the vote for any length of time, it was to prove difficult for its members to be seen as full citizens worthy of representation since they lacked the ability to reward and punish elected officeholders.

Following the Quebec Act of 1774 and the Constitution Act of 1791, property-qualified French and Irish Roman Catholic males held the vote on an equal basis with Anglo-Celtic Protestants. In this sense, long before Confederation voting rights in British North America rested on a multicultural foundation. As J. Tassé told the Commons in 1883, Canada was "prepared to assist the British Government in giving to the Irish people the land which they could not possess in their own country, the peace which they could not find, and the Home Rule for which they are agitating. In fact, our Dominion is broad enough to make a landlord of every Irish peasant."[74] With Loyalist ancestors, property-qualified African Canadians males as "sons of Canada" could also claim the voting franchise and the right to protection from discriminatory legislation. In 1906, for example, H.S. Clements proudly claimed a large number of his constituents as Black.

> We are proud of the coloured people in that section of the country. They are intelligent, respectable and thoroughly good Canadian citizens ...I feel it my duty as a representative of that section of the people to advocate their interests here and I trust these people will be represented as well as other nationalities in this Dominion.[75]

Notwithstanding his often restated view that natives were biologically inferior, Sir John A. Macdonald accepted that under the British doctrine of *jus soli*, they were "sons of the soil." Accordingly, male natives who were property-qualified should have the right to vote. This was a controversial move and natives only held the vote for three federal elections – 1887, 1891, and 1896. Over the objections of some parliamentarians who testified that the natives had proved excellent voters, the Laurier government stripped them of their vote in 1898.

Chapter 3 argues that the loss of the franchise was enormously important to natives as it denied them a significant point of leverage against the 'wardship' imposed on them by an increasingly powerful federal bureaucracy whose mission was to "civilize" them. Natives were cast as "children" who needed constant supervision and correction and they could only access parliament indirectly through sympathetic members who from time to time volunteered to take on ombudsman roles with Indian Affairs on their behalf. No one could have stated the bleak situation of natives more clearly than Mohawk Chief F. McD. Jacobs in his 1914 letter recorded in Hansard: "...we are not recognized as citizens. The basis and scope of our Indian Act is wrong, and injurious to us, because it interferes with our enjoyments of natural and inherent rights. We have no voice whatever in legislation. We are often opposed to it and suffer from its effect..."[76] It is difficult not to think that the history of natives in Canada would have been significantly different if the 1885 suggestion of S.J. Dawson that "the whole Indian race, from the Atlantic to the Pacific, should have some sort of representation in this House" had been followed perhaps through the creation of several designated native seats.[77]

Waves of immigrants from eastern and southern Europe began to arrive at the turn of the twentieth century. For the most part they were welcomed by the political establishment and it was assumed that they would be in time assimilated into the political values of British subjecthood and take up their responsibilities as voters. In 1899, Minister of the Interior Clifford Sifton explained to the Commons that Canada needed "industrious, careful and law-abiding" immigrants who were assimilable.

> ...I do not care what language a man speaks, or what religion he professes, if he is honest and law-abiding, if he will go on the land and make a living for himself and family, he is a desirable settler for the Dominion of Canada; and the people of Canada will never succeed in populating Manitoba and the North-west until we act practically upon that idea... Our experience of these people [Galicians] teaches us that they are industrious, careful and law-abiding, and their strongest desire is to assimilate with Canadians.[78]

Or as R.G. Macpherson put it, "the white man may not be just exactly the kind of man that you would like to invite into your parlour; he may not talk the language or understand it, but his boys and girls are going to school, they are given education along the required lines and they are singing 'God save the King' and 'Rule Britannia' within six months after they come here."[79]

Although, as noted above, racial determinist arguments were employed by the Borden government in 1917 to take away the vote of those who had emigrated from the German or the Austrian Empires and had been naturalized in Canada less than fifteen years, there was to be no attempt to extend the voting ban beyond one election. Not only did their MP's continue to represent German and Austrian Empire Canadians as constituents and complain loudly on their behalf in parliament, they had also enjoyed the unqualified support of the Official Opposition. Laurier energetically denounced what he said was an unprecedented breach of trust declaring that "…the Germans and Austrians are voters, and they have been voters from the time they were naturalized. The object of my hon. Friend is to take away from these men of foreign origin the rights and privileges of British subjects, which have been freely granted to them… That is what I blame my hon. Friend for today. He is introducing a new principle…"[80] "The War-time Elections Act," R. Lemieux told the Commons, was "nothing else but a Hunnish and Kaiser-like measure."[81]

There was to be nothing temporary about the removal of the federal votes of Chinese Canadians by Macdonald's government in 1885. For Macdonald this was a logical extension of the biological determinist side to his thinking. As he explained to the Commons, if the Chinese "…came in great numbers and settled on the Pacific coast they might control the vote of that whole Province, and they would send Chinese representatives to sit here, who would represent Chinese eccentricities, Chinese immorality, Asiatic principles altogether opposite to our wishes; and, in the even balance of parties, they might enforce those Asiatic principles, those immoralities… which are abhorrent to the Aryan race and Aryan principles, upon this House."[82] B.C. member J.A.R. Homer raised a similar spectre warning that "if allowed to vote, the entire control of the Province will be in the hands of the Chinese..."[83]

Disenfranchising Chinese Canadians caused a real stir in the Commons. Several members were scandalized by this assault on the rights of British subjects. There was also the question of regional politics. It was argued that "prejudice" against the Chinese was a fancy of British Columbia "whites" and that provincial opinion should not be allowed to override the Dominion principle of equal rights for all British subjects including the right to vote for all property-qualified males. "It is not right or fair that a broad question of principle should be decided by the passion or prejudice of those who come from one section of the Dominion alone," L.H. Davies declared.[84]

One of the effects of the 1896 Laurier government abandoning the federal electoral list in favour of using provincial lists in federal elections was that the issue of the franchise for Asian Canadians was no longer the responsibility of Ottawa. B.C. members could now give their undivided attention to pressing the federal government to exclude Asian immigration, a task which they took up with considerable gusto as Chapter 5 records. But the matter did not end there. The South Asian migrants that began to appear in noticeable numbers in British Columbia in 1907 and 1908 were British subjects. Employing the leverage of India's massive military contribution to the Empire during World War I, the Indian government pressed Canada to grant South Asian Canadians their full rights as British subjects and enfranchise them.

But British Columbia members resisted angrily any talk of giving votes to South Asians. A.W. Neill claimed that this was the thin edge of a dangerous wedge. If South Asian British Columbians were given the vote, how could it "logically and with any sense of decency" be denied to Chinese or Japanese Canadians who were born in Canada. The "Hindu" vote alone could "swing perhaps two or three seats" and so the character of politics in the province would be forever changed. This was a potentially perilous situation that the federal government must avoid if it did not want to "create a canker in British Columbia" that would threaten the stability of the nation.

> I said at the beginning that this was not the place to discuss this question, and it is not. It is not a Dominion matter. It is a British Columbia problem. Render unto Caesar the things that are Caesar's. Let us settle this problem in British Columbia. It has no more to do with the other provinces than if I were to interfere with some of the local customs and traditions of the province of Quebec... I would ask this House, therefore, not to force upon us in British Columbia a thing which is unconstitutional, and is against our customs and bitterly against our desires. There is no precedent for it whatever. Talk about creating a sore spot. Do this and you would create a canker in British Columbia that we as a nation would never recover from.[85]

Mackenzie King had been dealing with the belligerent racism of British Columbia MP's for a decade and a half having been sent during 1907 by the Laurier government to Vancouver to investigate the anti-Asian riots and to London to work out a formula to prevent South Asian immigrants from landing in British Columbia. He had no intention of rocking the regional boat and creating "a canker." And so, he explained to the Commons, that "it was very doubtful how any situation of unrest in one part of the British Empire could be improved by creating a new condition of unrest in another part.[86]

As with the case of native Canadians, we are left to imagine how different Canada's twentieth century might have been if, nearer its beginning, Asian Canadians had been able to secure the right to vote and to have their concerns represented directly in parliament. Would, for example, Japanese Canadians still have faced pressure in 1942 and 1943 from a B.C. parliamentary caucus united in demanding their internment? Or with the vote and the legitimacy of full citizenship could their situation have more resembled that of the experience of German and Austrian Empire Canadians during World War I when parliament was divided on the issue of placing limits on their political rights? As it turned out, of course, all parties supported internment and no parliamentarian was to speak out in the Commons against any of the wide range of discriminatory policies that targeted Japanese Canadians.

Notes

1. Canada, House of Commons, *Debates*, July 2, 1885, pp. 3006-3007.
2. Lowry, "The crown, empire loyalism and the assimilation of non-British white subjects," *The Journal of Imperial and Commonwealth History*, 31:2, 2003.
3. Commons, *Debates*, February 17, 1890, p. 746 and June 18, 1917, pp. 2402-2403.
4. Ibid., August 24, 1896, p. 33.
5. Ibid., June 14, 1906, p. 5317.
6. Ibid., February 25, 1913, p. 3995.
7. Ibid., March 4, 1896, pp. 2854-2855.
8. Ibid., p. 2878.
9. Ibid., March 11, 1919, p. 376.
10. Ibid., May 4, 1885, p. 1583.
11. Ibid., July 31, 1899, p. 8993.
12. Ibid., July 7, 1899, p. 6850.
13. Ibid., April 20, 1886, pp. 809-810.
14. Ibid., May 4, 1885, p. 1582.
15. Ibid., March 2, 1914, p. 1252.
16. Ibid., May 30, 1914, p. 4533.
17. Ibid., March 2, 1914, p. 1245.
18. Ibid., September 10, 1917, p. 5584.

19. Ibid., March 2, 1914, pp. 1240-1241.
20. As John Stuart Mill put it in Chapter 2 of his *Utilitarianism*, first published in 1863: "In the golden rule of Jesus of Nazareth, we read the complete spirit of the ethics of utility. To do as you would be done by, and to love your neighbour as yourself, constitute the ideal perfection of utilitarian morality." See also Waldron, *God, Locke, and Equality: Christian Foundations of John Locke's Political Thought* and Larry Siedentop, *Inventing the Individual: The Origins of Western Liberalism*. London, Allen Lane, 2014.
21. Commons, *Debates*, June 25, 1900, pp. 8166-8167.
22. Ibid., March 2, 1914, pp. 1252-1253.
23. Ibid., June 25, 1900, pp. 8190-8191.
24. Ibid., May 4, 1885, p. 1586.
25. Ibid., July 14, 1903, pp. 6576-6577.
26. Ibid., February 14, 1890, p. 670.
27. Ibid., June 10, 1885, pp. 2426-2427.
28. Ibid., May 9, 1883, pp. 1107-1108.
29. Ibid., June 22, 1908, p. 11056.
30. Ibid., March 29, 1883, p. 327.
31. Ibid., June 25, 1900, p. 8198.
32. Ibid., May 8, 1922, p. 1546.
33. Ibid., May 4, 1885, p. 1582.
34. Ibid., May 8, 1922, p. 1572. When B.C. member T.G. McBride opined that "...when the good Lord made the orientals and the white race he put the Pacific ocean between them to keep them apart," Woodsworth sarcastically interjected "May I ask if red men were not put in this country rather than the white?" April 2, 1925, p. 1826.
35. Ibid., June 29, 1917, p. 2866.
36. Ibid., June 28, 1917, p. 2804.
37. Ibid., March 29, 1883, pp. 329-330.
38. Ibid., December 16, 1907, p. 700.

39. Ibid., April 26, 1921, p. 2595. See also May 8, 1922, p. 1548.
40. Ibid., November 21, 1910, p. 21.
41. Ibid., December 17, 1912, p. 1304.
42. Ibid., February 14, 1890, p. 670.
43. Ibid., May 25, 1917, pp. 1764-1765.
44. Ibid., April 30, 1883, p. 905; May 9, 1883, p. 1101; May 4, 1885, p.1589.
45. Ibid., May 5, 1880, p. 1991.
46. Ibid., May 4, 1885, p.1589.
47. Ibid., May 12, 1882, p. 1477.
48. Royal Commission on Chinese Immigration, Honourable Commissioner Chapleau's Report, p. xcix.
49. Commons, *Debates*, June 25, 1900, pp. 8203-8204.
50. Ibid., December 16, 1907, p. 729.
51. Ibid., pp. 722, 726.
52. Ibid., January 22, 1909, pp. 35-36, 46.
53. Ibid., May 8, 1922, p. 1516.
54. Ibid., April 2, 1925, p. 1825.
55. Ibid., April 30, 1923, pp. 2309-2310.
56. Ibid., April 30, 1883, pp. 894-895.
57. Ibid., February 14, 1890, pp. 690-692.
58. Ibid., p. 667.
59. Ibid., March 12, 1901, p. 1292 and April 9, 1907, pp. 6182-6183.
60. Ibid., April 9. 1907, pp. 6146, 6155.
61. E.L. Marsh, *A History of the County of Grey*. Owen Sound: Fleming Publishing Company, 1931. p. 322.
62. Commons, *Debates*, July 14, 1903, pp. 6591-6592, 6594.
63. Ibid, March 13, 1905, p. 2366.
64. Ibid., February 17, 1890, pp. 729, 745.
65. Ibid., April 9, 1907, pp. 6190, 6192.

66. Ibid., August 5, 1904, pp. 8619-8620.
67. Ibid., March 12, 1901, p. 1291.
68. Ibid., June 18, 1917, p. 2409.
69. Ibid., June 19, 1917, p. 2474 and July 5, 1917, p. 3039.
70. Ibid., July 3, 1917, p. 2931.
71. Ibid., June 18, 1917, p. 2399.
72. Ibid., September 10, 1917, p. 5585, 5617-5618.
73. Ibid., September 14, 1917, p. 5851.
74. Ibid., April 30, 1883, p. 894.
75. Ibid., July 9, 1906, pp. 7503-05.
76. Ibid., April 3, 1914, pp. 2394-2395.
77. Ibid., April 30, 1885, p. 1491.
78. Ibid., July 7, 1899, p. 6859.
79. Ibid., April 8, 1908, p. 6445.
80. Ibid., September 10, 1917, p. 5573.
81. Ibid., April 22, 1918, p. 980.
82. Ibid., May 4, 1885, p.1589.
83. Ibid., May 4, 1885, p. 1582.
84. Ibid., p. 1585.
85. Ibid., June 29, 1923, p. 4647.
86. Ibid., pp. 4665-4666.

INDEX

African Canadians 27, 143, 188, 239-246, 275
Alberta 99, 102, 168, 177-178
Ames, H.B. 52, 266
Amyot, C. 257
Anglo-Celtic 28, 83, 94, 98, 101, 105, 112, 120, 124
Anglo-Japanese Alliance 204, 249
Anglo-Saxon 47, 49, 51, 88-94, 128, 143, 210, 213, 226, 272
anglo-saxonism 19-26, 266-267, 270-271
Anti-slavery campaign 17
Arendt, Hannah 36
Armstrong, J.E. 174-175
Arthurs, J. 116
Aryan, Arian 47, 88, 194, 199, 238, 241-242
Assimilate, assimilable 43-44, 89-90, 95, 97, 99, 101, 103, 123, 126, 132, 134, 136, 138, 155, 189, 197, 203, 208-210, 216-217, 219, 224, 258, 267-269, 271, 276

Australia 6, 43, 47, 50-51, 71, 80, 113, 134, 192, 194, 206, 214, 227
Austrian Empire 91, 106-112, 120, 127, 274, 277, 279
Avery, Donald 137
Avery, M. 103

Backhouse, Constance 26
Ball, R.J. 107
Banerjee, Sukanya 189
Bannister, Robert C. 38
Baptist 47, 130
barbarian, barbarism 16, 18-19, 65, 144-147, 154-156, 160, 195, 198, 205, 212, 261, 263, 266, 268
Barnard, G.H. 210
Baum, Bruce 18
Baxter, J.B.M. 269-270
Beasley, Edward 12-13, 38
Belgium 97, 271
Bell, David B.J. 45
Bell, Duncan 21, 25
Belliveau, Robert M. 32

Bennett, R.B. 46, 49, 53, 101-102, 109, 256, 274
Berger, Carl 25, 41, 66
Bernier, François 13
Best, J. 172
biological determinism 18-19, 22-24, 27, 44, 62, 145-146, 195, 198, 266-274
Black, G. 217
Blake, Edward 92
blood 69, 79, 89, 94, 96, 105, 108-111, 117-118, 120-121, 126, 128, 143, 185, 203, 206, 216, 257-258, 262, 270-271, 273-274
Blood Nation 177
Boer War 49, 56, 81, 112, 273
Bonilla-Silva, Eduardo 12
Borden, Robert 53, 55, 65, 108
Boulay, H. 121
Bourassa, Henri 67-68, 86, 94, 96-97, 99-100, 113-115, 135-137, 271-273
Boyer, Gustave 87, 115, 273
Bradbury, G.H. 162, 164, 166
British Columbia, B.C. 2-11, 27, 32-34, 43-44, 54, 106-107, 111, 122, 128, 147, 152, 169, 190-193, 195, 197-204, 206-211, 213-219, 222-227, 230, 232, 235-239, 246-250, 260-261, 269, 277-279
British liberty, freedom 46-49, 53, 62-66, 71, 74, 79-82, 85, 93, 95, 100, 105, 112-113, 125, 143, 205, 212, 220, 256-259, 261
British navy, naval power 48, 50-56, 68
British subject 20-21, 25, 46, 54-55, 58, 67, 79-83, 88, 92-93, 95, 96, 102, 105, 108, 110-111, 122-123, 133, 142-146, 150, 155, 158-159, 188-189, 193, 197, 199-203, 205, 215, 224-230, 237-238, 240, 243, 256-260, 263, 270, 274, 276-278
Bryce, Dr. P.H. 178
Buchignani, N. Indra, D. and Srivastava, R. 27
Buckner, Phillip 42, 75
Buddhist 46-47, 257
Bunster, A. 190
Bureau, J. 115, 120
Burgess, Michael 25
Burnham, J.H. 56, 259, 261

Cameron, D.M. 60, 171
Cameron, M.C. 156
Canadian Pacific Railway 58, 76, 190, 203
Cardin, P.J.A. 119
Caron, Adolphe 157
Cartwright, Richard 68
Casey, G.E. 69, 94, 153, 200
Casgrain, P.B. 156
Caucasian 43, 99, 209, 242, 258
CCF Party 3, 32-34
Celts 24, 91

Champion, C.P. 41
Chapleau, Joseph-Adolphe 192, 195-198, 254
Charlton, J. 50, 73, 89-90, 155, 206, 263, 267, 271
China 44, 54, 56, 190, 192-193, 195, 200, 202, 204, 208, 217, 234, 247, 260-262
Chinese Canadians 1, 44, 101, 190-208, 214-216, 221, 247-248, 264
Christian, Christianity, Christ 11-17, 22, 27-28, 36, 99, 103, 121, 148, 150, 193, 197, 204-205, 207-208, 212, 214, 220-221, 255, 261-264
Christie, T. 204-206, 262
civilisation, civilise 22, 60, 145, 148, 154, 156, 159, 197
civilization, civilize 62-63, 65, 69, 81, 96-99, 111-113, 142, 144, 146, 148-150, 156, 160-161, 163, 167-169, 175-176, 179-180, 191, 195-198, 205, 208, 212, 217, 219-222, 224, 226, 232-235, 262-263, 265, 267-268, 276
Clements, H.S. 106, 122-123, 242, 275
Cockburn, G.H.R. 50
Cockshutt, W.F. 45, 55, 63-64, 172, 259, 272
Cohn, Werner 34
Coldwell, M.J. 9
colony, colonies, colonial 12, 18-20, 25-26, 40-41, 49-51, 53-54, 57, 60-62, 65-66, 76, 79, 83, 91, 94, 98, 100, 113, 120, 134, 144, 189-190, 203, 208, 229, 257, 259-260, 262
color, colour (and race) 2, 4, 10, 13, 15, 33, 37, 53, 79, 144-145, 151, 155-156, 164, 190, 194, 198, 201, 211, 221-222, 239-240, 242-245, 247, 258-259, 265, 267, 275
Confederation 4, 19-20, 81, 83-88, 96, 100, 104, 134-135, 193, 258, 265, 270
conscription 62, 87, 115-116, 121, 139, 273
Conservative Party 6, 9, 59, 112, 153, 158, 177, 183-184, 203, 208, 211, 228, 246, 272, 274
continentalism 70-71
continuous passage 226-231
Cook, Ramsey 135
Cooper, R.C. 107
Coote, G.G. 177
cosmopolitan 106, 111, 125, 265
Cronyn, H.B. 131-132
Currie, J.A. 109, 117, 274

Daniel, J.W. 243
Daniels, Roger 35
Darwin, Charles 14-15, 38, 266
Davies, Alan 39
Davies, Louis Henry (L.H.) 69, 201, 258, 278
Davis, Christina L. 249

Davis, F.L. 108
Dawson, S.J. 154-155, 276
de Cosmos, Amor 191
de Gobineau, Arthur 14
development (social and political) 18-19, 22, 25, 28, 52-53, 87, 143-146, 185, 250, 266
Dickason, Olive Patricia 185
Dickie, C.H. 216
Diefenbaker, John 2, 31-32
diplomacy, diplomatic 40-41, 50, 53, 68-69, 204, 213, 217, 226, 228, 249, 253
Doherty, C.J. 35, 121
dominions 54, 56, 65, 123, 189, 208, 214, 232-233, 235, 259, 267
Doukhobors 87-98, 104, 111, 120, 175, 272

education 58, 72, 96-97, 99, 125, 129, 145, 147-148, 154, 159, 167-169, 172-176, 179-180, 189, 196, 207, 250, 263, 267, 271, 277
Edwards, J.W. 51, 64
Edwards, W.C. 204, 261
Egypt 48-49, 129, 226
enemy aliens 34, 104, 107-108
enfranchise 111, 145, 155-157, 159, 184, 237, 278
English-speaking 25, 51, 69, 82, 107, 112, 115, 118, 128
Enlightenment 11, 13, 16, 18, 23, 26

equality 3-5, 9, 11, 16-17, 27-28, 33, 40, 46, 79-80, 86-87, 92-93, 96, 133, 143-144, 189, 199, 203, 206, 224, 240, 246, 255-260, 264-265
Ethier, J.A.C. 264
Euler, W.D. 257
evolutionary 12, 15, 25, 43
expatriate, deport, expulsion 2, 5-6, 8-9, 123

Ferguson, Naill 14-15, 17, 23, 38
Fisher, Sydney Arthur (S.A.) 144-145, 212
flag 46-49, 53-55, 58, 68, 81-82, 97, 112-113, 119, 123, 183, 211, 220, 227, 240, 256-257, 266
Forke, Robert 131, 159
Foster, G.E. 48, 61, 113, 117, 173-174, 194, 240-241, 265
France 5, 65, 94, 97-98, 100, 108, 116-119, 124, 130-131, 154, 271-273
franchise (voting) 4, 110-112, 144-145, 153-160, 171, 175, 180, 182-184, 189, 198-203, 236-239, 241-242, 246, 250, 258, 260, 275
Freeman, Edward Augustus 88
French Canadians 67, 80-83, 85-95, 98, 105, 113-114, 116-120, 122-124, 143, 166, 257, 264-265, 270-271, 273

Galicians 97-98, 101-102, 104, 108, 111-112, 272, 274, 276
Galliher, W.A. 210, 224, 230
Gault, M.H. 199, 201, 248
Gauthier, L.J. 82
geostrategic 51, 54, 66, 69
German Canadians 10, 85, 93, 96, 98, 101-102, 104-111, 120, 131, 133, 143, 198, 210, 257-258, 265, 270, 272, 274, 277
Germany 47, 54, 63-66, 76, 85, 87, 98, 110-112, 123
Gillis, Clarence 33
Gillmor, A.H. 192-193, 202, 262
Gilmour, Julie F. 34
Good, W.C. 178
Gordon, G. 165
Gorman, Daniel 143
Gourley, S.E. 114-115
Granatstein, J.L. and Hitsman, J.M. 139
Grant, J. 50
Greer, Allan 134
guns 52-56
Guthrie, H. 160
Gwyn, Richard 2

Haggart, A. 229
Hansard 63, 163, 223, 276
Hansen, R.B. 9
Hatamiya, Leslie T. 31
Hawkins, Mike 38
Hazen, J.D. 56

head tax 39, 43, 195, 203-207, 220, 261-262
heathen 17, 71, 220, 264
Heathorn, Stephen J. 24
Heyd, C.B. 103, 157-158, 184
Hindu 25, 47, 209, 214, 223-225, 227-232, 234, 236-239, 260-261, 278
Hocken, H.C. 52, 107, 127
Hockin, Thomas A. 32
Homer, J.A.R. 199, 201, 278
Horsman, Reginald 21-22
Hudson, Nicholas 36-37
Hudson's Bay Company 20, 181
Hughes, Sam 48-49, 231
Hunt, James 18, 23
Huttenback, R.A. 189

immigration 1, 12, 43-44, 56, 72, 77, 97-99, 101-102, 120, 126, 128-133, 136-137, 189, 191-192, 194-198, 203, 206, 209, 213-216, 218-220, 222-223, 227-231, 233-235, 239, 241-243, 245-246, 249, 252-253, 268, 270-271, 278
Imperial War Conference 233-235
imperialist, imperialism 20-21, 25, 36, 41, 45, 112-113, 115, 210, 232-233, 259, 273
India 25, 47-50, 67, 86, 189-190, 222-228, 233-235, 259-261, 278
Indian Affairs Department 59,

146, 160, 163, 165-171, 173, 176-178, 180, 186, 263, 276
instinct, racial/race 15, 25, 88, 97, 108-109, 119-120, 146-147, 198, 200-201, 208-209, 266, 274
intermarriage 91, 148, 197, 209, 216, 269-270
internment 2-3, 5, 10, 31-32, 34-35, 279
Irish Canadians 52, 80, 85, 93, 96, 98, 104, 120, 128, 133, 190, 198, 270, 275
Italian Canadians 103

Jackson, J.P. and Weidman, N.M. 38
Jacobs, Chief F. McD. 163-164, 276
Jacobs, S.W. 129, 131, 141, 238-239
Japan 4-5, 44, 56, 63, 114, 208-209, 212-214, 217, 228-229, 234, 250, 264
Japanese Canadians 2-11, 31-34, 111, 208, 210, 217, 219, 221, 223, 237-238, 260, 278-280
Jeannotte, H. 95
Jews, Jewish Canadians 1, 11, 16, 33, 39, 88, 97-98, 103, 130, 136-138, 141, 237, 272
jingo 62-63, 67, 123, 232, 265
jus soli 144, 180, 188, 199, 275

Kaufmann, C.D. and Pape, R.A. 17
Kelley, N. and Trebilcock, M.J. 132, 137
Kennedy, Paul 38
Kidd, Colin 12, 16, 37
King, William Lyon Mackenzie 5-9, 34, 216-220, 226-227, 235-236, 279
Knowles, Stanley 33
Knowles, W.E. 225, 259-260
Knox, Robert 14, 23
Kohn, Edward P. 77
Kranz, Hugo 104
Kymlicka, Will 133-134

Lambertson, Ross 32
Lamonde, Yvan 139
Lancaster, E.A. 165
Landry, P-A 201
Langevin, Hector 83-84, 104, 270
Lapointe, Ernest 266
Larivière, A.A.C. 82-83, 167
Laurier, Wilfred 34, 43-44, 46, 57, 60-62, 65, 70, 72, 80-81, 93, 96, 99, 101, 103-104, 110, 118-119, 122, 138, 142, 157-159, 162-164, 185, 204, 206-207, 211-213, 218, 226-227, 229-230, 233-234, 243, 249-250, 256, 258, 269, 272-273, 275, 277-279
Lavergne, Armand 97, 137, 271-272

Lavergne, Joseph 257
Lemieux, Rodolphe 70, 100, 112, 115, 123, 130, 213-214
Levin, Michael 18-19
Lewis, E.N. 71, 77
Liberal Party 3, 6, 60, 68, 92, 101, 151-153, 157-159, 170, 177, 182-184, 203, 208, 213, 225, 246, 249-250, 272
liberalism, liberal values 3-5, 8-10, 18-19, 27-28, 65-66, 74, 100, 113, 137, 145, 158, 192, 204-205, 215, 221, 243, 246, 261-262, 264-266
Ligue nationaliste 113, 137, 139, 271
Linnaeus, Carl 13
Lister, J.F. 158
Locke, John 18, 40
Lopez, Ian F. Haney 12
Lorimer, Douglas 23-24
Lowry, Donal 79-80, 133, 256
Loyalist 70-71, 240, 275

Macdonald, E.M. 243
Macdonald, John A. 1-2, 21, 58-61, 92, 104, 144-151, 170-171, 180, 182, 184-186, 194-195, 198-201, 203, 206, 241-242, 256, 258-259, 263, 267-268, 275, 277
Macdonell, A.C. 103
MacInnis, Angus, Grace 3-4, 32-34
Mackay, George Leslie 39
Maclean, W.F. 54, 65, 70-71
Macpherson, R.G. 99, 209, 225, 231, 269, 276-277
Magrath, C.A. 162
Mahdi 58, 76
Mandler, Peter 22
Manitoba 101, 108, 145, 154, 221, 276
Manion, R.J. 59, 179
Maori 47, 182
Marcil, C. 81, 119
Martens, Jeremy 247
Martin, Médéric 121
McBride, T.G. 215, 237, 239, 269, 281
McCarthy, D. 88-89, 91-93, 135-136
McCoig, A.B. 244
McCraney, G.E. 111, 123
McCrea, F.N. 115
McIntyre, W. 99-100
McKenzie, D.D. 58
McLean, H.H. 51, 54, 62
McMaster, A.R. 128
McMurray, E.J. 127
McNeil, A. 67, 69, 91, 271
McQuarrie, W.G. 214-216, 218, 269
Meighen, Arthur 108-109, 111, 115, 126, 128-129, 168-170, 177-179, 185-186, 217, 259-260, 274
Mennonites 102, 111
Métis 58, 86, 159, 184
Miki, Roy 31

militarism 59, 62, 64-65, 67, 105, 114, 222
Mill, John Stuart 18-19, 23, 40, 145, 281
Miller, Carman 139
Miller, J.R. 135-136
Milloy, John S. 173, 182
Mills, David 151-152, 189, 241-242
miscegenation 14, 38, 43, 208, 216, 239, 241-242, 246, 266-268
Mitchell, Peter 199-200, 264
Mohawk Nation 163, 276
Mongolian 43, 99, 147, 194-195, 201, 206, 258
mongrel race 97, 199, 206, 269, 271
monogenesis, polygenesis 16, 22, 131, 241
Montgomery, Malcolm 183-184, 187
Morris, J. 117, 139
Morrison, A.M. 207
Morton, Desmond 34-35
Mulroney, Brian 2-3, 31
multicultural 2-3, 11, 26, 28, 30, 74, 80-81, 84, 133-134, 255-256, 270, 275

Narvey, Kenneth M. 181
Natal Act of 1897 189-190, 207, 217
naturalized 107-108, 111, 139, 189, 198-201, 215, 237, 258-260, 274, 277
Neill, A.W. 5, 8, 10, 33, 169-170, 236-239, 264, 278
New Brunswick 116, 192, 200
New Zealand 6, 47, 80, 134, 182, 214, 231, 259
Nordic 132
Norman (ancestry) 24, 88, 91, 94, 271
North-West (Territories) 20, 58-59, 61, 73, 88, 90-91, 96-97, 99, 101, 145-149, 152, 155, 157, 276
Nova Scotia 20, 240, 244

Oliver, Frank 57, 59, 102, 161-162
Ontario 1, 80, 104, 115-116, 121-124
Orange Order 80, 115, 272-273
Osiander, Andreas 36
Osler, E.B. 68
Ottawa 1, 8, 42, 61, 136, 161, 164, 166, 169, 174, 177, 203, 223, 242, 270, 278

Parker, C.J.W. 88
Paterson, William 152-154, 183-184
peace, peaceful 53, 57, 59, 61-64, 70, 73, 85, 87, 94-95
Peguis Nation 162, 185
philology 14, 88
Pitts, Jennifer 19

Poland, Polish Canadians 102, 129
Porter, Bernard 22-23
prejudice 10-11, 29, 33, 43-44, 93, 102, 105-106, 116, 193-194, 196-198, 200-201, 206, 211, 215, 221, 223, 238-239, 242, 246, 255-256, 264-265, 268, 278
Presbyterian 39, 47
Prior, E.G. 98, 101
Progressive Party 131, 218
Protestant 17-18, 46, 80, 88, 92-93, 95, 257, 275
Prussia, Prussian 97, 105, 112, 120, 123, 143, 272
pseudo-science (racial) 14, 16, 18, 88, 133, 198, 222, 241, 246, 255, 266-267, 270, 274
Pugsley, W. 64, 116, 243

Quebec 80, 82-84, 86, 88-89, 106, 112-113, 115-116, 118-120, 122-124, 133-134, 143, 192, 265, 273, 275, 279
Queen Victoria 50, 85, 189, 224

race-thinking 14, 16, 27-29, 36
racism 11-15, 26-30, 143
Read, G. and Webb, T. 76
realpolitik 52, 259
Redman, D.L. 129-130
Reid, J.D. 98, 243
Reid, T. 4
representation (political) 4, 83, 155-157, 159, 182, 203, 236, 250, 274-280
republic (U.S.) 61, 66, 70-71, 73, 91, 240
reserves (native) 144, 147, 149-152, 155, 159-160, 162, 167-169, 171, 173-174, 177, 180, 263
residential schools, boarding schools 148-149, 167-169, 174-175, 185, 263
responsible government 20, 48, 80, 82, 134-135
Riel Rebellion 58-60, 76, 86, 146, 171, 182
Roche, J. 228
Roebuck, A.W. 10
Rogers, Robert 235
Roman Catholic 21, 47, 80, 82, 86, 133, 256-257, 275
Rowell, N.W. 124, 140, 183
Roy, Patricia 34, 247-248
Royal Commission on Chinese Immigration 195-198, 202, 268
Russia 65, 76, 85, 98, 100, 114, 129, 136-137, 204, 212, 272

Saskatchewan 5, 103, 111, 123, 178, 260
savage, savages 60, 145-148, 154, 159, 167, 173-174, 181, 258
Scientific Revolution 11

Scotland, Scotch 96, 98-100, 120, 128, 133, 190, 270, 272
Scott, Duncan Campbell 178
Scott, T.W. 103-104, 272
Scramble for Africa 20
scum 96-97, 271
Séguin, Paul Arthur (P.A.) 106, 119-120
Serrano, S. K. and Minami, D. 31
Shakespeare, N. 192, 200
Shaw, J.T. 169
Shepard, R. Bruce 252-253
Shuchat, Rabbi Wilfred 141
Siedentop, Larry 281
Sifton, Clifford 101, 167, 276
Sikh 47, 67, 251
Silver, A.I. 83-84, 86-87
Sinclair, J.H. 66
Six Nations 152, 158, 163, 172, 183-184, 187
slavery, slave 12, 16-17, 39-40, 48-49, 129, 207, 240-241
Sloan, W. 208-209, 269
Smedley, Audrey and Brian D. 12
Smith, Helmet Walser 77
Smith, R. 265
Smits, Katherine 40
Snow, Jennifer C. 17-18
social Darwinism 15, 17, 21, 23, 44, 62, 64-65, 115, 117, 222, 246, 267, 273
Songhees Nation 162-163

South Africa 47, 50-51, 56, 66, 102, 112-113, 214, 222, 227, 259
South Asian Canadians 27, 143, 188-189, 218, 223-239, 241, 246, 259-260, 278-279
Sproule, T.S. 97-98, 231, 264, 272
St. Peter's Reserve scandal 162-163, 185
Stacey, F.B. 128
Stainton, Michael 39
Steele, Michael 116, 125
Stevens, H.H. 215-216, 218, 223-226, 260, 266
Stewart, Charles 169-170, 177-180, 270
Stoney Nation 168-169
Sueuchi, Keiko 187
Sutherland, D. 116-117, 171-172

Tassé, J. 82, 87, 275
Teuton 22, 24, 88
Thoburn, W. 241, 243
Thompson, A. 46-47
tolerance, toleration 7, 40, 47-48, 73, 85-86, 90, 92, 99, 121, 126, 134, 214, 256
treaties, treaty 20, 39, 44, 60-61, 70, 84, 149, 151, 164-165, 171, 177, 207-208
Treitschke, Heinrich von 64-65, 77

Troper, Harold 27, 42-43, 245, 253
Trudeau, Pierre 2, 31
tuberculosis 178-180
Tupper, Charles 20, 56-57, 68-69, 84-86, 158-159
Turks, Turkey 77, 88, 120

United States 25, 31, 35, 51-52, 59-61, 66-74, 82, 103, 111-112, 146, 148-149, 155-156, 174-176, 191, 203, 206, 216, 231, 240-241, 243-244, 253, 263
utilitarian 18, 281

Vancouver anti-Asian riots of 1907 6, 34, 211, 219, 226-227, 249
Varouxakis, Georgios 40
von Bernhardi, General Friedrich 15, 63-65
voting, votes 4, 144, 153, 157, 180, 184, 238, 241, 246, 259, 274-275, 277

Waite, Peter B. 182

Waldron, Jeremy 39-40, 281
Walker, James W. St G. 43-44
Ward, Alan J. 134-135
Ward, Peter 33-34, 249-250
wardship 161, 167, 176, 180
Wartime Elections Act of 1917 108, 112, 274
Weaver, Sally M. 184
Wedgewood, Josiah 17
Weichel, W.G. 65, 104-105, 124-125, 265
Whidden, H.P. 125, 130-131
white Canada 6, 211-212, 237, 246, 249-250, 269
White, J. 153
Wilcox, O.J. 53
Wilson, C.A. 112, 124
Winks, R.W. 240
Woodsworth, J.S. 43, 221-223, 237-238, 264, 281
Woodworth, D.B. 202
Wright, A.A. 102-103
Wright, Alonzo 93-94, 136

Yarwood, A.T. 233
yellow peril 209, 212, 269

ABOUT THE AUTHOR

Glen Williams is Professor Emeritus at Carleton University, Ottawa, having held the rank of Professor of Political Science for two decades and serving two terms as Chair of his Department. He authored *Not For Export: The International Competitiveness of Canadian Manufacturing*, (Third Edition) as well as co-editing and contributing chapters to two field-defining textbooks: *Canadian Politics in the 21st Century*, now in its seventh edition (with Michael Whittington), and *The New Canadian Political Economy* (with Wallace Clement). With a wide range of intellectual interests, Williams has taught across several subfields in his discipline – Canadian and comparative public policy; Canadian politics and foreign policy; Canadian and international political economy; as well as war and sovereignty in international relations.

ALSO BY GLEN WILLIAMS

Not For Export: The International Competitiveness of Canadian Manufacturing, Third Edition, McClelland and Stewart, 1994.

From the Publisher:

First published in 1983 and widely recognized as a definitive work in Canadian political economy, *Not for Export* examines the history of Canadian industrial development, from John A. Macdonald's National Policy of 1879 to Brian Mulroney's regional free trade agreements. This completely revised and updated edition looks at present Canadian industrial performance and future potential for an improved economy.

Review of the First Edition:

Williams' international perspective, his clear-headedness about Canada's position in the world economy, and his analysis of the relative autonomy of the Canadian state in industrial policy should recommend this extended essay to all students of Canadian political economy. – H.V. Nelles, *Canadian Historical Review*

Review of the Third Edition:

For students who may be coming to this work for the first time, the author offers a rigorous analysis of the development of industrial policy in this country which is as cogent as it is depressing... Williams skillfully highlights not only why certain policies and approaches were favoured but how each step was conditioned by past practices and attitudes and, in turn, influenced future developments. One is provided with a tapestry of Canadian political economy which does justice to the leading events in our economic past. – David Johnson, *Canadian Journal of Political Science*

www.ingramcontent.com/pod-product-compliance
Lightning Source LLC
Chambersburg PA
CBHW032028290426
44110CB00012B/722